Lacan, Discourse,
and Social Change

Also by Mark Bracher

Being Form'd: Thinking through Blake's "Milton"
Critical Paths: Blake and the Argument of Method (coeditor)
Lacan and the Subject of Language (coeditor)

LACAN, DISCOURSE, AND SOCIAL CHANGE

A PSYCHOANALYTIC CULTURAL CRITICISM

Mark Bracher

Cornell University Press

Ithaca and London

First published 1993 by Cornell University Press.

International Standard Book Number 0-8014-2784-3 (cloth)
International Standard Book Number 0-8014-8063-9 (paper)
Library of Congress Catalog Card Number 92-31172
Printed in the United States of America
Librarians: Library of Congress cataloging information appears on the last page of the book.
⊗The paper in this book meets the minimum requirements of the American National Standard For Information Sciences— Permanence of Paper for Printed Library Materials, ANSI Z39.48-1984.

For Nancy and Elizabeth

CONTENTS

Preface   ix
Introduction: For a Response-Centered Psychoanalytic
Cultural Criticism   1

PART I. Theory

1. Desire in Discourse   19
2. Social Change and the Ethics of Critical Discourse   53

PART II. Practice

3. Pornography   83
4. Antiabortionist Discourse   103
5. Political Campaign Rhetoric   119
6. *Heart of Darkness*   138
7. "To Autumn"   168
   Epilogue   190
   Works Cited   193
   Index   199

PREFACE

This book grows out of my conviction that literary and cultural studies have the potential to be of considerably greater human benefit than they have been up to now. On this score I find myself in sympathy with the growing sentiment that the present state of the humanities represents a betrayal of the public trust; after all, millions of students each year are required to spend their time and money for the privilege of discussing and writing about books that someone has decided are important for them to read, when in fact no one seems to know exactly what the benefits of such a study might be. At the same time, however, I have little sympathy with the assumption that the basic function of the humanities should be to indoctrinate students into a monolithic system of ideals, values, knowledge, and belief. My purpose here is thus to propose an aim and focus for the analysis of literature and other discourses which will make our scholarly and pedagogical activities more valuable—for ourselves, our students, and society in general— without turning literary and cultural studies into indoctrination.

What I propose is a shift in the type of knowledge that critics pursue and disseminate. Currently, most of our professional activity involves the production and distribution of knowledge about texts and their contexts. However satisfying this knowledge might be to those who produce it and consume it, I am not convinced that it is of great use, apart from its obvious value as professional currency. I think it would be more beneficial for us to pursue knowledge of how various texts and discourses affect those who use them, and how teachers and institutions might operate on and with different types of discourse in ways that challenge students to grow without imposing preestablished ideals or values on them. It is this sort of knowledge that I attempt to provide in this book.

My desire, then, to help make the study and teaching of literature and other discourses more valuable in human terms has led me to construct the model of response-oriented Lacanian psychoanalytic cultural criticism presented in this volume. On the most general level, my aim coincides with that of other modes of cultural criticism—namely, to help foster a better society, in which suffering and injustice are reduced and enjoyment and fulfillment are increased. My focus on audience response or reception rather than on cultural artifacts per se, or on their production or their context, follows directly from this aim, for if we are going to promote benign social change through cultural criticism, we need to intervene in some way in the psychological effects that cultural phenomena have on those who consume them.

My reason for employing psychoanalytic theory derives from its ability to explain the nature and significance of such psychological effects and from its capacity to explain how we can intervene in such effects in a beneficial and ethically defensible manner through our teaching and writing about literature and other discourses. I use Lacan's formulation of psychoanalytic theory because I believe that it provides the most comprehensive account available of the roles played by discourse in the psychic economy and therefore constitutes one of the most effective conceptual apparatuses available for promoting benign psychological change on a collective scale through the discourse of cultural criticism.

I owe an immeasurable debt to Marshall Alcorn, who first persuaded me that psychoanalysis was crucial to my interests and with whom I coauthored an article, "Literature, Psychoanalysis, and the Re-Formation of the Self," which articulated many of the concerns underlying this book. I have also benefited greatly from the friendship and support of Bob Bamberg, the founder and director of the Center for Literature and Psychoanalysis here at Kent State University, who, in addition to providing moral and logistical support throughout the writing, made it possible for me to go into training as a research candidate at the Cleveland Psychoanalytic Institute. For the clinical aspects of my training, which figure in important although indirect ways in this book, I am particularly indebted to William Adams, Elizabeth Daunton, Murray Goldstone, Kay McKenzie, and Joanne Naegele.

I am grateful as well to other friends and colleagues for offering suggestions, encouragement, and helpful questions and criticisms during the various stages of this project: Jennifer Berkshire, Marie-Hélène Brousse, Ron Corthell, Rick Feinberg, Doris Kadish, Juliet Flower MacCannell, Jacques-Alain Miller, Eve Moore, Gayle Ormiston, Diana Rabinovich, Paul Smith, Ellie Ragland-Sullivan, Renata Salecl, Greg Shreve, Colette Soler, and Slavoj Žižek. I also benefited appreciably from the responses and good humor of the students in my fall 1990 graduate seminar on Lacan and cultural criticism, who read and discussed an earlier version of this book in manuscript form: Arlene Lawson, Mary Lazar, Lisa Martinez, Masahiko Narita, Joanne Scarvell, Helen Sharpe, Rachel Tucker, and Woody Tyrrell. I thank David Wagenknecht for providing an extremely helpful critique of an earlier version of Chapter 7. The most valuable suggestions for improving the manuscript in its entirety came from two anonymous readers for Cornell University Press, to whom I am very much obliged.

To Morris Eaves and Michael Fischer, directors of a National Endowment for the Humanities Summer Seminar in which I participated in 1984, I owe the opportunity to pursue these concerns in a way that first led me to the study of Lacan's work. My thanks also to the NEH for this opportunity, as well as for a summer stipend in 1990 which allowed me to do much of the research for Chapter 1. A summer stipend in 1988 from the Kent State University Research Council enabled me to do substantial research for Chapter 2.

For permission to reprint material that originally appeared in their journals, I thank the editors and publishers of the *American Journal of Semiotics*, which first published a version of Chapter 3 titled "On the Interpellative Power of the Discourses of Ronald Reagan and Jesse Jackson" (7, no. 12 [1990]: 89–104) and a version of Chapter 5 titled "Writing and Imaging the Body in Pornography" (8, no. 4 [1991]: 105–30), and the Trustees of Boston University, who published a version of Chapter 7 titled "Ideology and Audience Response to Death in Keats's 'To Autumn'" in *Studies in Romanticism* 29, no. 4 (1990): 633–55.

Finally, I owe my deepest gratitude to my wife, Nancy, and my daughter, Elizabeth, whose love, affection, and patience have sustained me in and beyond this project.

MARK BRACHER

Kent, Ohio

Lacan, Discourse,
and Social Change

FOR A RESPONSE-CENTERED PSYCHOANALYTIC CULTURAL CRITICISM

The Aim of Cultural Criticism

All critical and interpretive activities, like the cultural artifacts on which they operate, ultimately take their value from the difference they make in people's lives. Historically, most cultural criticism has made little discernible difference, directly or indirectly, in the lives of most people. Nor have most critics been particularly interested in the question of whether—and if so, exactly how—either cultural criticism or the cultural artifacts critics focus on make a difference in people's lives. Although most critics have long acknowledged that certain cultural artifacts have historically made a substantial difference in the lives of some people—*The Sorrows of Young Werther*, for example, by precipitating a rash of suicides among European youth, or *Uncle Tom's Cabin* in striking a powerful blow for the abolition of slavery—critics have rarely focused on such effects. Even more rarely have they pursued the question of what effects cultural artifacts might have on those who read or study them today. Rather than encouraging systematic reflection on and intervention in the psychological, social, and political effects that various texts and discourses might produce in those who receive and consume them, humanities scholars have variously ignored, denied, or even celebrated the inconsequential nature of their own critical activity, resting content with platitudes about liberal education while perpetuating its relative inconsequentiality through curricula that emphasize consumption and analysis of literary texts as objects of knowledge. Nor has theory, for all the difference it has made

1

in the lives of some professional readers within the academy, had much effect on the lives of nonprofessionals (e. g., undergraduate students), for when it has entered the classroom as anything other than the unexamined prejudices of instructors, theory has usually functioned simply as one more means of attaining knowledge about texts (or contexts) as such—as another way of doing homage to verbal icons or of providing a sense of mastery for its practitioners—rather than as a means of revealing and intervening in the effects that texts and discourses can have on the human subjects who encounter them.

Although this state of affairs has by no means disappeared, significantly more humanities scholars and teachers are turning their attention away from texts as objects of investigation in and of themselves and toward the psychological and social significance of these texts. Reader-response approaches—such as Georges Poulet's and Wolfgang Iser's phenomenological analyses, Norman Holland's and David Bleich's psychoanalytic investigations, and Stanley Fish's affective stylistics, as well as Hans Robert Jauss's reception aesthetics, to name but a few of the more prominent examples—have made an important contribution in this regard, as has the increasingly sophisticated and growing body of Marxist theory and criticism, such as the work of Terry Eagleton and Fredric Jameson. Perhaps the most significant cause of this change of focus has been feminism, with its dual insistence on the political significance of art and on the social responsibility of the teacher and critic. As a result of these and other forces, the 1980s saw the emergence of a large and multifarious body of "cultural criticism" characterized in all its diverse forms by a concern with the social significance of culture and by a desire to make criticism itself socially significant.

This attempt to make the criticism of culture socially significant involves some basic changes in the aims, interests, and methods of criticism. As Mary Poovey observes, "Cultural criticism . . . changes the basic paradigm of our interpretive practice: as a consequence, the nature of the questions we ask changes, as do the forms in which they are posed and the kinds of answers that will be considered adequate or even relevant" (617). Jonathan Arac makes the same basic observation when he notes, "There are different ways of using cultural objects. To take this seriously requires that we reconceptualize the books and authors we study" ("Struggle" 127). As Giles Gunn explains, such criticism "reconceiv[es] texts not only as, in deconstructionist terms, undecidable objects, nor as, in variants of Marxist criticism, ideological templates, but also as sites of effective action, as scenes of forceful statement—'with consequences,' as [Edward] Said writes, 'that criticism should make it its business to reveal' " (16).

Ultimately, then, as critics are increasingly recognizing, making criticism socially significant means focusing precisely on the effects produced by cultural artifacts in the subjects who consume them. "For [cultural studies] to matter," Patrick Brantlinger declares, "the connections of texts and histories with our own lives and experiences must be recognized and become part of what we analyze" (*Crusoe's Footprints* ix). In Louis Montrose's formulation, cultural criticism should emphasize the capacity of specific discourses "to impact upon the social formation, to make things happen by shaping the subjectivities of social beings" (23). And in Poovey's words, a socially significant criticism is one that "describes culture as the ensemble of categories and signifying systems that provide the terms through which humans understand our world, from which we derive our identity, and in which we formulate and express desire" (617).

Terry Eagleton is even more explicit, insisting that if cultural criticism is to be socially beneficial, it must focus on the effects of discourses on those who consume them. "What would be specific to the kind of study I have in mind," Eagleton explains, "would be its concern for the kinds of *effects* which discourses produce, and how they produce them. Reading a zoology textbook to find out about giraffes is part of studying zoology, but reading it to see how its discourse is structured and organized, and examining what kind of effects these forms and devices produce in particular readers in actual situations, is a different kind of project" (205–6).

Richard Johnson, in perhaps the most systematic and comprehensive account of cultural criticism yet produced, also emphasizes the importance of focusing on effects. "The two key sets of questions to which cultural studies—rightly—continually returns," he remarks, have to do with the effects of cultural artifacts and discourses:

The first set concerns "popularity," pleasure and the *use value* of cultural forms. Why do some subjective forms acquire a popular force, become principles of living? . . . The second set of questions concerns the *outcomes* of cultural forms. Do these forms tend to reproduce existing forms of subordination or oppression? Do they hold down or contain social ambitions, defining wants too modestly? Or are they forms which permit a questioning of existing relations or a running beyond them in terms of desire? Do they point to alternative social arrangements? (72)

Displacements of the Aim of Cultural Criticism

Despite such widespread recognition of the need to focus on effects, however, cultural criticism has repressed this aim in practice and, as a result, has fallen significantly short of its goal of helping to transform society. According to some critics, the currently most prominent form of cultural criticism, new historicism, is successful only in giving its practitioners the illusion that their work is socially transformative, while in fact taking them in the opposite direction. Frank Lentricchia, for one, asserts that the supposed subversiveness of new historicism is limited to the aesthetic sphere and has no significant impact on larger social realities: "Hating a world that we never made, wanting to transform it, we settle for a holiday from reality, a safely sealed space reserved for the expression of aesthetic anarchy, a long weekend that defuses the radical implications of our unhappiness" (241). Alan Liu is equally skeptical about the supposed social efficacy of new historicism. According to Liu, "the only subject and action still possible" for the new historicist is "the critic . . . thinking about subversion" ("Power" 746).

The Formalist Displacement

One reason cultural criticism has so often failed to focus on effects is that its aim has been displaced by the formalist habit, which takes as its primary object of scrutiny the cultural icon per se rather than the process of reception of the artifact by human subjects. This formalist diversion has been noted by a number of critics. Catherine Gallagher observes that "the actual procedures of many new historicist analyses are often not very different from those of left formalists" (44). Elizabeth Fox-Genovese remarks of new historicists that "their considerable skills are devoted to the decoding of intertwining messages with little attention to sources or consequences" (221), while Alan Liu declares that new historicism "is our newest version of . . . formalism," whose objects of analysis "are finally only very delimited wholes—like schoolyards—designed to allow formal thought to play safely" ("Power" 739–40). Vincent Pecora finds that the new historicists' Geertzian emphasis on "local knowledge" "induces tendencies toward a new kind of formalism, trapping the critic inside the semiotic systems he or she would wish to explain. . . . The result is a fairly widespread trend in literary studies, not to make such studies more political or engaged, but to make them less so" ("Limits" 272).

The Historicist Displacement

A second instance of displacement from the analysis of effects is contextualization, which derives in part from the realization that the formalist focus on the cultural artifact per se is inadequate and that, if cultural criticism is to be socially significant, the artifact needs to be related to social realities outside itself. As Arac observes,

> The crucial contemporary agenda is elaborating the relations that join the nexus of classroom, discipline, and profession to such political areas as . . . gender, race, and class, as well as nation. . . . The current movement from "literary" to "cultural" studies, from "literary criticism" to "criticism," shows this direction. . . . Postmodern critics . . . can carry on a significant political activity by relating the concerns once enclosed within "literature" to a broader cultural sphere that is itself related to . . . the larger concerns of the state and economy. ("Introduction" xxx)

Such contextualization, however, actually explains very little, as Liu notes:

> Historical "context" and literary "text" . . . now confront each other and interpenetrate directly—the desideratum of the New Historicism— but with the disturbing corollary that they do so in what seems an unthought and unregulated manner. . . . A New Historicist paradigm holds up to view a historical context on one side, a literary text on the other, and, in between, a connection of pure nothing. ("Power" 742–43)

The unthought relation between text and context is covered over by the valorization of historicizing per se. Brantlinger, who remarks on the trend toward greater contextualization and historicization, defends the latter as an activity whose virtue he takes to be obvious:

> Calls for more and better contextualization in literary studies are certainly one symptom if not a cure for the current crisis in the humanities. Sometimes these calls seek little more than a return to old-fashioned historical scholarship. There is nothing wrong with this: despite attacks by deconstructionists and others on history, empiricism, reference, and seemingly plodding kinds of research, history will always be an absolutely essential activity. (*Crusoe's Footprints* 22)

But essential for what, precisely? What remains unthought is how historical contextualization can improve the lives of people who are alive today or those who have yet to be born. It is merely assumed that historicizing is somehow in and of itself socially beneficial.

Some critics, like Montrose, go beyond tacit assumption and explicitly assert that history is important for the lives of those in the present. "A primary task for the teacher of a new historical criticism," Montrose declares, "must be to disabuse students of the notion that history is what's over and done with; to bring them to understand that they themselves live *in* history, and that they *live* in history" (25). But this assertion, too, fails to indicate how studying history will make students' lives or anyone else's better.

Brook Thomas is a bit more specific. "The authority of a new historicism," he states, "rests on the faith that knowledge of the past matters for the present. . . . [S]o long as we believe that we are empowered by knowledge of our situation in the world and so long as we believe that that situation has in part been determined by the past, the most empowering study of the past will be the one that comes as close as possible to telling how it really was" ("New Historicism" 201). But this faith that knowledge of the past empowers us in the present depends on a sleight of hand that substitutes "knowledge of our situation" for knowledge of what has in part determined that situation. Such a view is like assuming that knowledge about how one came to be arrested and imprisoned is the same as knowledge of the intricacies of the legal system and thus of how one might obtain one's release. Knowledge of how one came to be imprisoned can, of course, in some cases be indispensable in obtaining one's release, but this is not always the case. And in any case, the knowledge crucial for empowerment is knowledge of one's situation in the present, without which no amount of knowledge of the past will be of use for materially ameliorating one's present situation.

The same criticism holds for Poovey's defense of historicization:[1]

> [The post-structuralist model] suggests that cultural critics should abandon the goal of devising "complete" interpretations of individual texts in favor of analyses that reconstruct the debates and practices in which texts initially participated. . . . This kind of analysis, then, will most typically have a historical component (although the kind of comparative work anthropologists do is also relevant). The historical component is important because one is initially trying to describe how and under what determinant conditions entities and concepts acquired coherence. (23)

What seems valuable about the historical approach as conceived by Poovey is not the historical nature of the knowledge that it produces but rather (as indicated by her parenthetical gesture toward comparativism) the awareness of alternative subject positions—modes of being, conceptual categories, values, and so on—that the study of history can provide.

This search for alternative subject positions is also behind Donna Przybylowicz's assertion that "it is important to stress an historical approach to the question of gender and class" (269). "It is the critic's task," Przybylowicz explains, "to investigate the transformative possibilities of exposing hidden ideologies or suppressed voices" (267). Once again, however, we are left without an answer to the question of why texts from the past should necessarily be the best source of viable alternative subject positions for subjects alive today (or in the future). And even if they were the best source, we would still need to determine what such texts could do to get people to assume (or reject) these alternative positions. In short, identifying forms of power in the past does not *necessarily* tell us anything about how oppression and injustice are operating in the present, and even if it does tell us something about oppression and injustice in the present, that knowledge by itself doesn't necessarily change things for the better.[2]

---

[1]See also Giles Gunn (5) and David R. Shumway (86).

[2]For change to occur, analysis of collective history, like the analysis of personal history in psychoanalysis, would have to lead to the reexperiencing of past conflicts in the present, through transference. Historicist cultural criticism must provide engagement of

The Epistemological Displacement

A third major displacement that has befallen contemporary cultural criticism is a diversion present not only in formalist and contextualist/historicist criticism but in most of the relatively rare analyses of reception as well. This displacement is the focus on knowledge, which is assumed to be virtually the sole factor in both text and subject that is socially significant. The prevailing assumptions in cultural criticism are that a subject position is basically reducible to knowledge and that this knowledge is derived from the representations that a subject encounters. Although the first assumption is usually tacit, it is sometimes indicated quite clearly, such as in Nancy Hartsock's formulation of a basic goal of cultural criticism. "The question I want to address," Hartsock states, "is what sorts of *subjectivities*—in this case, oppositional *consciousnesses*—can grow out of these experiences [of being marginalized and devalued]? Put differently, what are the *epistemological features* characteristic of marked as opposed to fictionally unmarked subjectivities?" (24; emphasis added). Here subjectivity is reduced to consciousness and thence to "epistemological features." This reduction of subjectivity to cognition is also present in much reception theory and reader-response criticism. It is found, for instance, in Jauss's notion that a work that promotes social change does so by frustrating one's expectations and thus "compell[ing] one to a new perception of things" (41). A similar reduction occurs in Iser's focus on the reader's activity of filling in gaps in narrative, description, and characterization.

The second assumption, often more explicit, is that the "epistemological features" (or knowledge) that supposedly determine subjectivity are produced by representation. Pecora observes, for example, that new historicism "emphasizes the degree to which representation . . . itself plays a formative, determining social role" ("Limits" 243).[3] In Judith Newton's words, "Those engaged in 'new historicism,' assume, finally, that representation 'makes things happen' by 'shaping

---

and insight into the present identities and desires of human subjects in order for it to have the capacity of promoting collective psychological change and thereby social and political change.

[3]The passage continues as follows: "The question of 'representation' is thus crucial to the argument, but even a brief glance at new historicist writings will reveal a wide divergence in the uses to which this term is put. In the 'cultural materialism' of certain English critics . . . , cultural representation works primarily, even simultaneously, as

human consciousness'" (152). Montrose asserts the importance of representations by explaining that "representations of the world in written discourse are engaged in constructing the world, in shaping the modalities of social reality, and in accommodating their writers, performers, readers, and audiences to multiple and shifting subject positions within the world they both constitute and inhabit" (16).

If one assumes, in this manner, that representation is the central factor in the effect that culture has on human subjectivity, it follows, as Brantlinger explains, that the primary task of cultural criticism is to identify and correct misrepresentations:

> As Said contends, understanding and working to change the ideological processes of *misrepresentation* are the main tasks of the "oppositional critic." Most accounts of the shift from literary to cultural criticism in both U.S. and British universities stress analyzing and rectifying the dominant culture's *misrepresentations* of workers, women, Afro-Americans, and other "subaltern" groups. . . . [The notion of hegemony] suggests that culture is a field of struggle in which the stakes are accurate, just, and direct *representation* by groups and individuals instead of *misrepresentations* by others. Better than "ideology," . . . "*representation*" is a term which makes room for the fact that there are degrees of justice and accuracy as well as of distortion and illusion in all forms of culture. . . . The particular forms of *mis*representation or ideology can then be distinguished by comparison with alternative forms of more accurate or more truthful *representation*. *The role of the cultural critic is to make such distinctions.* (112, 104; all emphasis added)

This focus on (mis)representation not only entails a return to a more limited notion of ideology as false consciousness—as a discrepancy between awareness and reality—it also implies that such a false consciousness can be induced merely by presenting consciousness with distorted pictures of reality. The focus on epistemology is thus doubly

---

ideological 'consolidation, subversion and containment.' . . . Yet in much American new historicism, . . . 'representation' has become a code word for the denial that any distinction whatsoever exists between a non-signifying 'real' and some realm of cultural production that 'reflects,' or reflects upon, it. . . . [S]ince everything is always already 'representation,' representation is where all the 'real' action has been all along" (Pecora, "Limits" 243–44). Thus although critics use the term 'representation' in different ways, each type of representation refers to the fact that representation is always essentially misrepresentation.

misleading. In the first place, it ignores important elements of subjectivity (ideals, values, fantasy, desire, drives, and jouissance) that are just as essential in determining a subject position as knowledge is. And in the second place, it overlooks important interpellative forces of the text or discourse that cannot be reduced to a function of representation/misrepresentation. Moreover, as Gunn notes in criticizing Sacvan Bercovitch, such a view "conflates the notion of ideology, or political templates for *changing* reality, with the concept of worldview, or metaphysical templates for *describing* reality" (9; emphasis added). In short, pointing out misrepresentations does not necessarily even identify the major forces of interpellation, much less constitute a significant intervention in those forces.

The Role of Psychoanalysis in Cultural Criticism

But if the formalist, historicist, and epistemological biases so clearly divert cultural criticism from its professed aim of being socially significant, why, we might ask, have they persisted? There are several reasons, I think. One is professional inertia: individuals and institutions continue to produce and to support the kinds of analysis that they are familiar with and most adept at, and which thus provide the sense of mastery and narcissistic satisfaction that is one of the rewards of all intellectual activity. Another reason is the partial efficacy of these foci: the properties of a text, including its representations and its contexts, obviously play an essential role in the process of reception, and thus formalist, historicist, and epistemological concerns are by no means irrelevant to the effects cultural artifacts produce on human subjects. But perhaps the most significant reason for the persistence of these diversions is the existence of a crucial gap in our theory of culture. As Richard Johnson notes, there are four major aspects or moments of culture: (1) the moment of production (e.g., writing a poem and publishing it); (2) the product produced (the "text"); (3) the reception or consumption of the product ("reading"), and (4) "lived culture" (i.e., the meanings, values, identities, enjoyments, desires, and so on of the human subjects who inhabit a given culture). In practice, however, Johnson observes, only three of these aspects tend to be analyzed: production, text, and lived culture (71). What is largely left out of account in current cultural criticism is the moment of reading, the reception of cultural artifacts and its effect on lived culture. The ultimate reason for this crucial omission, Johnson contends, is "the absence of an adequate post-structuralist (or should I say post–post-structuralist) *theory of subjectivity*" (63).[4]

The most pressing need of cultural criticism is thus for a theory of subjectivity that can explain how cultural artifacts affect people. Johnson and others have noted the great potential, as yet unrealized, of psychoanalysis to provide such a theory. As Johnson puts it, "There is a huge potentiality, for cultural studies, in the critical use of Freudian categories" (68). Eagleton also comments on the potential of psychoanalysis for cultural criticism, a potential he locates in the fact that "psychoanalysis is a science committed to the emancipation of human beings from what frustrates their fulfilment and well-being [and thus] . . . is a theory at the service of a transformative practice, and to that extent has parallels with radical politics" (192).[5]

Similarly, Michael Ryan has noted the value of the unique orientation of what he refers to as "psychotherapy" toward a transformative practice, and he suggests that this uniqueness puts psychotherapy in position to function as a kind of paradigm for cultural criticism. "Psychotherapy," Ryan observes, "is a good example of how scientific knowledge can be directly practical. The therapeutic cure occurs through an increase of knowledge and through the practice of discovering and communicating knowledge" (101). Given this orientation of psychotherapy, Ryan proposes to "take psychotherapy as a model" for a "critical cultural science": "as in psychotherapy, such a science would seek to increase knowledge not for the sake of expanding the academic inventory, but instead for the sake of having the direct practical effect of helping to bring about what for want of a better word

4See also Brantlinger *Crusoe's Footprints* (84).

5Eagleton goes on to note: "The problems of literary value and pleasure would seem to lie somewhere at the juncture of psychoanalysis, linguistics, and ideology, and little work has been done here as yet. We know enough, however, to suspect that it is a good deal more possible to say why someone enjoys certain arrangements of words than conventional literary criticism has believed. More importantly, it is possible that by a fuller understanding of the pleasures and displeasures readers reap from literature, a modest but significant light may be cast on some rather more pressing problems of happiness and misery" (192–93). "One reason why we need to enquire into the dynamics of pleasure and unpleasure," Eagleton continues, "is because we need to know how much repression and deferred fulfilment a society is likely to tolerate; how it is that desire can be switched from ends that we would value to ends which trivialize and degrade it" (192–93).

might be called a 'cure,' and by that I mean the construction of a good society" (101–2). What is crucial in Ryan's observations is the recognition that knowledge must be taken as a *means* of promoting change, rather than as an end in itself. Knowledge about the properties of texts (formalism) or about historical contexts (historicism) is valuable only if it can be used to promote beneficial social change.

The Contribution of Lacanian Theory

My conviction is that Lacanian theory can provide the sort of account of subjectivity that cultural criticism needs. Lacan's theory of subjectivity is capable of serving as a foundation for the kind of socially significant criticism so many critics are calling for. It offers a comprehensive model of the human subject that includes what is in my view the fullest account available of the various roles that language and discourse play in the psychic economy and thereby in human affairs in general. Other theories, such as semiotics, offer a richer topography of the phenomena of language and discourse, but these systems are not as helpful as Lacanian theory when it comes to explaining how linguistic and discursive phenomena affect specific elements of subjectivity and thus *move* people. Umberto Eco's *Theory of Semiotics* and Robert Hodge and Gunther Kress's *Social Semiotics*, for instance, are valuable for understanding certain dimensions of discourse as such but have less to offer when it comes to explaining the psychological impact of the multifarious elements and aspects of discourse they identify.

Other psychoanalytic theories of language and discourse are also limited. Of such theories, the examples of Julia Kristeva and Holland are particularly instructive. Students of Kristeva may find it puzzling that I have chosen to develop my model on the basis of Lacan's work rather than Kristeva's, when the concerns of the latter (especially in her early works, such as *Revolution in Poetic Language*) are much closer to my own than Lacan's are. The reason is that I have found Lacan to offer a richer array of conceptual tools and materials for constructing a model of the multiplicity of ways in which discourses intervene in and at times alter subjectivity. The conceptual tools employed by Kristeva are limited on several counts. First, only rarely does she focus on the *reception* of discourse: her focus is usually on the speaking subject rather than on the receiving subject. Second, her discussion of the effects of discourse on subjectivity is limited largely to the way in which certain discourses can supposedly disrupt or destroy a subject's established identity, an effect that is both too vague and too sanguine, in my view. I am thus unable to follow Kristeva's path because she is concerned with a rather limited array of effects, because she does not examine the microscopic level of the relations between text and subjectivity that produce these effects, and because her conclusion that these effects are immediately or even necessarily revolutionary is questionable.

The case of Holland is in some respects similar. In general, I have felt that accounts based in Lacanian theory more comprehensively explain the full range and specificity of discursive elements and subjective factors as they interact when subjects consume cultural artifacts. In addition, I find Holland's early work (as articulated in *The Dynamics of Literary Response*) flawed by what Johnson describes as the "cost" exacted by many present psychoanalytic attempts to "bridge text and reader": "the radical simplification of the social subject, reducing him or her to the original, naked, infant needs" (68). Holland's later works (for example, *The I, Poems in Persons*, and *Five Readers Reading*) are characterized by a different and in some ways even more problematic "radical simplification of the social subject": Holland's almost exclusive focus on the idiosyncratic elements of individual responses and the reader's transformation of texts and consequent replication of the reader's established identity, to the exclusion of texts' formation or transformation of readers. Lacan's account of subjectivity, in contrast, accords great emphasis to the social, collective aspects of subjectivity, to the point that the individual and the social cannot be separated.[6] As Jacques-Alain Miller has noted, Lacan's understanding of the role played by what he calls the Other in the formation of the subject makes the Lacanian subject social in its very foundations.

In short, because it best explains how discourse affects the collective aspects of subjects' subjective economies (and hence also their actions), Lacanian theory offers the possibility of understanding and intervening in the social effects of culture with considerably more efficacy than other theories have enabled us to do. This perception has led me to

[6]Lacan's emphasizing social and collective aspects of subjectivity is, of course, not the same as claiming that all subjects are identical or that subjects have no dimension of singularity. Lacan emphasized the singular, individual aspect of subjectivity through his elaboration of the concept of the symptom, which involves the unique ways in which a subject has historically found meaning and enjoyment.

employ Lacanian theory as the means of pursuing my objectives in this book. I do not mean to imply that other approaches could not also be profitably employed to this end, nor do I mean to present these reflections as the rudiments of some sort of deductive argument designed to convince other critics of Lacan's superiority in this regard. The proof, after all, is in the pudding, and readers will judge for themselves, after reading this book, whether the choice of a Lacanian framework has been a judicious one.

Prospectus

My aim, then, is first to sketch (in Part I) some of the basic contours of Lacanian theory, but detailing and elaborating only those aspects of it which seem to me to be most crucial for understanding the effects that cultural artifacts and discourses have on human subjects. In Chapter 1 I attempt to account for the ways in which discourses interpellate subjects by operating on and through subjects' desires and identifications in the three registers that Lacan designates as Symbolic, Imaginary, and Real. More specifically, in this chapter I explain and exemplify how signifiers, images, and fantasies can each operate in such a way as to elicit from an audience four different modes of desire (passive narcissistic, active narcissistic, active anaclitic, and passive anaclitic), one of which (the active narcissistic) produces identifications. Explanations and examples are provided to indicate how these twelve different forms of desire operate within discourse in order to exercise an interpellative force on the subjective economy of those who receive the discourse.

In Chapter 2 I endeavor to explain how these discursive forces of identification and desire operate—in different ways, according to four different structures of discourse identified by Lacan—to produce different types of psychological effects. These different structures of discourse and their respective forms of psychological change are correlated with different modes of cultural criticism. I conclude the chapter by sketching out an analytic strategy for a discourse of cultural criticism modeled on the structure of the discourse of the Analyst that promises to be most effective in promoting collective psychological change and thereby social change.

In Part II, I apply this analytic strategy to a variety of texts and discourses from both "high" and popular culture, including discourses that have overt political aims and demonstrable political results, as well as literary discourses the political significance of which has been in dispute. My project in these analyses is not to offer a reading of the works in question but rather to read certain specific *readings* of these texts in such a way as to explain the psychological impact of the discourses on readers who have responded in the particular manner that I happen to be investigating. I am thus concerned neither with purely idiosyncratic aspects of response to a given work nor with universal responses (impossible to find) but rather with a cluster of responses shared by a large enough group of people so that these responses can be deemed socially significant.

In Chapter 3, I analyze how heterosexual men are aroused by pornography, a discourse that is the subject of heated debate concerning its social significance. The threefold aim of this analysis is to reveal the specific desires through which pornography operates on heterosexual men (traditionally the primary audience for pornography), the subjective changes produced by this operation, and the social and political ramifications of these subjective changes.

In Chapter 4, I examine the way antiabortionist discourse operates on the desires of those who embrace its cause. I attempt to explain what forces are driving those who crusade against abortion, and what more general psychological and social effects are produced by these forces.

In Chapter 5, I look at how the political campaign speeches of Ronald Reagan and Jesse Jackson were able to arouse such passionate responses in the two large groups of people who embraced each of these very different candidates, and I explain the respective subject positions to which those who embraced each candidate were interpellated.

In Chapters 6 and 7, I analyze certain typical responses, and the accompanying psychological effects and consequent political ramifications, promoted by two "high culture" classics, Joseph Conrad's *Heart of Darkness* and John Keats's "To Autumn." The major ideological forces involved here, I argue, have been overlooked by critics, even those purporting to critique the ideologies of these works. By examining crucial common denominators in a wide range of critical responses, I attempt to demonstrate that the most common responses indicate that these works operate on the subjective economies of readers in ways that have more profound and troubling ideological consequences than have heretofore been recognized.

The trajectory of these analyses as a group is at once from the present to the past, from "low" culture to "high" culture, from discourses evoking obvious (even physical) responses to those producing less overt and more purely mental responses, and from overtly ideological to supposedly more ideologically neutral forms of discourse. My aim in arranging the analyses in this order is to suggest how some of the more disturbing forces operating in the more overtly ideological "low culture" discourses being produced today (particularly the patriarchal thrusts of pornography, antiabortionist propaganda, and political demagoguery) are underwritten by some of the "great works" that are often assumed to be empowering and ennobling rather than oppressive and degrading, but which, analysis reveals, function for many readers to promote the institution of what Lacan called the paternal metaphor.

It is my conviction that the type of cultural criticism formulated and enacted in these pages can aid literary studies in particular and humanistic studies in general as they venture further from their ivory towers and engage in a struggle where the stakes are not merely interpretive dominance and academic prestige but the more substantial sufferings and enjoyments of human beings in the world at large.

PART I

THEORY

CHAPTER ONE

DESIRE IN DISCOURSE

Desire in Discourse

If culture plays a role in social change, or in resistance to change, it does so largely by means of desire. Insofar as a cultural phenomenon succeeds in interpellating subjects—that is, in summoning them to assume a certain subjective (dis)position—it does so by evoking some form of desire or by promising satisfaction of some desire. It is thus desire rather than knowledge that must become the focal point of cultural criticism if we are to understand how cultural phenomena move people.[1] And if we hope to intervene in the interpellative forces of culture, we must understand, first, the various forms and roles of desire in the subjective economy and, second, the various means by which culture operates on and through these different forms of desire.

The key to understanding desire in the subjective economy and in its cultural aspect can be found in Lacan's dictum that desire is the desire of the Other. Three crucial ambiguities in this formulation index three bases for distinction within the field of desire.[2] First, "desire" can take the form of either the desire to *be* or the desire to *have*, corresponding

[1]Knowledge is often an important factor in such motivation; indeed, it is always at least implicit in desire and jouissance. But knowledge cannot account for the position assumed by subjects within that knowledge, for position within knowledge is a function of identification or desire, or the ground of desire: being and its lack.

[2]The three ambiguities and the resulting taxonomy of desire that I am presenting here were not developed systematically by Lacan in each of the three registers. Each of the three ambiguities in his formula for desire was, however, emphasized and elaborated on by Lacan himself in various ways and in various contexts. His distinction among Imagin-

to Freud's distinction between narcissistic and anaclitic libido.[3] The narcissistic form of desire manifests itself as love and identification, while the anaclitic form involves desire for a jouissance that is fundamentally indifferent—and often even inimical—to the well-being both of oneself and of the other person. Second, the word "of" functions in Lacan's formulation as both subjective genitive and objective genitive, indicating that the Other can be either the subject or the object of desire, a distinction that Freud formulated as the difference between active and passive aims of the libido.[4] And third, "the Other" can be either the image of another person in the Imaginary register, or the code constituting the Symbolic order, or the Other Sex and/or the object *a* of the Real. The respective objects of desire in these three registers are thus images, signifiers, and instances of that magical object or special substance that Lacan calls the object *a*. We can thus identify twelve basic forms of desire operating in discourse, four in each of Lacan's three registers:

1. Passive narcissistic desire. One can desire to be the object of the Other's love (or the Other's admiration, idealization, or recognition).
2. Active narcissistic desire. One can desire to become the Other—a desire of which identification is one form and love or devotion is another.

---

ary other, Symbolic Other, and Real Other is, of course, well known. The distinction between being and having is developed by Lacan in the context of the Symbolic phallus, where the "masculine" position is characterized by having the phallus and the "feminine" by being the phallus (see *Selection* 281–91). This distinction corresponds to the opposition Freud establishes between anaclitic and narcissistic libido (see *Standard Edition* 14:73–102). The distinction between active and passive is taken over by Lacan directly from Freud (see *SE* 14:133–34, 126–37) and is developed most fully in his discussion of fantasy, $ \diamond a$, where the subject can assume either the position of the active, desiring subject ($) or the passive object (*a*), of the Other's desire.

[3] In his essay "On Narcissism," Freud speaks of "an antithesis between ego-libido and object-libido[:] [t]he more of the one is employed, the more the other becomes depleted" (*SE* 14:76). Narcissism, or the direction of libido to the ego, is seen as being primary: "there [is] an original libidinal cathexis of the ego, from which some is later given off to objects, but which fundamentally persists and is related to the object-cathexes much as the body of an amoeba is related to the pseudopodia which it puts out" (*SE* 14:75). Freud goes on to characterize active anaclitic or attachment "object-love" as typically masculine, and passive narcissistic object-love as typically feminine (88–89), although he also admits "that there are quite a number of women who love according to the masculine type" (89). For a discussion of the complex interrelations of narcissistic desire, identification, and anaclitic desire, see *SE* 14:237–58.

[4] See *SE* 14:126–27, 133–34.

3. Active anaclitic desire. One can desire to possess the Other as a means of jouissance.
4. Passive anaclitic desire. One can desire to be desired or possessed by the Other as the object of the Other's jouissance.

Identification in Discourse

The second form of desire indicated here, identification, is particularly important in culture and deserves some elaboration before we consider the various types of desire in their specific manifestations in the three registers of subjectivity. For identification is one of the major ways in which subjects are interpellated and their subjectivities changed by discourse. That identification plays a significant role in audience response is at one level quite obvious and widely acknowledged: people commonly speak of identifying with a particular character when they read a story or watch a movie. That such identification can have important social consequences is also a familiar notion, constituting as it does the basis of censorship from Plato to contemporary parents and educators concerned about television violence. Nor have such identifications been seen as only negative. Percy Bysshe Shelley, for example, asserted that "the sentiments of the auditors must have been refined and enlarged by a sympathy with [Homer's characters], until from admiring they imitated, and from imitation they *identified* themselves with the objects of their admiration," with the result that "the poems of Homer and his contemporaries . . . were the elements of that social system which is the column upon which all succeeding civilization has reposed" (117; emphasis added).[5]

But despite a venerable tradition asserting the importance of identification in the reception of discourse, understanding has been lacking

[5]More recently, Hans Robert Jauss has argued that social effects of art overlooked by formalist and Marxist approaches can be profitably illuminated by examining the various identifications that specific works or discourses elicit from their audiences (153–54). To this end, Jauss proposes a model of analysis consisting of five "interaction patterns of identification with the hero" (159) based on five different "modalities of reception" (154). Jauss cautions, however, that his model is "provisional" and that it lacks "the foundation that a theory of the emotions would give it" (158). He observes that although one might logically expect psychoanalysis to provide such a foundation, "the practitioners of [psychoanalysis] feel that the problem of identification has been only inadequately solved and the question of identification under conditions of the aesthetic attitude barely touched upon" (158).

concerning three major questions regarding its operation: (1) precisely what elements of a discourse promote identification in an audience, (2) what psychological processes or structures are involved in identification, and (3) what lasting changes are promoted in the subjective economy of those who engage in identification? Despite Shelley's observations, made over a century and a half ago, the analysis of literature, and of discourse in general, still lacks an adequate account of the role that language plays in forming the foundational, structural identifications that constitute the basis of our identities and producing ad hoc identifications with characters or positions in discourse, identifications that can prompt us to feel or act in certain ways and that can also re-form or alter our foundational, structural identifications and thus change our subjectivity and our behavior as well.

Lacan's explanation of the roles played by identification and desire in the constitution and functioning of subjectivity provides a foundation for addressing this deficiency. When Lacan speaks of identification in relation to desire, he often emphasizes the conflictual nature of the two phenomena: when an identification becomes established as our identity, it functions to repress all desires that are incongruent with this identity. But as Lacan himself indicates, identifications also function as both causes and effects of desire. Their role as the cause of desire can be seen in the way subjects strive to fully actualize the qualities they have identified with, while their role as the effect of desire can be seen from the fact that identifications are always *motivated*—that is, they respond to a want-of-being. Given this close interaction between desire and identification, I have decided to treat identification as a mode of desire, since it is this active, dynamic aspect of identification that is crucial to interpellation.[6]

Interpellation through Master Signifiers

Identification, along with the other forms of desire, operates in each of the three registers of subjectivity: Symbolic, Imaginary, and Real.[7] In

[6]The account of identification included here is thus by no means meant to be a comprehensive sketch of Lacan's thinking on the subject; by limiting myself to a discussion of those aspects of identification that play a central role in interpellation and thus in my argument, I must leave aside a wealth of material that could easily be (and has been, in fact) the subject of an entire book (see, for example, *Les identifications et le désir*).

[7]These three registers can be distinguished from each other by their different relations to language. The Symbolic order refers to that dimension of the human subject essen-

culture, these three registers manifest themselves, respectively, in signifiers, images, and fantasies. Of the three, it is the signifier that holds
the key to desire. As Lacan puts it, "It is as a derivation of the signifying chain that the channel of desire flows" (*Ecrits: A Selection* 259).
The question then becomes, how exactly does the signifying chain,
based in the Symbolic Other, operate with desire? First, signifiers
themselves functions as the objects of desire—in four basic ways,
deriving from the four modes of desire identified above.

Passive narcissistic desires of the Symbolic order involve the wish
that the Symbolic Other—the ultimate authority or source of meaning
constituted by the Symbolic order and epitomized in our notions of
Nature, Society, God, and so on—loves the subject in some way, that
is, values, cares about, recognizes, or even just takes account of the
subject. And subjects are loved by the Symbolic Other because of the
signifier they embody, as indicated, for example, in the belief that God
loves "the meek," in the notion that Nature loves "the wise and pure"
(Coleridge, "Dejection"), and in the conviction that Society (i.e., "everybody") loves "a winner." Political and religious discourses frequently offer love or recognition (which Lacan says is the original
object of desire) as a means of enticing subjects to assume a specific
position. Obvious instances of such love or recognition can be found in
the Christian affirmation, "God loves you"; in the military's assertion,
"Uncle Sam wants you"; and in the poet's declaration that "Nature
never did betray / The heart that loved her" (Wordsworth, "Tintern
Abbey," lines 122–23).

Lacan calls such identity-bearing words "master signifiers." The
way in which such signifiers function as bearers of our identity can
easily be seen from our reactions when someone attempts either to
damage one of our identity-bearing signifiers (e.g., disparages a signifier bearing our familial, national, ethnic, racial, or sexual identity)
or to deprive us of one of these signifiers (e.g., by calling us a girl if we
are a boy or vice versa.[8] Master signifiers arise from "*m'être à moi-*

tially identical to language—the subject insofar as it has identified with certain
signifiers—while the Imaginary and Real registers refer, respectively, to what are, in a
certain logical sense, preverbal and postverbal aspects of the subject. The Imaginary is
constituted by schemata of memory and cognition that are dominant before the child
learns to speak, while the Real in the subjective economy is constituted by those aspects
of the subject's being that have been excluded from the categories of language.

[8]The constitutive effect of the Symbolic order is produced well before a child learns to
speak or even understand language; in fact, it begins even before birth. The meaning
language gives, for instance, to "male" and "female," structures and directs the

même" (XVII 60),[9] from the urge to master (*maître*) myself by "being myself" (*m'être*) to myself—to have an identity in which I can recognize myself and be encountered and recognized by others. The result of this urge is the establishment of a cluster of master signifiers as the ego ideal, which originates in the child's attempt to be desired and loved— that is, recognized (passive narcissistic desire)—by the Other (which at the beginning of life is typically the mother, then both parents, later one's peers, and finally any number of bodies or figures of authority, including God, Society, and Nature). Being this signifier allows subjects to feel good about themselves and also provides the sense of temporal continuity and coherence essential to identity, since the signifier can be reproduced and communicated.[10]

Master signifiers are thus one of the main elements that give discourse purchase on a subject. Since master signifiers are any signifiers that a subject has invested his or her identity in—any signifiers that the subject has identified with (or against) and which thus constitute powerful positive (or negative) values—they are what make a message meaningful, what make it have an impact rather than being like a foreign language that one cannot understand. They are, as Lacan puts it, what make a discourse readable (XVII 218). This readability derives

---

thoughts, feelings, perceptions, and hence actions of the various caretakers through whom the infant gains its first (preverbal) experience of itself and the world. Thus even though the infant cannot speak or even understand the language, that language has already structured the infant's experience via the effect it has on the behavior of the infant's caretakers. In addition, there are stories—familial and cultural "myths," as Lacan calls them—that surround the child from before birth and serve to fix the child, in the minds of the family and the community at large, at certain positions in the Symbolic order. These include various cultural and familial discourses that establish certain subject positions as possible for human habitation and situate the child in some of these possible positions rather than others—not only directly but also indirectly, by situating the persons the child identifies with and the persons whose behavior has a formative impact on the child.

[9]Citations with roman numerals refer to Lacan's seminars. Seminars I, II, and XI have been translated and published in English, the latter as *The Four Fundamental Concepts of Psychoanalysis.* Seminars III, VII, and XVII have been published in French but not yet in English. The English in these cases is my own translation, as it is in the cases of Seminars VI and IX, which have not yet been officially published in French. Citations referring to *Ecrits* designate my own translations from the French edition, while citations referring to *Selection* are from the English *Ecrits: A Selection.*

[10]Lacan emphasizes the manner in which the ego ideal produces a sense both of permanence and self-esteem in his description of the primordial form of the ego ideal, the "unique-unifying trait" (*trait unaire*). The *trait unaire,* the "simplest form" of the signifier (IX 72), is a kind of notch that the Other makes on the child (e.g., through

from the fact that, whereas other terms and the values and assumptions they bear may be challenged by one who receives a message, master signifiers are simply accepted as having a value or validity that goes without saying. Senders of messages treat master signifiers in a similar manner: they use them as the last word, the bottom line, the term that anchors, explains, or justifies the claims or demands contained in the message.

Master signifiers are able to exert such force in messages because of the role they play in structuring the subject—specifically in giving the subject a sense of identity and direction. But the identity-bearing function of master signifiers is ultimately not qualitatively different from the function of any other signifier, for "a signifier," Lacan says, "is that which represents a subject for another signifier" (XI 207). The word "represent" here means not "to be a represen*tation*, depiction, or portrayal of the subject" but rather "to be the subject's represen*tative*, stand-in, or avatar." Just as a nation can achieve the unity and identity necessary for conducting its affairs with other nations only through its ambassadors, envoys, or elected officials—i.e., through its representatives—so too can an individual subject attain a unity and identity only through its representatives: signifiers.

The ramifications of this notion of the signifier for cultural studies are great. If, when I encounter another human subject, it is really our representatives, our signifiers, that are communicating and negotiating with each other, then whenever these representatives get together, my fate as a subject is in some way at stake. That is, what happens to our sense of being or identity is determined to a large degree by what happens to those signifiers that represent us—our master signifiers—particularly the alliances they form with and the wars they wage on other signifiers.

---

approbation or disapprobation) when the Other gets (or misses) its target in relation to the child (XI 256). This notch provides the means for that counting, that repetition of the same (with a difference) that is at the basis of the subject's sense of identity. The human subject, that is, as a phenomenon having some sort of identity from one moment to the next, is constituted by the effect of the signifier, the signifier serving to mark a certain state of affairs as the repetition of an earlier state of affairs. And repetition of the *trait unaire* as the subject's identity is the motive force beneath the workings of both conscious and unconscious systems: "What the subject seeks at the level of both these systems is the identity of thoughts; what philosophy attempts, the organization of our world, the efforts of logic—all are properly speaking to reduce the diverse to the identical, to identify thought with thought" (VI 155).

A basic desire motivating all subjects in their reception of culture is thus the passive narcissistic desire of having these identity-bearing signifiers repeated. Such attempts at repetition of our master signifiers are operating continuously, not only in all of our verbal discourse but in our other behavior as well. We can see these attempts at repetition most clearly when we behave in ways that embody these master signifiers (e.g., "masculine" or "feminine," "fair" or "honest," "smart," "pretty," or "tough,") and thus elicit, either tacitly or expressly, the Other's recognition. Common collective master signifiers would include, in religious discourse, words like "God," "Satan," "sin," "heaven," and "hell," and in political discourse, terms such as "American," "freedom," "democracy," and "communism."[11] Such signifiers, as well as our proper name, give us a sense of substance, significance, and well-being when we manage to ally ourselves with them (or oppose ourselves to them) in the eyes of the Other, satisfying our passive narcissistic Symbolic-order desires.

Master signifiers thus account for much of the interpellative force, both immediate and enduring, that discourses have. The first major way that culture operates on our Symbolic-order desire is by either allowing or preventing us from enjoying the passive narcissistic gratification of dwelling within circuits of discourse controlled by our master signifiers. As we have seen, what we seek is the repeated dominance of those signifiers that represent us. Discourses that offer this dominance usually give us a sense of security and well-being, the sense that we have a definite identity, that we are significant, that our existence matters. Discourses that fail to provide a reassuring encounter with our representatives tend, in contrast, to evoke feelings of alienation and anxiety and responses of aggression—including rejection of the discourse, or indifference toward it. This effect is most easily observed in our responses to overt insults, which often bear quite directly on our sexual, racial, ethnic, religious, class, or political identifications.

The fact that what the Symbolic Other loves is always (implicitly, at least) a signifier (e.g., the "American," the "patriot," the "meek")

---

[11]Lacan also indicates that the names of well-known authors function as master signifiers (XVII 201), and he observes that one well-known author, Freud, produced a number of master signifiers, which analysts can't get clear of. "It is not so much Freud that they hold on to," Lacan observes, "as a certain number of master signifiers: the unconscious, seduction, trauma, fantasy, the ego, etc." (XVII 115).

leads the subject to *active narcissistic desire*, that is, to identification. Passive narcissistic desire for recognition and approval by the Symbolic Other, that is, often entails the active narcissistic desire to identify with the Symbolic Other to the extent of embodying certain signifiers given pride of place in the code constituting this Other. To achieve such recognition and the sense of identity that accompanies it, the child identifies with and thus attempts to embody those signifiers (qualities or attributes) valued by the Other and imposed by the Other's approbation. A girl, for example, who is reprimanded for acting "like a baby" and praised for being "a big girl" will seek (all other factors being equal) activities, situations, and objects that allow her to embody the latter signifier and escape the former, and she will identify with other subjects who have succeeded in winning the Symbolic Other's love and recognition.

Since the Symbolic Other extends beyond individual authority figures and is ultimately coextensive with the Symbolic order itself, the signifiers one desires to embody in order to achieve recognition by the Other are, in the final analysis, those signifiers given pride of place by the system of language as such. And the subject desires to embody not only the operative signifier itself (such as "manly") but also any other signifier bearing a metonymic or metaphoric relation to the operative signifier—any signifier that functions as a synonym, attribute, or even associate of the master signifier (e.g., "strong," "virile," and "big" as attributes of "man"). That is, we gravitate (in active narcissistic desire) toward positions and identify with persons, characters, and images linked with one or more of the master signifiers constituting our ego ideal. One important manifestation of this phenomenon at a collective level can be seen in the way we often identify almost automatically with athletes or soldiers bearing the insignia of our nationality, whether or not we would find the individuals bearing these insignias worthy of support if the insignias were absent.

These observations indicate the second major way in which culture operates with master signifiers: defining certain master signifiers in terms of (or in opposition to) the specific attributes or actions embodied in other, secondary signifiers, and thus evoking the desire to identify with —that is, to embody—these secondary signifiers as a way of attaining the recognition offered by the master signifiers to which they are attached. Discourses that get us to change our position are discourses that coerce us to give up some of our representatives and/or embrace new ones—often in order to retain and solidify the services of others that are even more central to our identity.

This process can be seen clearly in a text such as Martin Luther King's "Letter from Birmingham Jail," where King deftly subverts identifications that his audience has *against* certain key signifiers—with which they have characterized King—by linking (a process that Lacan refers to as metonymy) these signifiers with signifiers that the audience has identified even more strongly *with*. For example, acknowledging that his audience is opposed to his strategy of creating tension in Birmingham, King declares, "I am not afraid of the word 'tension.'" He then proceeds to undermine the opposition between the word "tension" and the ego ideal of his audience by allying "tension" with certain signifiers that his audience is strongly allied with: for example, "constructive," "nonviolent," "growth," and "Socrates." King uses this same basic technique in relation to words like "law," "civil disobedience," and "extremist." Of the latter, he says:

> You speak of our activity in Birmingham as extreme. At first I was rather disappointed that fellow clergymen would see my nonviolent efforts as those of an extremist. . . . But though I was initially disappointed at being categorized as an extremist, as I continued to think about the matter I gradually gained a measure of satisfaction from the label. Was not Jesus an extremist for love. . . . Was not Amos an extremist for justice. . . . Was not Paul an extremist for the Christian gospel. . . . Was not Martin Luther an extremist. . . . And John Bunyan. . . . And Abraham Lincoln. . . . And Thomas Jefferson. (861)

By the time King is through, the opposition of his primary audience (the clergy to whom he wrote the letter) to the word "extremist" and thus to King himself has been shaken, if not overthrown.

The interpellative force of a discourse like King's derives from the impact it has on a subject's sense of identity. As Lacan explains, a discourse that is to move or even interest a subject must say, explicitly or implicitly, "You are this," or "You are that." In the case of King's audience, the message is: "You are followers of Jesus, admirers of Lincoln and Jefferson," and so on. If "Jesus," "Lincoln," or "Jefferson" is a master signifier for the subject, the subject's position is affected: "This 'you are this,'" Lacan observes, "when I receive it, makes me in speech other than I am" (III 315). In King's discourse, acceptance of the interpellation as followers of Jesus and the others makes the audience accepting of King's "extremism," thus exemplifying Lacan's description of interpellation (without naming it, at this point) as "that by which I make pass into the other the faith that is mine" (III 343).

Interpellation does this by operating through "the reciprocal relations of 'you' [e.g., King's primary audience of clergymen], foreign body [e.g., extremists], with the signifier that pins, buttons down the subject [e.g., Jesus]" (III 315). The signifiers that "button down" (*capitonnent*) a subject—signifiers that Lacan at this point in his thinking (1956) terms *points de capiton* (literally, "upholstery buttons")—are crucial elements in the interpellative effect of discourse. They are the master signifiers that determine whether a subject assumes or rejects the signifying part of a sentence—the "foreign body" or attribute tied to it that one is attempting to make the receivers of one's discourse assume as their own (III 318). Being interpellated, for example, as followers of Jesus thus entails the subject's active narcissistic desire to assume all the attributes of Jesus (e.g., extremism) and to divest oneself of all qualities that are incompatible with these attributes (e.g., opposition to extremism). In order to accept the interpellation as followers of Jesus, King's audience must give up their opposition to "extremists" in general and King in particular because only such a move allows them to retain their sense of identity—the passive narcissistic gratification deriving from the Other's recognition—not only within King's discourse but also (after reading King's letter) within the more general discourse of their (Judeo-Christian) culture. Such is the interpellative action of active narcissistic desire in the Symbolic order.

Active anaclitic desire in the Symbolic order involves the desire to possess, as a means for one's jouissance, an object that embodies a specific signifier. This form of desire also responds powerfully to master signifiers. The most obvious instance of this type of desire is found in a man's sexual desire for "woman." As we will see in the section on images, the bodily image of the other plays a crucial role in active anaclitic desire (e.g., in sexual arousal), but the image is ultimately subordinate to the signifier. For a quick intuitive grasp of how this is so, consider the case of a heterosexual man ogling a shapely woman in a bar. The man becomes sexually excited as he fantasizes an encounter with this woman. He indicates his desire to his buddies, only to be told by a friend that the "woman" is really a "man"! Immediately his lust will evaporate and even turn to disgust—even if his friend was putting him on and the "woman" really is a female.[12] The crucial role of the signifier in desire is here unmistakable: in the moment of lust and the moment of deflation, the image and the anatomical reality of the other person remain the same; only the signifier changes, and this change causes a reversal of desire. Thus although an image of the female body may be an important factor in the production of heterosexual male desire, it is not by itself sufficient to produce such desire. In order for sexual desire to be produced, the image must be coupled (explicitly or implicitly) with the proper signifier.

This aspect of Symbolic-order desire derives in part from active narcissistic desire: in coming to embody certain signifiers, the subject also adopts certain specific desires, since some of these signifiers desired by the Other govern active anaclitic desire. Thus in assuming the identity of man or of woman—the only two possibilities provided by the Symbolic Other—a subject also submits to the (usually unconscious) coercion to desire objects embodying certain specific signifiers rather than others, and to desire them in ways that enact certain signifiers rather than others. This coercion comes about through the system of alliances and oppositions established between master signifiers of sexual identity such as "masculine" and "feminine," on the one hand, and specific attributes—such as active, passive, hard, soft, strong, weak—on the other hand. One cannot be recognized as masculine or feminine by the Other (or by oneself) unless one embodies certain specific attributes (signifiers), central among which are those attributes concerning the nature, manner, and objects of one's desire. For example, in most traditions, being "a man" requires that one have genital desire of an assertive sort and that it be directed toward "women," a signifier that then effectively determines which objects will be desired by certain subjects (i.e., "men").

The passive anaclitic form of Symbolic-order desire involves a subject's desire to be desired by the Symbolic Other as bearer of one of the

---

[12]The signifier here can be Imaginary as well as Symbolic. An example of an Imaginary signifier playing the key role can be found in the instance in which a heterosexual man is attracted to a person with long blond hair and shapely legs in tight jeans only to encounter, when the person turns around, a full beard, an imaginary signifier of "man."

master signifiers (such as a man's desire to be desired as "man," by "woman"). Culture operates on this desire whenever it promises that possessing a certain quality or attribute will make one a real "man" or "woman" and thus the object of the Other Sex's desire. Many advertisements play to this desire, promising, implicitly or explicitly, to make one more of a "man" or a "woman," signifiers that evoke desire in the opposite sex or the same sex, depending on the other's orientation. The difference between this desire and the active narcissistic form of desire is that here the identity-bearing signifier is expected to arouse *desire* in the Other rather than love.

Interpellation through Images

While manipulation of signifiers representing the subject as well as the objects of its desire accounts for much of the impact of a given text or discourse, two other powerful features—images and fantasies—also operate in discourse as part of its total interpellative power. Images derive their power from what Lacan calls the Imaginary order, which is based on our sense or image of our preverbal bodily identity (III 20). The Imaginary order never exists in complete independence from the Symbolic order, since the child's experience is indirectly structured by the Symbolic order from before birth. And as the child learns to speak, Symbolic hegemony is attained, with the Symbolic order massively restructuring the child's psychic economy, interrupting the immediate, dual relation of subject to object (both human and nonhuman) and interposing a third term, the signifier. The Symbolic cannot be eliminated from the Imaginary; "the imaginary economy has meaning, we gain some purchase on it, only in so far as it is transcribed into the symbolic order" (II 255).

But the Imaginary schemata of organization do not disappear (II 306); images form the foundation upon which the Symbolic order is erected in individual subjectivity, the trunk onto which the signifiers of the child's newly acquired language are grafted. Human language is structured around "choice images which all have a specific relation with the living existence of the human being, with quite a narrow sector of its biological reality, with the image of the fellow being. This imaginary experience furnishes ballast for every concrete language, and by the same token for every verbal exchange" (II 319), "and [this imaginary dimension] is what gives human language its weight, its resources, and its emotional vibration" (II 306).

The Imaginary order is composed of the schemata of meaning that arise from our bodily experiences as infants, before we learn to speak. The awareness, the image, that we form of our own body, Lacan says, "is the ring, the bottle-neck, through which the confused bundle of desire and needs must pass in order to be [us]," that is, in order to be felt by us to be part of ourselves—part of our preverbal, Imaginary sense of ourselves (I 176). The Imaginary order thus plays a crucial role in the construction of identity and desire, and discourse can affect one's desire and sense of identity by operating in the Imagnary register. The effect of such operations is quite familiar in certain forms, such as the "emotional vibration" (to use Lacan's phrase) produced by powerful imagery. But the precise way in which images operate on one's sense of bodily mastery and identity in order to evoke and direct significant desires (including identifications) has not really been understood or even investigated.

Imaginary Identification and the Body Ego

The *active narcissistic form of Imaginary desire* involves loving and admiring the image of the other person—to the point of desiring to become corporeally like that person. Our earliest sense of ourselves—our desire as well as our ego—results largely from such an identification, which has its prototype in the mirror stage. Such identification is responsible for constituting a central element of the most rudimentary sense of unified being or self: the ideal body ego, which is the image of oneself in which one feels most fully oneself, and which constitutes the first form of the ego. The mirror stage refers to that set of experiences in which the infant, despite the fact that it has not yet attained an interior, subjective unification of its own bodily movements and sensations, nonetheless manages to attain a sense of itself as a unified being of some sort, by perceiving its own body and its movements from the outside, either in a literal mirror or in the virtual mirror of another person's face and body. Conflations of this sort between (external) image and (internal) sense of identity can be seen quite clearly in a child's interaction with other children. "It is [the] captation by the *imago* of the human form," Lacan says, "which, between the ages of six months and two and a half years, dominates the entire dialectic of the child's behaviour in the presence of his similars" (*Selection* 19). Of particular significance in this regard is the phenomenon of transitivism:

> The child who strikes another says that he has been struck; the child who sees another fall, cries. Similarly, it is by means of an identification with the other that he sees the whole gamut of reactions of bearing and display, whose structural ambivalence is clearly revealed in his behaviour, the slave being identified with the despot, the actor with the spectator, the seduced with the seducer. (19)

Such responses—and particularly the child's experience of jubilation in response to its image—demonstrate, Lacan says, that "the mirror stage [is] *an identification*, in the full sense that analysis gives to the term: namely, the transformation that takes place in the subject when he assumes an image" (*Selection* 2; emphasis added). Thus, concludes Lacan,

> the mirror stage is a drama whose internal thrust is precipitated from insufficiency to anticipation—and which manufactures for the subject, caught up in the lure of *spatial identification*, the succession of phantasies that extends . . . lastly, to the assumption of the armour of an alienating identity, which will mark with its rigid structure the subject's entire mental development. (4; emphasis added)

Imaginary-order identification can also involve the acquisition of desire, through adopting the desire of the other person. "Before desire learns to recognise itself . . . through the symbol," Lacan says, "desire exists solely in the single plane of the imaginary relation of the specular stage, projected, alienated in the other" (I 170). Just as the child's sense of identity is derived from her or his perception of bodily unity in an other (in the mirror stage), so the child's attainment of a definite desire with specific aim and object is achieved only by perceiving that desire outside herself or himself in another: "It is within the see-saw movement, the movement of exchange with the other, that man becomes aware of himself as body, as the empty form of the body. In the same way, everything which is then within him in a pure state of desire, original desire, unconstituted and confused, which finds expression in the wailing of the child—he will learn to recognise it through its inversion in the other" (I 170). One comes to apprehend and thus to constitute the wishes and impulses that are *inside* oneself only by perceiving those impulses *outside* oneself in the desire of the other—a desire which, we might say, is manifested by the other's "body language."

The ramifications of this aspect of Imaginary desire for the impact of culture are great. The fact that one originally attains one's own desire only by means of the bodily images of another person means that like the Imaginary identification of the mirror stage, Imaginary-order desire is from the beginning a social and even fictional phenomenon—a metaphor, we might say, that substitutes for an inchoate group of amorphous urges a more definite impulse with an aim toward a specific object. This fictional, metaphoric nature of desire means that there is no intrinsic, essential, or absolute content to desire in the Imaginary order any more than in the Symbolic order and that desire in the Imaginary order is produced through the operation of images in cultural artifacts.

This active narcissistic form of Imaginary desire can be evoked by various cultural employments of the image of the human body. Fashion and cosmetics are perhaps the most obvious arenas in which such desire operates, with consumers buying the products because they desire to look like the fashion models they see in magazines. Other powerful instances of such desire can be found in the effects produced in spectators by various athletic performances, including dance, where the integrity and mastery of the body are quite pronounced. In watching models, athletes, and dancers, spectators often find themselves wishing that the capabilities and appearances of their own bodies were like those of the performers. And they also often find themselves experiencing the same desire that is manifested in the movements of the performers. Sports fans, for example, often tense their bodies and even move in ways similar to the movements of an athlete as they share the athlete's desire to score on an opponent or perform some other feat. Viewers of such dancers as Fred Astaire and Ginger Rogers sometimes become entranced by the desire projected by the movement of the bodies on the screen and dance along with them, or sway back and forth in their seats imagining that they are dancing.

More subtle instances of such identification with the other's bodily form and the desire manifested by that form can be found in the responses of an audience watching actors in a play or a movie and also in responses to painted and sculpted human figures, where the static representation of the human form provides a sense of balance and proportion (as in classical Greek sculpture), or a threat to such a sense (as in Cubist paintings of the human form).

Similar responses can be evoked verbally. For instance, a feeling of pleasure or sense of well-being can often be produced in an audience through depiction of bodily mastery or integrity, as in H.D.'s description of a shellfish in "The Walls Do Not Fall":

> . . . that flabby, amorphous hermit
> within, like the planet
> senses the finite,
> it limits its orbit
> of being. . . .
>
> . . . .
>
> I sense my own limit,
> my shell-jaws snap shut
> at invasion of the limitless,
> ocean-weight; infinite water
> can not crack me, egg in egg-shell;
> closed in, complete, immortal.

The body ego of an audience can also be operated on through the active narcissistic desire evoked by verbal accounts of bodies, as well as by descriptions of the spatial aspects of a scene, architectural structure, or action, insofar as these spatial aspects are related to the categories or dimensions of the human body. Such an effect occurs because every perceptual tableau includes somewhere within itself, if only by implication, an image of the human form (II 166–67). This results from the fact that the same sensorimotor schemata that constitute the image (i.e., the unified sense) of our own body also constitute the basis for our perception of the external world and its objects. "The corporeal image," Lacan informs us, "gives [the subject's] *Umwelt* its form, in as much as he is man and not horse. It makes up the unity of the subject, and we see it projecting itself in a thousand different ways" (I 125). As a result, "the object [of perception] is always more or less structured as the image of the body of the subject. The reflection of the subject, its mirror image, is always found somewhere in every perceptual picture, and that is what gives it a quality, a special inertia. . . . [Thus] perception is a total relation to a given picture, in which man always recognizes himself somewhere" (II 166–67).

The Imaginary schemata make perceiving somewhat like looking througha pane of glass and seeing both ourselves in the glass and the objects beyond the glass, without being able fully to distinguish the two. It is precisely this coincidence of body image with images of objects that makes objects recognizable, meaningful, substantial. "If the picture of the relation to the world is not made unreal by the subject, it is because it contains elements representing the diversified images of his ego, and these are so many points of anchorage, of stabilisation, of inertia" (III 166–67).

The construction of one's image of and investment in the world takes place via a series of identifications with objects: "Normally, the subject finds for those objects of his primitive identification a series of imaginary equivalents which diversify his world—he draws up identifications with certain objects, withdraws them, makes them up again with others, etc. . . . But these comings and goings will give its framework to that infinitely more complex real which is the human real" (I 69). In other words, one's image of the world takes shape when the first objects of one's identification and desire, such as the breast, feces, and urine, are equated in the Imaginary order with different, more neutralized objects from the external world. Thus it is "through the possibilities of play in the imaginary transposition that the progressive valorisation of objects comes about, on the plane that we commonly designate as affective, through a diversification, a fanning-out of all the imaginary equations." It is this process of Imaginary substitution that makes the human being "the only animal to have at his disposition an almost infinite number of objects—objects marked with the value of a *Gestalt* in his *Umwelt*, objects isolated as to their forms" (I 83).

Cultural artifacts, particularly poetry and fiction, operate quite powerfully with this identificatory connection between body ego and objects of perception. An explicit instance of such conflation (identification) between body ego and external object is described in—and for some readers, also evoked by—Whitman's "I Saw in Louisiana a Live-Oak Growing":

I saw in Louisiana a live-oak growing,
All alone stood it, and the moss hung down from the branches;

Without any companion it grew there, uttering joyous leaves of dark
    green,
And its look, rude, unbending, lusty, made me think of myself.

Lacan's comments suggest that such identification operates unconsciously in virtually every encounter with visual images, including
visual images in discourse. We can thus surmise that the force exerted
on subjectivity by images in discourse derives from the fact that one's
body ego and Imaginary-order desire are in some way, to some degree,
put at stake whenever one encounters images. This is the case even
when we do not identify with the objects described, as in the following
passage from Ernest Hemingway's *The Sun Also Rises*:

> The bus climbed steadily up the road. The country was barren and rocks
> stuck up through the clay. There was no grass beside the road. Looking
> back we could see the country spread out below. Far back the fields were
> squares of green and brown on the hillsides. Marking the horizon were
> the brown mountains. They were strangely shaped. As we climbed higher
> the horizon kept changing. As the bus ground slowly up the road we
> could see other mountains coming up in the south. Then the road came
> over the crest, flattened out, and went into a forest. It was a forest of cork
> oaks, and the sun came through the trees in patches, and there were cattle
> grazing back in the trees. We went through the forest and the road came
> out and turned along a rise of land and out ahead of us was a rolling
> green plain, with dark mountains beyond it. These were not like the
> brown, heat-baked mountains we had left behind. These were wooded
> and there were clouds coming down from them. (108)

The primary Imaginary-order identification of most readers here is
probably not with any of the objects described but rather with the
speaker, whose position and movement through the landscape affects
attuned readers by producing subtle sensations of corporeal effort,
vulnerability, alienation, and desolation, followed by sensations of reduced effort and increased security and succor.

The *passive narcissistic form of Imaginary-order desire* is the desire
to be admired or idealized for one's physical appearance, to the point
of being loved or identified with. Such desire can frequently be observed in models and performers, many of whom desire to be admired
or emulated by their audience. But this desire is often evoked in specta-

tors as well, and it often forms the motivation behind spectators' active narcissistic Imaginary desire to be or be like the model or performer. That is, many spectators identify with the performers because they wish to be objects of admiration and emulation just as the performers are.

Passive narcissistic Imaginary-order desire is also engaged by any description of a situation involving narcissistic mirroring, aggressivity, parade, or prestige—any situation in which a figure's bodily well-being is at stake, even if only indirectly. Anything that affirms and reinforces our body image thus provides a narcissistic gratification, a sense of security and self-worth, which has its roots in a sense of bodily integrity and mastery. And conversely, anything (whether an external force or an impulse from within) that might damage the armor constituted by this body image represents a threat to our sense of self and is thus met with opposition and aggressivity. Hence, "aggressivity [is] one of the intentional co-ordinates of the human ego" (*Selection* 25), and at its most fundamental level, aggressivity is motivated and directed by "imagos of the fragmented body": "images of castration, mutilation, dismemberment, dislocation, evisceration, devouring, bursting open of the body" (*Selection* 11). Representations of sickness, physical injury, or other incapacity embody both the fear of what can happen to oneself and the aim of the aggressivity, motivated by this fear, that is directed toward the other.

Thus while images of bodily mastery provide a sense of well-being and enjoyment, images of bodily deficiency either feed one's sadistic, aggressive impulse or evoke a fundamental aversion and anxiety. Hamlet's duel with Laertes, Lacan points out, is one well-known instance of the former. An instance of the latter effect is produced for many readers by the following lines from Wilfred Owen's "Dulce et Decorum Est":[13]

> He plunges at me, guttering, choking, drowning.
> If in some smothering dreams you too could pace
> Behind the wagon that we flung him in,
> And watch the white eyes writhing in his face,
> His hanging face, like a devil's sick of sin,
> If you could hear, at every jolt, the blood

[13] I am indebted to Lisa Martinez for this example.

Come gargling from the froth-corrupted lungs
Obscene as cancer, bitter as the cud
Of vile, incurable sores on innocent tongues.

The degree of discomfort that a reader experiences upon reading these
lines indicates the extent to which the imagery constitutes a threat to
the reader's body ego.

The image of the human body is also at the basis of *anaclitic desire*,
both *active and passive*. This is most obvious in the role played by the
image of the body in arousing active sexual desire. As Lacan puts it,
"The libidinal drive is centred on the function of the image" (I 122).
"The primary imaginary relation," Lacan says, "provides the fundamental framework for all possible erotism. It is a condition to which
the object of Eros as such must be submitted" (I 274). On the Imaginary level, the human sexual response resembles in certain ways that of
animals: sexual desire can be aroused by an image of the human
gestalt. "The basic mainspring determining the setting into motion of
the gigantic sexual mechanism," Lacan observes, "isn't the existence of
the sexual partner, the particularity of one individual. . . . [Rather,]
the mechanical throwing into gear of the sexual instinct is . . . essentially crystallised in a relation of images" (I 121–22).

The most powerful instances of the cultural production of such
desire involve the use of the female body in pornography to arouse
heterosexual male desire, evidence for the power of which can be seen
in the response of heterosexual males to the images of nude women in
magazines like *Playboy*—a response that can go as far as ejaculation.
Magazines like *Playgirl*, which feature nude photographs of men, can
produce similar desires in heterosexual women, and the images in
these same magazines can serve a similar function for homosexual
women and men, respectively. That sexual desire can also be produced
by verbal portraits of the human body is demonstrated by the existence
of such descriptions in pornographic stories and novels. Less flagrant
production of such desire can be found in many responses to images of
the human form represented by films, paintings, sculptures, advertisements, and various other visual and verbal discourses, the most notori-
ous examples of which involve the use of images of the female body to
sell everything from cars to cigars.

The *passive anaclitic form of Imaginary desire* involves the wish to
be the body that the other person desires as a means of jouissance. It

too, like the active anaclitic form, is often embedded in the active narcissistic form of desire, the desire to be corporeally like the other person. In fact, often the desire to be corporeally like one person is motivated by the desire to be corporeally desired by another person—which, in turn, often serves as a means of making the other person available as an object of one's own jouissance. Here again, one of the cultural discourses that evokes such a desire most clearly is the phenomenon of fashion, which offers corporeal images that subjects can conform with in order to satisfy their desire to be attractive to others—that is, desired as objects of jouissance by others. All advertisements that promise to make one's body more attractive to another person—for example, by making parts of the body bigger or smaller, or by making one's hair more luxurious or one's skin smoother—are operating on the audience's passive anaclitic desire in the Imaginary order.

Interpellation through Fantasy

Desire in the order of the Real is a little more complicated than in the Symbolic and Imaginary orders, for here we must distinguish between the Real as the organic substrate of subjectivity constituted by our body, where drives are grounded, and the Real as the (psycho)logical effect of the subject's accession to the Symbolic order, the irreducible lack that is the heart of subjectivity and to which fantasy responds. Slavoj Žižek explains this dual nature of the Real as follows:

> [First,] we have the Real as the starting point, the basis, the foundation of the process of symbolization . . . , the Real which in a sense *precedes* the symbolic order and is subsequently structured by it when it gets caught in its network: this is the great Lacanian motif of symbolization as a process which mortifies, drains off . . . the fullness of the Real of the living body. But the Real is at the same time the product, remainder, leftover, . . . the excess which escapes symbolization and is as such produced by the symbolization itself. In Hegelian terms, the Real is simultaneously *presupposed* and *posed* by the symbolic. In so far as the kernel of the Real is *jouissance*, this duality takes the form of a difference between *jouissance*, enjoyment, and *plus-de-jouir*, the surplus-of-enjoying: *jouissance* is the basis upon which symbolization works, the basis emptied, disembodied, structured by the symbolization, but this process produces at the same time a residue, a leftover, which is the surplus-enjoying.

The Real is the fullness of the inert presence, positivity; nothing is lacking in the Real—that is, the lack is introduced only by the symbolization; it is a signifier which introduces a void, an absence in the Real. But at the same time the Real is in itself a hole, a gap, an opening in the middle of the symbolic order—it is the lack around which the symbolic order is structured. (169–70)

The Object a

Desire in the Real is an effort to attain the missing part of one's own being or jouissance either through possessing what Lacan calls the object *a*, a precious object or substance associated with the Real body, or through being oneself the object *a* that the Other wants to be or to have. The object *a*, which functions as the ultimate object around which the drive turns and upon which fantasy is constructed, "designates precisely what of the effects of discourse presents itself as the most opaque and . . . misunderstood, though essential" (XVII 47).

In other words, the object *a* figures in discourse as the return of the being or jouissance that is excluded by the master signifiers.[14] "All forms of the object *a* that can be enumerated," Lacan says, "are the representatives" of "what is subtracted from the living being by virtue of the fact that it is subject to the cycle of sexed reproduction" (XI 198). Such exclusion and return of jouissance derive primarily from the cultural Symbolic-order definitions of what it means to be a man or a woman. Drives are thus the product at the level of the Real of one aspect of the demand of the Symbolic Other: they are the result of the

---

[14]At the very moment that we come into being as a subject by virtue of identifying with a signifier, we are solidified, petrified, by the signifier, reduced in a way to being nothing more than the signifier that represents us (VI 76; XI 199, 207). Thus, Lacan says, "through his relation to the signifier, the subject is deprived of something of himself, of his very life" ("Hamlet" 28). The lost part of life—the part that disappears behind the signifier—is the object *a*. This situation produces the divided subject $, whose division is the effect of the master signifier and which the master signifier has the function of covering over. The $, the divided subject, is operative in all of the various ways in which we fail to identify ourselves, grasp ourselves, or coincide with ourselves. These can all be grasped as relations among signifiers. One manifestation is the gap between thinking and being. The "I" that I think about never coincides completely with the "I" that does the thinking; the urges and characteristics that I take to be mine never exhaust or even adequately represent the forces that constitute my being and drive my thought and action—forces, moreover, that are themselves conflictual and self-contradictory. As Lacan puts it, " 'either I do not think, or I am not.' There where I think, I don't recognize myself; there where I am not, is the unconscious; there where I am, it is only too clear that I stray from myself " ("Hamlet" 92).

fact that the Other demands certain responses, including certain desires, from the subject's body. Drives are constructed in the Real of the subject's body by the unconscious chains of signifiers established by the demands of the Symbolic Other (parents, peers, and Society in general).

These signifying chains, which we embrace when we identify with the signifier "man" or "woman" (see XI 204), effectively dissect our bodies and render parts of them dead to our enjoyment. That is, when one is represented (to oneself as well as to others) by the signifier "man" or the signifier "woman," one is prohibited—by both internal and external forces, and in the great majority of cases, very effectively—from enjoying, or even using in specific ways, certain parts of one's own body and the other's body. This sacrificed enjoyment persists, however, and manifests itself in various ways, including through the partial drives—the largely unconscious enjoyments that we get from those bodily parts and functions that are proscribed as focal points of enjoyment. Such enjoyments are usually subordinated to the genital drive as aspects of sexual foreplay, or they operate only in disguised or sublimated form. This includes most oral, anal, scopic, and auditory activities for most people.

Fantasy

The objects *a*, or all the guises of breast, feces, gaze, and voice, are not only an occasion for surreptitious enjoyments of the Real body; they also represent metonymically the totality of the being that was lost by the subject when it faded behind the signifiers that were elected to serve as its representatives in the ego ideal. Thus in addition to being the object around which the partial drives and their jouissances turn, the object *a*, as the representative of our lost immortality and vitality in general, is the cause of all desire, desire being precisely a function of our lack of being. "Something becomes an object in desire," Lacan says, "when it takes the place of what by its very nature remains concealed from the subject: that self-sacrifice, that pound of flesh which is mortgaged in his relation to the signifier" ("Hamlet" 28). The failure of the gestalts of the Imaginary other, the desire of the Symbolic Other, and the demands of the Real Other to provide absolute regulation of jouissance/*jouis-sens* by means of a transcendental gestalt, signifier, or object, in relation to which the subject could take his or her bearing, is one of the fundamental causes of fantasy, in which the subject seeks the object *a* or *plus-de-jouir*.

The other fundamental cause of fantasy is the positive content of the *a*, which derives from the traces of jouissance left by the often contingent and arbitrary action of the Imaginary, Symbolic, and Real Others on the subject. Such tacit, forbidden modes of jouissance are unwittingly and inevitably established by the parental Other, in particular. One way is through the parent's function as Symbolic Other, by forbidding, explicitly or implicitly, particular acts or behaviors (see *Selection* 243). Another way is by appearing nude to the child, or otherwise stimulating the child in a visual way as an Imaginary other. A third way in which parents establish forbidden modes of jouissance in children is as the Real Other who stimulates bodily jouissance in the infant and young child through caring for it—by feeding, bathing, dressing, holding, and playing, for example. It is from the jouissance produced by such care, in fact, that some children, according to Freud, later construct fantasies of having been seduced.

Subsequently, in mandating a certain image of bodily integrity, as well as certain desires and drives, the Symbolic Other decertifies those modes of jouissance in the Real of the subject's body that are at odds with the Imaginary sense of bodily integrity and with the central desires of the Symbolic Other in the ego ideal. As is the case with Imaginary desire, such decertified being persists and insists in the form of unconscious jouissances that we get from those bodily parts and functions that are proscribed as focal points of enjoyment. The desire for this lost jouissance or being runs counter to conscious desire: here, "what [the subject] desires presents itself to him as what he does not want" (*Selection* 312), a prime example being the unconscious homosexual and/or nongenital sexual desires of "normal" heterosexual adults.

These forbidden modes of jouissance are inscribed in the subject in the form of fantasy, $ \$ \diamondsuit a $, which stages the desire ($ \diamondsuit $) of the subject ($\$$) for the *plus-de-jouir* (*a*), a surplus of jouissance over and above what the subject currently attains. Fantasy thus not only promises ultimate jouissance for desire (either having or being the object *a*), it also protects the subject from being engulfed in the abyss of nonmeaning at the basis of human existence. Fantasy fills this dual role in a number of ways. As with desire in the Imaginary and Symbolic orders, in fantasy the subject can take one of four positions with relation to the object *a*, and culture is full of phenomena offering subjects the object *a* in one or more of these four basic forms.

Active anaclitic fantasy involves possessing, as a means for one's own jouissance, the object *a* embodied in another person, thing, or activity. Obvious instances are the fetish object and the collector's object, both of which are pursued by the subject as a way of filling up the lack of being and/or recovering that (mythical) lost jouissance that would be totally fulfilling. More generally, the role of the object *a* can be filled by whatever appears to offer the possibility of producing this lost jouissance.[15] In discourse, anything that functions for an audience as an object of desire or a precondition for jouissance has assumed, in some manner and to some degree, the role of the object *a*, the fundamental cause of desire. Obvious instances that are more or less universal in our culture include money, which promises to fill all lack, and many of the products represented in advertising, a paradigmatic instance of which can be found, as Žižek points out, in ads for Coca-Cola which, in claiming that Coke is "the real thing," or that "this is it," present Coke as "the unattainable X, the object-cause of desire" (Žižek 96).

Passive anaclitic fantasy involves embodying the object *a* that the Other desires to possess as a means for jouissance. This type of fantasy is present in a similarly diverse array of cultural phenomena, most notably in passive sexual fantasies of being that something beyond image or signifier that gives the Other jouissance. The most striking instances of this are sadomasochistic fantasies, which play in complex ways with being the instrument of the Other's jouissance—for example, advertisements suggesting that a certain fragrance can make one the mysterious object of the other's passsion.

Passive anaclitic fantasy is to be distinguished from the *passive narcissistic fantasy*, which is the fantasy of being the object of the Other's love, the object that will fill the Other's lack. One of the most powerful forms of this fantasy is found in such phenomena as nationalism and

---

[15]Woman (i.e., Woman, object of male fantasy), insofar as she is desired by man, assumes the role of object *a* (XVII 161), a role that can also be taken on by a pet (XVII 180), by capital (XVII 189), and by other things. Early in life the role is filled primarily by various body parts and functions—our own as well as those of other people. For the infant, the breast of the mother, as well as her voice and her gaze, comes closest to filling the lack or stopping the gap (XVII 50). For the mother (and father), the baby itself may serve this function.

racism, where groups of people conceive of themselves as embodying something extra that makes them valued more highly by the Other (Nature, God, Global Society) than other groups, and in religion and philosophy, where humans often take themselves to be the crown of creation. Children who are the apple of their parents' eye or the teacher's pet experience this sort of jouissance. In fact, most of us begin life in this position, Lacan notes, insofar as our birth is desired by our parents.

Active narcissistic fantasy involves loving or admiring the object *a* in another and attempting to unite with it or identify with it. This form of desire can be seen in the attempt of subjects (perhaps most overt in children and adolescents) to assume the voice, gaze, or certain mannerisms or styles of subjects who seem "cool" or outrageous. These objects of identification are "stars," iconoclasts, or "outlaws" of some sort, who appear to have transcended the limits of the Symbolic order and thus to have access to unlimited jouissance. Their object *a* might be a gun, drugs, money, a car, speed, or music—that is, a certain look a certain sound, or some other piece of the Real.

The Other's Lack

However, these forms of fantasy are no more capable of providing complete fulfillment for the subject than is the image of one's own bodily integrity and mastery, or the overt values and direct paths of meaning of the Symbolic order. This failure of the Other, a failure that is normally unconscious, can at times be experienced consciously—for instance, as a form of sadness or emptiness produced as the aftereffect of jouissance resulting from drive gratification, or as a more general angst or depression—and it is engaged in powerful ways by cultural artifacts. Much literature involves confrontation with this lack in one form or another, and such a confrontation is often explicit and pervasive in tragedy and in lyric poetry. Thomas Hardy's "Hap" offers one of the purest expressions of the Symbolic Other's lack—its failure to provide ultimate meaning—in relation to, and in distinction from, the Real deficiencies of existence:

> If but some vengeful god would call to me
> From up the sky, and laugh: "Thou suffering thing,

Know that thy sorrow is my ecstasy,
That thy love's loss is my hate's profiting!"
Then would I bear it, clench myself, and die,
Steeled by the sense of ire unmerited;
Half-eased in that a Powerfuller than I
Had willed and meted me the tears I shed.
But not so.

In tragedy, the Other's deficiency is signified not only by the action but also quite explicitly by famous utterances, such as Shakespeare's "[Life] is a tale / Told by an idiot, full of sound and fury, / Signifying nothing." Poems like Wordsworth's "Peele Castle," Coleridge's "Dejection" ode, and Arnold's "Dover Beach" articulate the failure of both the Symbolic Other (Nature, Society, God) and the Real Other (the physical world, one's own bodily sensations, and one's own deepest impulses) to provide completely fulfilling jouissance/*jouis-sens*, or being. These particular poems suggest that solace is to be found in the Imaginary other—the other person as friend, confidant, or lover. Whether a discourse interpellates an audience toward a particular solace such as this or not, any invocation of the Other's lack evokes in the audience a desire for that lack to be filled up, obliterated, or somehow compensated for. Presenting the Other's lack can thus serve to intensify the interpellative force of a particular desire elicited by a discourse. In gauging the interpellative force of a given text or discourse, then, one must take account not only of the different objects and positions offered to an audience's desire but also of the evocation and/or repression of the Other's lack.

Chains of Signifiers

It is also essential to take into account the connections and conflicts that occur among different desires and, hence, among the interpellative forces underwritten by these desires. Two basic relationships are possible: desires (including identifications) can either support and reinforce each other, or they can oppose and subvert each other in various ways. Fantasy, for instance, supports a master signifier when its action is congruent with the quality signified by the master signifier—such as when gratification of the scopic drive (voyeurism or exhibitionism) is presented as concomitant with being a real "man" or a real "woman." For example, exhibitionistic desires are usually incompatible with a conservative woman's sense of her identity, that is, with the master signifier "lady" in her ego ideal—and are therefore repressed and unconscious. But Marabel Morgan's account of the "total woman" meeting her husband at the door clad in nothing but Saran Wrap unites exhibitionistic fantasy and ego ideal ("total woman") and thus allows a conservative female reader to indulge in and even act out her unconscious fantasies of exhibitionism while maintaining her sense of identity as a very proper woman (and also her Imaginary-order sense of bodily integrity and mastery). In such instances, the ideal ego, the ego ideal, and the fantasy are all reinforced, and both the subject's unconscious fantasy and her preexisting sense of identity are gratified.

In many cases, however, different desires oppose and subvert each other. This occurs, for example, when the object a is linked with a signifier that is incompatible with one or more signifiers of the ego ideal. Such would be the case were Marabel Morgan's conservative female reader to encounter a novel about a female stripper. In this case, the exhibitionistic action would be connected with signifiers totally incompatible with the master signifiers constituting this reader's ego ideal. In such instances, one of two things can happen: either the ego ideal can prevail, in which case the fantasy is suppressed, repressed, or altered (e.g., sublimated), or the fantasy can win out, in which case the ego ideal undergoes a change, with one or more of its old signifiers being decommissioned and new signifiers (which represent, in part at least, the object a of fantasy) being elected in their place.

Conflict and the Unconscious

Such conflicts among different interpellations, and consequently, among the respective subject positions to which they lead, occur not only among the different registers (Symbolic, Imaginary, and Real) but also among different chains of signifiers operating within the same register, which can interpellate a given subject or group of subjects into contradictory positions.[16] But the most prominent conflict underlying all specific conflicts is between master signifiers and fantasy, or ego

[16]Such conflict is, in fact, ubiquitous. As Lacan observes, "Every human drama, every theatrical drama in particular, is founded on the existence of established bonds, ties, pacts. Human beings already have commitments which tie them together, commitments

and unconscious, each of which is constituted by an entire network of signifiers. The ego, which is structured around the master signifiers of the subject's ego ideal, opposes any interpellation to positions that are incompatible with its master signifiers and their entailments.

The unconscious is composed of positions that we have in some way embraced—because we have experienced that these positions offer a particular Real jouissance or an aspect of our Imaginary sense of mastery or even Symbolic recognition—which *are in themselves antithetical* to the positions we have set up in our ego ideal, or which *entail* (through the chains of signifiers established in the Symbolic order) *such antithetical positions*. Hence, "the unconscious is, in the subject, a schism of the symbolic system, a limitation, an alienation induced by the symbolic system" (I 196)—a schism produced by Imaginary or Real forces. In its Imaginary aspect, the "unconscious is made of what the subject essentially fails to recognise in his structuring image, in the image of his ego—namely, those captivations by imaginary fixations which are unassimilable to the symbolic development of his history" (I 283), that is, incompatible with the master signifiers and the fantasies, drives, desires, and jouissances mandated by these signifiers. In its Real aspect, the unconscious is composed of those jouissances—and their concomitant drives, desires, and fantasies, or the network of associations surrounding those jouissances—that are incompatible with the master signifiers and bodily images constituting one's ego, or sense of self.

Such unconscious inscriptions are often highly individual and idiosyncratic. But there are elements of the unconscious that are shared by groups of subjects—not because of common racial experience, as Jung would have it, but because of similar formative experiences attributable to inhabiting the same culture and discourses. Lacan indicates this "collective" aspect of the unconscious in his dictum that "the uncon-

---

which have determined their places, names, their essences. Then along comes another discourse, other commitments, other speech. It is quite certain that there'll be some places where they'll have to come to blows. All treaties aren't signed simultaneously. Some are contradictory. If you go to war, it is so as to know which treaty will be binding. Thank God, there are many occasions on which one doesn't go to war, and treaties continue to hold good, the slipper continues to circulate amongst people, in several directions all at once, and sometimes the object of a game of hunt-the-slipper encounters that of another game of hunt-the-slipper. Subdivision, reconversion, substitution take place. Whoever is engaged in playing hunt-the-slipper in one circle has to hide the fact that he is also playing in another" (II 197).

scious is the discourse of the Other," which means that "the unconscious is that part of the concrete discourse, in so far as it is transin-
dividual, that is not at the disposal of the subject in re-establishing the
continuity of his conscious discourse" (*Selection* 49). This transin-
dividual quality of the unconscious is due to the fact that it is constructed out of the common currency of cultural signifiers and discourses (networks of signifiers). While some of the links and circuits
thus established are idiosyncratic, others are quite common, particularly those circuits that derive from a common cultural experience and
are at the same time forcefully opposed by dominant master signifiers.

Cultural artifacts, then, in addition to eliciting desire, also guide it
toward some objects and aims and away from others, by means of such
networks of signifiers in the unconscious and in the ego. This occurs
by virtue of the alliances and oppositions established among signifiers
in the code constituting the ultimate Symbolic Other, the system of
language. It is these alliances and oppositions that determine that
subjects who, for example, have identified with signifier *A* will do all
they can to avoid identifying with signifier *B*, if *A* and *B* are established
as incompatible in the subject's Symbolic Other. Conversely, it will
determine that subjects will do all they can to embody *B* if *B* is coded
as entailed by *A* or otherwise allied with *A*. As Lacan puts it, "While
the subject doesn't think about it, the symbols continue to mount one
another, to copulate, to proliferate, to fertilise each other, to jump on
each other, to tear each other apart" (II 185).

Metonymy and Metaphor

Thus to have an effect, a discourse does not have to engage *directly* a
master signifier, image, or fantasy; such engagement can also be indirect, for negotiations among signifiers do not take place merely among
these primary representatives but also—to pursue the diplomatic
analogy—among members of the staffs of these representatives. Such
lower-level negotiations are, in fact, where the real work gets done, for
the position of a primary representative is held in place by its numerous alliances and oppositions to lesser signifiers, and without undoing
ties of this sort and instituting new ties, the position of the primary
representative remains unaltered. Thus, for example, altering a subject's identification as a "real man" would involve altering the subject's
relation to numerous lesser signifiers that are presided over by the

master signifier "real man"—for example, embracing signifiers like "dancer" or "tender," and becoming detached from signifiers like "tough." It is only by virtue of changes at this level that changes in the positions of the primary representatives of the subject's identity and desire can occur.

The two basic types of negotiation that occur among signifiers are metaphor and metonymy. Metonymy is the function by which discourses constitute alliances and oppositions among signifiers. Metonymy, in Lacan's usage, refers to the way in which signifiers are linked to other signifiers in a chain and ultimately an entire network that provides the pathways along which identification and desire operate. The simplest instances of the establishment of such associations among signifiers are sentences, where metonymy operates, for example, between subject and verb, verb and objects, and nouns and adjectives. It is such linkages that constitute the pathways of desire. Consider two examples: Real men don't eat quiche, and Roosevelt Grier knits. The first sentence, by establishing a disjunction between a certain subject and object, renders the object inaccessible to the desire of subjects who aspire to be "real men." The second sentence, in linking a subject, the former all-pro defensive tackle for the Los Angeles Rams and hence a "real man," with a verb, the activity of knitting, opens up an area of activity and desire that has been, for the most part, off-limits for men. The first sentence is an example of how metonymy establishes barriers to desire, and the second is an instance in which metonymy opens up new paths across barriers, by establishing alliances between signifiers that have been opposed. But metonymy is also operating in these two examples in an implicit way, by situating the key terms within the code constituting the Symbolic Other, with "real men" and "Roosevelt Grier" being linked with such signifiers as "big," "burly," "powerful," "hard," "heavy," "assertive," "robust," and "ravenous" and "knits" and "quiche" being linked to such signifiers as "feminine," "delicate," "light," "soft," "gentle," and "subtle"—many of them opposites of the signifiers linked to "real men" and "Roosevelt Grier." It is by virtue of simple metonymic connections, as well as infinitely more complex and indirect ones, that identity and desire are engaged, manipulated, and at times altered.

Such implicit metonymic chains also lie at the basis of metaphor, which is the substitution of one signifier for another. Such substitution produces a twofold effect. First, it effectively represses certain attributes of the signified—that is, certain metonymic links present in the first signifier are absent from the new, substitute signifier. Second, it effectively opens up new possibilities for identity and desire by virtue of the new metonymic linkages entailed by the new signifier. Metaphor, which Lacan says is the source of the *point de capiton* (*Selection* 303), is produced when a signification residing in the unconscious "inflects, commands the usage of the signifier, to the point that any sort of preestablished . . . lexical connection is untied" (III 248).

The Ur-example, in Lacanian theory, of this process is what Lacan calls the paternal metaphor, the substitution of the Name of the Father for the Desire of the Mother. The paternal metaphor, which refers to the subject's assumption of a position (and hence, sexual identity) within the Symbolic order, simultaneously opens up a vast array of new possible identities for the subject and closes off an equally vast array—those belonging to the opposite sex, for example—as well as wrenching the subject out of the passive narcissistic gratification experienced by the child in its apprehension of itself as primarily the object of the mother's desire. All metaphors engage in a similar twofold effect of commissioning certain paths for identity and desire and decommissioning others.

Unconscious desire makes its way along the underground paths constructed out of metaphor and metonymy (including, but not limited to, puns, rhymes, and other aspects of the materiality of the signifier)[17] in signifying chains constructed from the materials of the very Symbolic order that excludes such desires from recognition or overt enactment. And cultural artifacts can operate on this unconscious desire in various ways, offering surreptitious gratification of it, or evoking it as a threat to one's identity and narcissistic gratification. They do so by engaging the metaphoric and metonymic connections that the unconscious network establishes around this repressed desire.

In summary, then, discourses exercise force over a group of people by engaging, directly or indirectly, signifying circuits common to either the ego ideals, the body images, or the fantasies of members of the group. Through these often conflicting forces, subjects are pressured to relinquish previous desires (including identifications) and embrace

---

[17]The materiality of the signifier, which in early American appropriations of Lacanian thought assumed paramount importance, is in most discourses not the crucial factor. On the American academic overestimation of the importance of this aspect of the signifier, see Jacques-Alain Miller, "A and *a* in Clinical Structures."

new ones—or alternatively, to invest all the more completely in old ones. The vector of interpellation resulting from these multiple converging and conflicting forces of a discourse can be gauged by using the taxonomy of desire developed here to identify the various instances of desire evoked by a given discourse in a given audience and then tracing the metonymic paths and metaphoric bridges by which these desires are directed toward specific actions, aims, and objects. The value of this taxonomy of desire—four basic modes in each of three registers—lies not in its capacity to serve as a totalizing system for describing and categorizing the various elements of discourse. Its value lies rather in its demonstration of the multifariousness and complexity of desire and in its function as a kind of checklist prompting us to search a given text or discourse for interpellative forces that might not be immediately evident. Such identification of interpellative forces, moreover, is itself a primary means for promoting social change. How the identification of such forces might promote social change is what now requires explanation.

CHAPTER TWO

SOCIAL CHANGE AND THE ETHICS OF CRITICAL DISCOURSE

The Structure of Discourse

In order to formulate a strategy of cultural criticism that can operate in such a way as to promote social change in an ethical and effective manner, it is necessary to understand the various ways in which discourses can produce psychological effects in a large enough number of people to entail results at the social level. Such an understanding can be gained through Lacan's account of four fundamental structures of discourse (see XVII) which produce, respectively, four fundamental social effects: (1) educating/indoctrinating; (2) governing/commanding; (3) desiring/protesting; (4) analyzing/transforming/revolutionizing.

The differing effects produced by these discourses result from the differing roles or positions occupied in each discourse by four psychological factors—knowledge, ideals, self-division, and jouissance. These four major factors involved in the production and reception of any text or discourse are master signifiers (S1), the network of signifiers or system of knowledge (S2), the Real that is simultaneously excluded and produced by the system of knowledge and its master signifers (a), and the divided subject ($\$$), split between the identity to which it is interpellated (S1) and the *plus-de-jouir* (a), the jouissance that it sacrifices in assuming that identity.

The four positions that these factors can occupy are the following:

Speaker   Receiver

$$\dfrac{\text{Agent} \longrightarrow \text{Other}}{\text{Truth} \longleftarrow \text{Production}}$$

The left-hand positions designate the factors active in the subject who is speaking or sending a message, and the right-hand positions are occupied by the factors activated or elicited in the subject who receives the message. The top position on each side represents the overt or manifest factor, and the bottom position represents the covert, latent, implicit, or repressed factor—the factor that acts or occurs beneath the surface. More specifically, the top left position is the place of agency or dominance; it is occupied by the factor in a discourse that is most active and obvious. The bottom left position is the place of (hidden) truth—that is, of the factor that supports, grounds, underwrites, and gives rise to the dominant factor, or constitutes the condition of its possibility, but is repressed by it.

On the right, the side of the receiver, the top position is designated as that of the other, which is occupied by the factor in the receiving subject that is called into action by the dominant factor in the message. The activation of this factor is a prerequisite for receiving and understanding a given message or discourse. For example, if systematic knowledge is the dominant element of a discourse (occupying the top left position), receivers, in order to understand this discourse, must (for a moment, at least) be receptive to a preconstituted knowledge, which means emptying themselves of any knowledge that might interfere with the knowledge in the discourse and becoming an amorphous, nonarticulated substance (*a*) to be articulated by the discourse. What receivers are thus compelled to produce (implicitly and even unconsciously) as a result of their allowing themselves to be thus interpellated is represented by the position of production, the bottom right.[1]

---

[1]What is produced by the receiver in the bottom right position will ideally feed back into, or call for, the impetus, in the bottom left position, underlying the sender's original message. Unfortunately for the sender (and fortunately for the receiver), since no receiver is ever completely "empty," such coincidence is never more than partial: the interpellative force never positions the receiver at the point of demanding from the sender a repetition of precisely the original impetus (bottom left) giving rise to the original interpellation. Hence, the vector from the bottom right to the bottom left must be seen as interrupted—as, in fact, must the top vector, the force of which is also never more than partially successful.

Lacan's "Four Discourses" in Cultural Criticism

The Discourse of the University

We can use these schemata of the four discourses as a means of indicating the basic interpellative modes of the major types of cultural criticism currently being practiced and thus gauge the potential that each mode has for producing social change. Most cultural criticism that is written, read, or taught by academicians falls, as one would expect, into the category of what Lacan calls the discourse of the University, which has the following structure:

$$\frac{S2}{S1} \longrightarrow \frac{a}{\$}$$

We begin our academic careers as students, in the position of *a*, receivers of the system of knowledge (S2). Subjected in this position to a dominating totalized system of knowledge/belief (S2), we are made to produce ourselves as (alienated) subjects (\$) of this system.[2] Social effects of this discursive position of students are not hard to find. Alienation and rebellion are perhaps the most evident.[3] Students are in

[2]Our position as the *a* simply continues the position we are born into. Before we learn to speak—and even before we are born—we occupy the position of the receiver of speech, and we do so in the form of the *a*, as the as yet unassimilated piece of the Real that is the object of the desires of those around us, particularly our parents, for whom children often function as the object *a* that promises to compensate for the Other's lack and thus fill the subject's lack as well. As we have seen, our preverbal experience of ourselves and the world, mediated as it is by the actions and demeanor of our primary caretakers, is partially determined by the system of knowledge/belief, or language, inhabited by them, and by the position they attribute to us within that system, speaking and thinking of us, for example, as son or daughter, delicate or hearty, future beauty queen or athlete, etc. In the second instance, it means that when we begin to understand language and to speak it, we must fashion our sense of ourselves (our identity) out of the subject positions made available by the signifiers (i.e., categories) of the system S2. This discursive structure and, hence, the totalizing and tyrannical effect of the S2 are not limited, however, to our infancy or to education. They are also present in several other realms. Bureaucracy is perhaps the purest form of the discourse of the University; it is nothing but knowledge (XVII 34)—i.e., pure impersonal system: The System, and nothing else. No provision is made for individual subjects and their desires and idiosyncracies. Individuals are to act, think, and desire only in ways that function to enact, reproduce, or extend The System. Bureaucracy thus functions to educate, in the root sense of that term: it forms particular types of subjects.

[3]Lacan emphasizes to his audience, many of whom are students, that it is through the structure of University discourse and their position within it that "many things can be explained regarding the singular phenomena that are occurring at the present time [May 13, 1970] throughout the world" (XVII 172).

the position of the exploited (XVII 172), and what torments them, Lacan says, is not that the knowledge they are given isn't structured and solid, but that there is only one thing they can do: namely, weave themselves into the system S2 and thus serve as both the means of production and the surplus value (XVII 234–35) of The System. The surplus value that students are charged with producing is "culture" (XVIIA 176), an elaboration or extension of The System. Insofar as they produce culture—by means of their theses, for example (XVII 220)—they simply nourish The System (XVIIA 176), because the function of a thesis is to add to society's knowledge—to reinforce precisely the factor (S2) by which they themselves are exploited and alienated.

Science is a particularly obvious example of such production, but the human sciences, including the humanities, also function to this end. This operation is most evident in the so-called great books or liberal education courses in which students are required to assimilate the knowledge/belief embodied in certain canonical texts. The present neoconservative attempt (spearheaded by such books as Allan Bloom's *The Closing of the American Mind* and E. D. Hirsch's *Cultural Literacy*) to impose uniformity on cultural diversity is an excellent example of the discourse of the University in action. But the system of knowledge is also served, and its dominance reinforced, by the study of iconoclastic works, such as those of women and of ethnic and racial minorities, that do not simply repeat the knowledge and values to which we are interpellated by the dominant patriarchal strain of literature and the arts. For although the knowledge in such cases can be different—and in ways that are not psychologically or politically negligible—a preconstituted knowledge remains the goal of such education; hence, the student remains subordinated to a system of knowledge/belief, with "mastery of" (read: "mastery by") the system being taken as an end in itself rather than as a means to benefit either individual subjects or society in general.

The same disposition of forces prevails in such activities as the supposed "criticism" of culture that humanities scholars and their students produce in ever-increasing amounts. While here the subjects appear to be active producers of knowledge rather than mere passive receptacles, this activity functions in many cases primarily to make subjects all the more subservient to the system of knowledge, which in their active manipulation of its categories they accommodate much more thoroughly than when they are mere passive recipients of the system.

Most cultural criticism thus functions for its producers as well as its consumers as a means of forming them to be replicators of the system. This is true of any criticism to the degree that it takes knowledge as an end in itself rather than as a means to promote social change. This function is performed most purely by all modes of formalist criticism, where the aim of the discourse is limited to producing knowledge about the aesthetic object, with little concern for the significance of this artifact for either the producing or the receiving subjects. But much supposedly iconoclastic criticism (e.g., Marxist, feminist, psychoanalytic, and new historicist criticism) also falls into this category, even though its guiding concepts—whether existential, moral, psychological, or social—intrinsically bear on vital human concerns. For even in such criticism, the emphasis is on producing more knowledge rather than on further empowering human subjects, a goal that requires attention to fantasy, desire, jouissance, and ideals in addition to knowledge.

But even attention to these elements does not guarantee that one will escape from the mill of knowledge-for-its-own-sake. The present study, for instance, while focusing on ideals, desire, jouissance, and so on, remains inextricably involved in the production of knowledge about these phenomena and is therefore susceptible at every step to expropriation by the aim of producing knowledge as an end in itself— knowledge as a mode of jouissance. This is an outcome that I want to prevent, to the extent that it is possible to do so. That is, I do not want myself or my readers to rest content with the satisfaction produced by the knowledge presented or made possible by this book. Rather, I want this knowledge to serve as a means for promoting large-scale psychological change.

But to make such a result possible, we must be cognizant of just how difficult it is to achieve, due to our immersion, as academics, in the discourse of the University. That is, we must recognize that whenever we have acquired or developed a bit of knowledge, the satisfaction that we derive from inhabiting or possessing this knowledge will tempt us simply to dwell within it rather than to use it in the service of psychological and social change.

Counteracting University Discourse

Given the totalizing power of the discourse of the University, the System, it is crucial to understand what the most effective means of counteracting it are. According to Lacan, the most effective mode of opposition does not lie in traditional revolutionary strategies, such as an alliance of workers and peasants asserting their demands. This sort of alliance in the former Soviet Union, for instance, produced the reign of the discourse of the University (XVII 237)—that is, a society in which a totalizing, totalitarian system (S2) was dominant. As long as students continue to speak, they remain within the discourse of the University (XVII 237), where they inevitably search for a new discourse of the Master. The only place that such revolutionary desire can lead, Lacan says, is to a discourse of the Master (XVII 239), of which the discourse of the University is a perversion (XVII 212), serving, as it does, to propagate the master signifiers on which it is surreptitiously based. "What you aspire to as revolutionaries," Lacan told students in 1970, "is a Master. You will have one!" (XVII 237).

These observations of Lacan's are relevant not only for those who aspire to political revolution *tout court* but also for those who wish to promote social change through cultural criticism. The validity of his observations for this realm is borne out by the fact that the two critical approaches that have aimed most explicitly at revolutionary ends— Marxism and feminism—have often slipped from critique into a new discourse of the Master.

One factor that makes the discourse of the University so powerful and tyrannical is the force of its master signifiers, which operate, for the most part, surreptitiously. In the field of science, for example— and, as we have seen, in much cultural criticism—the major master signifier is knowledge itself. It is impossible, Lacan observes, not to obey the commandment—the master signifier or ultimate value—that is at the place of truth in the discourse of science: "Keep on knowing more and more." All questioning about the value of this master signifier is simply crushed (XVII 120): the notion that knowledge is valuable—especially scientific knowledge—goes without saying in this scientific age. This notion is also powerfully present in cultural criticism, as we saw in the Introduction.[4] Nor is this book immune from

[4]Lacan interrogates the ground of this master signifier and finds that it consists in an even more fundamental master signifier—that of an "I" that is identical to itself and

this danger since, like psychoanalytic theory itself, this work is deeply involved with a knowledge that aspires to be as comprehensive as possible. And whenever one is involved with such knowledge, there is always the danger that the knowledge, with its master signifiers, will become the end and human subjects the means of serving it, rather than vice versa.

Since the master signifier in this way dominates (clandestinely) the discourse of the University, this discourse is in a way subservient to the discourse of the Master (XVII 172). The university, insofar as the master discourse of overt law and governance is suppressed, functions as an avatar of the master discourse, promulgating its master signifiers hidden beneath systematic knowledge. This suggests that one step toward opposing the tyranny of University discourse would be to expose the master signifiers that underlie it and constitute its truth. The more fully these master signifiers are exposed, the less capable they are of exercising their mesmerizing power, as the work of deconstruction and various other forms of ideology critique have demonstrated.

The Discourse of the Master

The discourse of the Master, Lacan says, is known by us today only in a considerably modified form (XVII 203), but it is nonetheless active and visible in the various discourses that promote mastery—discourses that valorize and attempt to enact an autonomous, self-identical ego. The discourse of the Master promotes consciousness, synthesis (XVII 79), and self-equivalence (XVII 91) by instituting the dominance of master signifiers (S1), which order knowledge (S2) according to their own values and keep fantasy ($\$ \Diamond a$) in a subordinate and repressed position (XVII 124):

$$\frac{S1}{\$} \longrightarrow \frac{S2}{a}$$

transcendental. Thus the final root operation that establishes the discourse of the University is the assumption of such an "I." Anyone who enunciates scientific knowledge automatically assumes the position of subject of this coherent, totalized knowledge, a subject that must itself be stable, consistent, and self-identical. And the assumption of this subject position is neither more nor less than the assumption by the subject of the self-identical "I" as its master signifier (XVII 70–71).

As Lacan notes, the discourse of the Master is particularly evident in attempts to promote a particular philosophy or politics, which would include much philosophical and political criticism. All teaching, in fact, begins as a discourse of mastery (XVII 79), with the imposition of the basic concepts of a discipline—master signifiers that serve to ground and explain the procedure of a body of knowledge that constitutes the discipline. Lacan suggests that medical teaching, for example, sometimes consists basically of acts of reverence to terms considered sacred (XVII 25), that is, to master signifiers.

Philosophy is a clear instance of the discourse of the Master (XVII 20). As philosophers of the ordinary language school have realized for some time, philosophical works are ultimately nothing other than attempts to promote a certain way of speaking.[5] Lacan's identification of philosophy as a discourse of the Master allows us to see that, more specifically, the basic function of philosophy is to articulate and promote certain master signifiers. Ontology, for instance, attempts to see all phenomena in terms of its central master signifier, "being," and specific ontologies establish other master signifiers, such as "permanence," "presence," "becoming," and "entelechy," which function as the bearers of ultimate meaning and which thus bestow meaning and value on all other signifiers. Ethics, similarly, is concerned with signifying all action in terms of the master signifiers that it establishes as either attributes or opposites of "good," the central master signifier. And epistemology views all phenomena in terms of "knowledge," "truth," or "reality."[6] Philosophical criticism—including even deconstruction, which criticizes the master signifiers of philosophy— finds it very difficult to escape becoming another master discourse, as demonstrated by the proliferation in the 1970s and early 1980s of deconstructive master signifiers like "logocentric," "aporia," and "undecidability."

[5]What this school often fails to emphasize, however, is that such ways of speaking are never *merely* ways of *speaking*: they are also ways of thinking, feeling, desiring, and acting, and thus have real consequences for people's lives.

[6]Science, too, is in solidarity with the discourse of the master. "At the present time," Lacan says, "our scientific discourse is on the side of the master . . . ; it represents him/it as such" (XVII 174). Science, as we have seen, "is not at all an affair of the progress of understanding." Rather, it "is something that . . . always functions to the benefit of the discourse of the master" (XVIIA 174). In fact, "science is what constitutes, maintains in force, the discourse of the master" (XVIIA 176). The point here is that although science claims to be devoted to understanding the real through empirical research, it effectively

Psychoanalytic theory, including Lacanian theory, is also susceptible to becoming a discourse of the Master, a possibility that Lacan noted explicitly on a number of occasions and to which he responded by insisting (following Freud) that psychoanalysis is not a metaphysics or worldview or alternative religion. Insofar as Lacan's theory has at times been seen as a discourse of the Master, it is important to acknowledge this fact squarely and distinguish such usage of Lacanian master signifiers from the usage I am advocating. I do not mean to suggest that one can use Lacan's concepts without having them function as master signifiers; in fact, no discourse can operate without master signifiers. Rather, the question is what use we put Lacanian master signifiers to. My aim is to use these master signifiers as means to promote change rather than as holy words with which we might baptize or consecrate certain phenomena and thereby ascend to some state of blessedness. Maintaining this distinction between end and means is crucial, for like deconstruction, psychoanalytic theory (including this book) becomes a discourse of the Master whenever its master signifiers (S1) and system of knowledge (S2) function as ends rather than means, that is, whenever its concepts are used to institute its preconstituted knowledge in its audience and thus achieve closure—

$$\frac{S1}{\$} \longrightarrow \frac{S2}{a}$$

—rather than to promote a transformative practice, which, as we shall see in considering the discourse of the Analyst, entails radically different functions for the master signifiers and knowledge of psychoanalysis.

The discourse of the Master, Lacan indicates, also operates in the

---

functions to promote the various master signifiers that dominate it. That is, rather than using its encounter with the Real (in empirical research) to challenge the dominant paradigms (S1) of knowledge (S2), science uses this encounter to annex more and more of the Real into the territory ruled by the already established master signifiers. And these master signifiers are not limited to those that structure the explanatory paradigms of the scientific disciplines themselves; they also include the master signifiers that guide the larger social and political agendas of our society. These master signifiers, such as "strength," "freedom," "independence," "individuality," and "family," etc. not only determine which scientific enterprises receive major funding; they also determine what issues are identified in the first place as questions to be asked or problems to be solved. And above all, the discourse of science makes no provision for fantasy, desire, or jouissance.

realm of politics (XVII 99). "What I mean by that," Lacan says, "is that [the discourse of the Master] encompasses everything, even what is believed to be revolution. More exactly, by what is romantically called Revolution, with a capital *R*, this discourse of the Master accomplishes *its* revolution, in the other sense of the turning that buckles itself" (XVII 99). This revolution is not a military or governmental phenomenon but rather a revolving of the elements of discourse into the structure of the discourse of the Master, where the master signifier becomes overtly dominant and buckles the other elements of discourse so they can't move and disrupt its dominance. In the late 1960s when Lacan made this comment, almost everything had been politicized— particularly in Paris—producing a totalizing, totalitarian discourse of the Master. This effect was promoted above all by those advocating revolution, for it was precisely they who annexed all aspects of life into the discourse of politics, seeing all phenomena in terms of master signifiers like "imperialism," "domination," "freedom," "oppression," and "Revolution" itself. The elevation of "Revolution" to the rank of a master signifier, however, ironically served to promote not radical change but rather reinforcement—"buckling"—of the S1-S2 articulation of the discourse of the Master that underlay the tyranny of the present system (S2).

The same fate awaits cultural criticism when it aims directly at revolution in attempting to institute specific values, or in applying certain master signifiers as labels of approbation or condemnation. This can be seen, for example, in Foucauldian discourse, where the master signifiers "power" and "knowledge" are frequently used so ubiquitously and indiscriminately that they do little more than provide monolithic labels for a given discourse, leaving unexposed the minute details of its operation and therefore the mechanism of its power over human subjects.

The same master discourse structure can be found wherever the primary force of the criticism derives from its utilization of master signifiers of either approbation or disapprobation as a means of celebrating or condemning a particular position, practice, or state of affairs. Instances of this structure can be found, for example, in feminist criticism that relies primarily on notions of phallocentrism, or Marxist criticism that focuses primarily on alienation, as well as in those instances of Lacanian criticism whose primary goal is to pin the tail of a Lacanian master signifier (e.g., "master signifier") onto the donkey of a text.

In fact, the preceding sentence becomes an example of precisely what it is criticizing, if one emphasizes the disapprobation it expresses and rests satisfied in the pronouncement of such a verdict. What I want to emphasize, however—in that sentence, and throughout this book— is the role that Lacanian master signifiers (like "master signifier") play not in baptizing phenomena but in constituting a specific knowledge, which, in turn, I want to use not for the immediate production of the satisfaction of mastery but as the basis of a transformative practice. It is necessary to insist on such distinctions, because Lacanian master signifiers and knowledge—S1 and S2—like any others, as soon as they become the dominant factor in a discourse, constellate a discourse of the Master and a discourse of the University, respectively, unless subordinated to an alternative aim, which, as we shall see, the discourse of the Analyst provides.

Undermining the Discourse of the Master

The question of "how to stop this little mechanism" of the discourse of the Master (XVII 207) is thus quite difficult, for the answer does not lie in the rhetoric of revolution. The effect of Marx's discourse, Lacan says, has changed nothing concerning the stability of the discourse of the Master (XVIIA 175). Marxism has succeeded not in overthrowing the imperialism of the discourse of the Master but rather in simply altering slightly the distribution of its force, replacing a master signifier like "individual" (in capitalism) or "master" (in feudalism) with that of "worker" (XVII 195). Hence Lacan's warning that calling for political revolution is only asking for a master (XVII 237). The reason is that any mass movement, as Freud demonstrated, is based on idealization and thus "reproduces very exactly," Lacan says, "the resurgence of the discourse of the Master" (XVIIA 175). That is, the idealized object or its attributes function as master signifiers around which a new (totalizing, imperialistic) system is constituted.

But if revolutionary rhetoric and political movements simply repeat the discourse of the Master and its imperialism, how could it ever be possible to overturn this tyranny? The answer, according to Lacan, lies in promoting a discourse with the opposite structure—what he calls the discourse of the Analyst. To understand this discourse and to see how it can produce psychological change and thereby social change, we must first examine the structure of the discourse of the Master and then the intermediate structure between the Master and the Analytic discourses, the discourse of the Hysteric.

The most salient structural feature of the discourse of the Master—

$$\frac{S1}{\$} \longrightarrow \frac{S2}{a}$$

—is, as we have seen, the dominance of the master signifier S1. When one reads or hears such a discourse, one is forced, in order to understand the message, to accord full explanatory power and/or moral authority to the proffered master signifiers and to refer all other signifiers (objects, concepts, or issues) back to these master signifiers. In doing this, the receiver of the message enacts the function of knowledge (S2). And as a result of enacting this function, the receiver produces a, the plus-de-jouir, that is, the suppressed (i.e., beneath the bar) excess of enjoyment, no longer to be enjoyed, for which there is no place either in the master's subjectivity (\$-S1) or in the system of knowledge or belief (S2) enacted by the receiver in response to the master's S1. It is this a, this plus-de-jouir, that carries the power of revolution, of subverting and disrupting the system of knowledge (S2) and its master signifiers (S1).[7]

The discourse of the Master, however, restricts this a, the unsymbolized cause of desire, to the receiver (the slave, the one in the position of powerlessness), who has no voice (no legitimation of his or her own subjectivity). The speaker, or master, is oblivious to the cause of his own desire (a) and has even repressed his own self-division (\$) (XVII 124), as experienced in such subjective states as shame, anxiety, meaninglessness, and frustration. The speaker, that is, so successfully identifies with her master signifiers that she actually believes herself to be whole, undivided, and self-identical (XVII 102, 177–78).

But in thus filling the function of the master—in being m'être à moi-

---

[7]This is the element that Kristeva has elaborated in her notion of the semiotic, which interrupts and otherwise interferes with the Symbolic order and thus produces revolution—in poetic language and thereby also in society. As I have indicated in the Introduction, my view is that the connection between poetic revolution and social revolution is much less certain and direct than Kristeva assumes.

même—the speaker loses something (XVI 123): the *a*, the cause of his desire. Thus the essence of the position of the master, Lacan says, is to be castrated: a certain jouissance is forbidden to him (XVII 124). The discourse of the Master is unique in this regard; it is the only one of the four discourses to exclude fantasy, which consists precisely in the Symbolic order's taking into account the relation of *a* (nonsymbolized being or unauthorized jouissance) with the subject that is subjected to the signifier in ways discussed above. In the discourse of the Master, the speaker is totally unaware of the reason for promulgating her master signifiers—totally unaware, that is, of the lack of being, or cause of desire, that the master signifier attempts to plaster over. As a result, the major factor that sustains revolution or resistance is suppressed.

Such suppression is also the result of all cultural artifacts, including criticism, that exclude the *a*, the want-of-being. Philosophy provides the most obvious instance, often focusing on what, according to its master signifiers, is or should be and neglecting subjects' desires. Literature, while it usually involves desire in some way, often uses the evocation of desire as a means of interpellating the audience to embrace a particular master signifier or set of such signifiers and thus to exclude truly revolutionary or disruptive desire. And much criticism, as we have seen, also functions, in part, at least, to suppress the *a* by insisting on certain master signifiers. In addition to much generic moral criticism, many instances of Marxist and feminist criticism ignore their audience's want-of-being and focus instead on promulgating certain basic values—certain master signifiers—as the solution to the social problems they expose.

The Discourse of the Hysteric

It is only by confronting the lack in its relation to the cause of desire (*a*) that the impetus behind the S1 can be understood and, perhaps, redirected or displaced. Around this element that remains hidden, Lacan says, not only psychoanalytic discovery (XVII 101) but also the transformation of the social order takes place. By interrogating that part of subjects that is left out by master signifiers, it becomes possible to reclaim what has been repressed and thereby institute a new economy of the collective psychological and hence also the social structure.

If one wants to be subversive, Lacan suggests, one would be advised to approach "the hole from which the master signifier gushes" (XVII 218).

In cultural artifacts and also in the criticism of those artifacts, this approach has often taken the form of the discourse of the Hysteric, where the subjective division (\$) assumes the position of dominance:

$$\frac{\$}{a} \longrightarrow \frac{S1}{S2}$$

This discourse takes its name from the fact that its most obvious instance is hysterical neurosis, whose physical symptoms manifest in the most striking way possible the subject's refusal to embody— literally, to give his or her body over to—the master signifiers that constitute the subject positions that society, through language, makes available to individuals (XVII 107). In hysterical neurosis this refusal of the body to follow the master signifier manifests itself in symptoms like anesthesia, paralysis, and tics—disorders which, Freud discovered, derive not from neurological dysfunction but rather from representations of the body becoming caught up in conflicts between ideals and desire—in Lacanian terms, between S1 and a. The divided subject (\$) is thus a manifestation of the alienation that occurs as a result of the subject's accession to language—an alienation that is suppressed in the discourses of the Master and of the University but that gains expression and dominance in the discourse of the Hysteric.

The hysterical structure also characterizes other discourses involving resistance, protest, and complaint—from the plaintive anthems of slaves, to the yearning lyrics of poets, to the iconoclastic rhetoric of revolutionaries, to the fire-and-brimstone sermons of Puritan preachers railing against "sin" (one word that religion uses to designate the a). The hysterical structure is in force whenever a discourse is dominated by the speaker's symptom—that is, his or her conflicted mode of experiencing jouissance, a conflict manifested (in experiences such as shame, meaninglessness, anxiety, and desire) as a failure of the subject (\$) to coincide with, or be satisfied with, the jouissance underwritten by, the master signifiers offered by society and embraced as the subject's ideals.

In cultural criticism, certain forms of reader-response criticism and, to an even greater degree, deconstruction often appear to privilege the \$, but the division in such cases is located either between different master signifiers (in the case of reader-response criticism such as that of Wolfgang Iser or Stanley Fish) or within a given master signifier (in deconstruction). Such divisions serve to mask the more profound split between S1 and a, ideal and want-of-being, that characterizes hysterical discourse. It is in feminist criticism rather than deconstruction per se that one finds the most powerful instances of hysterical discourse structure. This is not surprising, since feminist criticism protests with verbal discourse what Freud's hysterical patients (most of them women) protested through the physiological discourse of their bodily symptoms: the exclusion of part of their being (desires and jouissances) by the master signifiers and the resultant subject positions of women imposed by the patriarchal system (S2). Feminism has led the way in freeing criticism from its enthrallment to master signifers and systems of knowledge by introducing the personal into the public, political arena, where System dominates, and thus confronting the S1 and S2 with the $, the experience of alienation, suppression, and exclusion.

Despite its refusal to follow specific master signifiers, however, the hysterical subject remains in solidarity with master signifiers as such (XVII 107). This solidarity manifests itself in the quest of desire for an object that will satisfy it, the wish of anxiety for security and stability, the search of meaninglessness for a meaning or identity, and the urge of shame to coincide with the ideal. It was this connection that Lacan had in mind when he told revolutionary students that what they were really asking for—and would get—was a master. Lacan's point is not that the hysterical subject should do without master signifiers; no subject can do that, and all discourses—including, as we shall see, the discourse of the Analyst—have a place for master signifiers. The problem with the discourse of the Hysteric lies in its demanding the master signifier from the other rather than producing it oneself.

As Lacan's schema indicates, the S1 in the discourse of the Hysteric lies on the side of the receiver, who is summoned to respond to the hysterical subject's message by providing a master signifier (S1), a secure meaning that will overcome anxiety and give a sense of stable, meaningful, and respectable identity. Such responses are given by counselors, therapists, and priests to distraught individuals; by advertisements and political speeches to the desiring masses; and by all sympathetic people to needy friends. But although such responses provide comfort, hysterics remain alienated in demanding master signifiers from others rather than producing such signifiers themselves.

And the receivers of the hysterical message are also alienated by being summoned to produce master signifiers and knowledge in response to the other's division ($) rather than in response to their own want-of-being (*a*).

This situation can be found in various artifacts of culture and instances of the criticism of those artifacts. Lyric poetry often presents a persona in the position of the divided subject, and also frequently interpellates the audience into an identification with that position, while at the same time providing master signifiers that promise to close up the division (a characteristic shared by the political rhetoric of Jesse Jackson, as we shall see in Chapter 5). Such solidarity with the master signifier is also evident in the essentialist solutions embraced by some feminists in response to the problem of sexual identity and difference, although feminist criticism is generally more sensitive to the dangers of such solidarity with master signifiers than many other modes of criticism are.

The Discourse of the Analyst

It is only with the discourse of the Analyst—

$$\frac{a}{S2} \longrightarrow \frac{\$}{S1}$$

—that the subject is in a position to assume its own alienation and desire and, on the basis of that assumption, separate from the given master signifiers and produce its own new master signifiers, that is, ideals and values less inimical to its fundamental fantasy and the desire embodied by that fantasy. It is thus the discourse of the Analyst which, according to Lacan, offers the most effective means of achieving social change by countering the psychological and social tyranny exercised through language. The discourse of the Analyst promotes psychological change by placing in the dominant position of the sender's message the *a* belonging to the receiver of the message or analysand—precisely what has been excluded from symbolization (XVII 48) and suppressed by the discourse of the Master. In this way the discourse of the Analyst interpellates the analysand to recognize, acknowledge, and deal with this excluded portion of being, to the extent of producing a new master signifier (S1) in response to it. That is, when a person enters analysis seeking help—usually because some aspect of life is unfulfilling or painful—analysis seeks the cause of the patient's malaise (and even of apparently "external" problems) in an internal conflict between, on the one hand, the identity (the S1) the patient has assumed and tries to maintain, and, on the other hand, an unconscious desire for a jouissance (the *a*) that is excentric to or incommensurable with (i.e., forbidden by) this assumed identity. The aim of analysis is to help the patient encounter, acknowledge, identify, and finally come to identify with this excluded part of his or her being, the *a*.

This process entails two basic steps, which Lacan refers to as alienation and separation and which involve dissolving and re-forming identifications in one or more of the three registers. The schema of the discourse of the Analyst focuses on the second step, that of separation from the alienating master signifiers. But for such separation to occur, another, logically prior step must take place: identifying or "mapping" those master signifiers that constitute the alienating identifications. These two processes together can be seen as moving the analysand through the four structures of discourse identified by Lacan.

Analysis often begins with the patient speaking the discourse of the University, relating personal history and reflections on that history, with knowledge occupying the position of dominance. Such discourse constitutes an attempt to cling to and consolidate one's ideal ego (the point from which one experiences oneself as lovable) by presenting oneself as someone worthy of the analyst's love and approval, a love which, were one to get it, would simply reinforce one's ideal ego by gratifying one's passive narcissistic desire and giving one a feeling of well-being.[8]

The analyst must refrain from providing the passive narcissistic gratification that analysands seek and instead help the analysands recognize the alienating effect of the ideal ego, that is, realize that everything that they like about themselves, all those attributes that they usually take as characterizing the core of their being, are to a significant degree an illusion, a sham, a travesty. With the Rat Man, for example, this would have involved his recognizing and accepting that whereas he had thought himself to be a dutiful son bearing nothing but love and respect for his father, in reality he harbored murderous aggressive impulses toward his father, as well as passionate sexual wishes for him.

---

[8]Some forms of treatment concentrate precisely on providing such gratification. This is the therapy of "I'm OK, You're OK," as the title of the best-selling pop-therapy book of the seventies put it.

Where his oedipal identification (S1) established him as an honorable man, his unconscious fantasy (\$ ◇ a)—the remnant of what Freud terms the negative oedipal complex, or the son's sexual desire for his father—positioned him, we might say, as dishonorable and as a woman. A fully successful analysis would have promoted separation from this ideal ego; it would have entailed his coming to recognize and acknowledge both his sadism and his homosexuality as parts of himself that were just as real (if not as powerful and as manifest) as his altruism and heterosexuality.

Achieving this type of separation, between ego and ideal ego, occurs commonly both within analysis and outside it.[9] It is at least incipient whenever there is guilt or shame—two prominent types of alienation. Outside analysis it is a phenomenon frequently found in conjunction with religious belief, in believers' sentiments that they are sinners and unworthy of God's love. Within analysis this particular sort of separation has often already occurred to a degree before the patient enters treatment, its most common form being simply the patient's feeling that something is wrong with him or her (and not just with his or her environment). Such a feeling of alienation throws into relief the subject's master signifiers—those ideals or values that the subject in this case fails to live up to—and thus constitutes the basis of mapping the subject's identifications.

[9]Patients often go to considerable lengths to avoid this alienation from the ideal ego and thus maintain their passive narcissistic gratification. For instance, when a patient fails to achieve passive narcissistic gratification from an analyst, her active narcissistic desire often comes into play, resulting in a new identification at the level of the ego ideal—the patient's identification with certain (presumed) qualities of the analyst which, she feels, will win the analyst's love. In identifying with the analyst, the patient gives up part of her old identity, her old ego ideal, in order to maintain her ideal ego, her sense of being worthy, lovable. Some forms of treatment actually promote this process. Such therapy operates through the power of suggestion and positive and negative reinforcement, which produces psychological change through the Other's importing of new master signifiers (values and ideals) into the ego ideal. Such alterations of the ego ideal can be found in all sorts of situations, from psychotherapy to religious instruction and from child-rearing to brainwashing. The operative discourse here is either that of the Master, which imposes its master signifiers through insistently repeating them, or that of the University, which also provides master signifiers, but less emphatically and in the context of a system of knowledge or belief (S2). The problem with the psychological change promoted by such discourses is that it ignores the patient's fantasy and unconscious jouissance and thus doesn't get to the root of the patient's difficulties, which often lie in a conflict between ideals, on the one hand, and unconscious fantasy on the other. There is, moreover, a significant ethical problem with such a psychotherapy, as Lacan indicates, a point to which I will return later in this chapter with regard to cultural criticism.

Such mapping, in turn, transforms the analysand's University discourse into a discourse of the Master, which brings the analysand's alienation to its peak and sets the stage for separation from the alienating master signifiers, which means recognizing the questionable, relative nature, and the debilitating effect, of certain values or ideals— master signifiers of the ego ideal—that one has been taking as absolute. In the case of the Rat Man, this would have meant separating from the position in which having homosexual or murderous impulses is a terrible thing.[10] To help the patient achieve such separation from the ego ideal, the analyst, in a sort of deconstructive moment, helps the analysand interrogate the analysand's Master discourse, the discourse of the self-identical ego, thus intensifying the alienating effect of the master signifiers until the division ($) beneath the analysand's monolithic identity (S1) is experienced. In other words, the analyst works to elicit from the analysand a discourse with a hysterical structure (XVII 35), in which anxiety and a sense of emptiness or meaninglessness often dominate.

In response to the analysand's hysterical discourse, the analyst does not offer the master signifier (S1) and knowledge (S2) that the analysand demands in order to assuage the anxiety and emptiness. Instead, the analyst reflects or refracts the analysand's demand in such a way as to reveal the a, cause of the analysand's desire, and thus to expose the underlying fantasy ($S \diamond a$), which functions as a bedrock meaning for the analysand. The analyst, that is, responds to the hysterical element in the analysand's discourse in such a way as to illuminate and emphasize what has been left out and repressed, the a.[11]

[10]But the Rat Man, like most other subjects, strongly resisted altering his ego ideal to accommodate his still largely unconscious desire, preferring instead (at times, at least) to give up his ideal ego (his sense of self-regard), such as when, after having a scandalous fantasy about Freud's daughter, he told Freud that Freud should throw him out (*SE* 7:283). Here, giving up identifications with the ideal ego functions precisely as a scheme for holding on to the ego ideal and setting up surreptitiously an alternative ego ideal. This strategy is perhaps most obvious in the case of the religious believer whose statement (*énoncé*), "I am a wretched sinner and not worthy of God's love," is based on a tacit enunciation that runs something like: "But since I share God's view of my unworthiness, he will love me anyway." Religious belief and some types of psychotherapy often help subjects avoid crossing the plane of the ego ideal, but psychoanalysis promotes the crossing.

[11]This response of the analyst may not involve any explicit interpretation at all; it may consist simply in a punctuation of the patient's speech produced by ending the session or uttering an exclamation at a particular point in the patient's speech. Or it may occur as the forebearance of naming—as the silent witness which the analyst bears to the patient's speech and to the transference elicited by the fact that the patient supposes the

Confronted with this discourse of the Analyst, the analysand, as receiver responding to his or her own *a*, is in position to produce a new master signifier (S1), which amounts to an alteration of the ego ideal, and this entails an altered sense of identity as well as new meanings and different values. Only by thus realizing how their present master signifiers alienate them from the *a* can analysands proceed to separation from the alienating position embodied in their master signifiers, the separation occurring as the analysands gradually become reconciled to their repressed elements and, in fact, come to accept these as more a part of themselves than the monolithic values embodied in their ego ideal.[12]

This final phase of analysis includes what Lacan calls traversing the fantasy, which itself involves a third, repressed level of identification—in the case of the Wolfman (and probably also the Rat Man), the repressed identification with his mother as the passive object of his father's sexual desire. While this repressed identification with the object *a* of the Other—the object of the desire or jouissance of the Other—constitutes much of the motive force for the analysand's separation from the ideal ego and the ego ideal, the analysand must also separate from this position. This process involves the recognition of the Other's deficiency, the realization that the unconscious fantasies that have been directing one's desire and contributing to one's suffering are both relative and doomed to remain unfulfilled and, hence, that there is no transcendental meaning to be found for one's existence, no ultimate object that will satisfy one's desire, and no single, fundamental jouissance that will of itself make life worth living. To the extent

---

analyst to have knowledge of why the patient suffers, what the patient desires, and what will answer to this suffering and/or desire. Whatever the specific response of the analyst, it will be efficacious to the extent that it brings the patient closer to what has been left out of discourse, the *a* (XVII 48), the cause of the patient's desire (XVII 205). It is the confrontation with this rejected element that produces the depth and intensity of self-division or alienation necessary for patients to want to separate themselves from some of the alienating master signifiers, which embody these patients' symbolic identifications, and to produce new master signifiers and identifications that are less exclusive, restrictive, and conflictual.

[12] As a result of producing a new master signifier, the analysand moves, in effect, into a new discourse of the Master. This discourse does not constitute a radical break with tyranny and an accession to freedom, for the subject remains in thrall to a master signifier (XVII 205), thus rendering the process circular rather than progressive (XVIIA 177). There is a crucial difference, however, in the discourse of the Analyst: its master signifiers are produced by the subject herself rather than imposed on the subject from

that this realization is established—by the repetitious process of working through—the analysand realizes the arbitrary, ungrounded nature, with regard to the Other, of this fantasy and accepts the fantasy as his or her own particular means of jouissance. Thus at the end of analysis, Lacan says, the fundamental fantasy becomes the drive: the repressed desire for an alien jouissance embodied in the fantasy achieves a more overt and direct expression as a result of a new master signifier that accommodates the previously repressed desire.

Culture and Psychological Change

Given this understanding of how individual subjects are changed through the discourse of the Analyst in psychoanalytic treatment, we can now sketch out a strategy by which cultural criticism can promote social change by engaging, in a significant number of individual subjects, some of the same basic processes as those operative in psychoanalytic treatment. Lacan himself hinted at this possibility when he indicated that the position of the analyst can be assumed in relation not only to individual subjects but also to society as a whole. Taking up such a position provides the only real chance, Lacan says, to "accomplish what truly merits the title of revolution in relation to the discourse of the Master" (XVIIA 176). This is the case because any real social change must involve not just changes in laws and public policy but alterations in the ideals, desires, and jouissances of a significant number of individual subjects—precisely the sorts of alteration that psychoanalytic treatment involves. The best thing to do to bring about revolution, Lacan suggested, is thus to be not anarchists but analysts, which means positioning oneself in such a way as to interrogate how culture participates in the position of mastery (XVIIA 176)—that is, exposing, and thus allowing subjects to work through, the knowl-

---

the outside. In this way, one "shifts gears," as Lacan puts it. The Analytic discourse, that is, enacts "a new loop, ring, buckle," and thus obtains "a staggering, a shifting of the zero," through which the master signifier might be a little less oppressive (XVIIA 177). The new master signifier should be less oppressive because it is of a different style (XVII 205)—a style that is less absolute, exclusive, and rigid in its establishment of the subject's identity, and more open, fluid, and processual: constituted, in a word, by relativity and textuality. The discourse of the Analyst is able to promote such a response and production because it is opposed to all will of mastery (XVII 79), engaging in a continuous flight from meaning and closure, in a displacement that never ceases (XVII 171).

edge/beliefs (S2), ideals (S1), want-of-being ($), and forbidden jouissance (*a*) that the various cultural discourses establish as dominant.

The fundamental strategy of a socially transformative psychoanalytic cultural criticism, then, would be to promote, in "readers" or consumers of culture, a twofold process of alienation and separation similar to that which constitutes the transformative efficacy of psychoanalytic treatment. This means that, first of all, the cultural critic would refrain from any attempt to produce an alternative reading of a cultural artifact, alongside of or in opposition to the received reading(s). To offer a new reading, even a Lacanian one, of a given text or discourse would constitute a discourse of the University or a discourse of the Master that attempted to impose its beliefs (S2) or ideals (S1) on readers. (I would thus emphasize that what I will *not* be doing in Part II of this study is offering new or better readings of cultural artifacts per se.)

What the cultural critic must interpret is not the *text* but rather *readings* of the text. The cultural critic must analyze responses to a given artifact or discourse in order (1) to map the fundamental identifications (and the concomitant desires) that are promoted in a certain number of subjects by the cultural phenomenon in question, thus emphasizing in the critic's readers the alienation entailed by these identifications, and (2) to expose the unconscious desires and fantasies that the cultural phenomenon is surreptitiously operating with and/or further repressing. Such an analysis of response can promote a process of separation in the critic's readers from the alienating identifications. Pursuing such a strategy entails three logical steps.

The first step involves identifying a particular *manifest, collective, subjective effect* produced in a significant number of people by a cultural artifact or discourse. This can be a fairly simple task when the response of a large number of people includes identical actions and more or less identical demonstrated feelings, such as when there is a passionate and massive reaction to a particular political speech or discourse, as was the case with the speeches of Reagan and Jackson (analyzed in Chapter 5), with antiabortionist rhetoric (Chapter 4), and with pornography (Chapter 3). It is also possible to identify manifest collective effects by looking for common denominators in reviews, critical articles, and other testimony (written or oral) of members of an audience of a given text or discourse, as with *Heart of Darkness*, "To Autumn," and antiabortionist discourse, analyzed in Chapters 6, 7, and 4, respectively. On the basis of such evidence—which, moreover, avoids the danger, courted by most response-centered analyses, of simply generalizing from the critic's own responses or from the critic's speculations about how everyone else responds—one can infer the potential of a social effect, without needing to assume that all, or even a majority, of those who respond to a cultural artifact share the particular sort of response that one is investigating. Thus in the analyses that follow in Part II, my only claim about the scope of the responses is that in each case the particular type of response that I have chosen to investigate is widespread enough to be of potential social significance.

The second step of the psychoanalytic cultural criticism that I am proposing involves identifying the *elements of the discourse* that are responsible for the manifest effects identified in the first step. Lacanian theory makes this procedure possible by explaining, as we saw in Chapter 1, the various ways in which subjects' identity, desire, and jouissance are determined by the fate of signifiers, thus allowing us to infer, from manifest effects in the receiving subjects' actions, opinions, or feelings, which specific configurations of images, signifiers, and fantasies in the given discourse must have produced these manifest effects. If the first step has determined that the overall response of a given audience to a given discourse was positive, then one examines the discourse for elements that would serve to gratify one or more forms of desire in the Imaginary, Symbolic, and/or Real registers and thus reinforce, respectively, the body ego, ego ideal, and/or fantasy of the audience. Conversely, if the overall response to the discourse was negative, one looks for elements that thwart the various forms of desire in each register.

Greater specificity either in the nature of the response (i.e., beyond simple like or dislike) or in the elements toward which the response is directed (e.g., a particular character, image, or scene rather than just the text or discourse as a whole) constitutes additional evidence of considerable value in identifying the particular psychological factors and textual/discursive elements operative in a given case. If the specificity is great enough in both areas, one should be able to pinpoint with considerable certainty precisely what textual elements are operating on what psychological structures to produce the observed responses in the audience. For example, if an audience exults in the success of one character and celebrates the demise of his or her opponent, we can be fairly certain that the audience is identifying with the first character on at least one level and that Imaginary-order rivalry and aggression are also involved.

The third logical task, occurring, in fact, simultaneously with the second step, is to identify the *nonmanifest* collective *subjective* factors—particular desires and specific contents of ideal ego (Imaginary), ego ideal (Symbolic), and fantasy (Real)—that are appealed to by those discursive elements that produce the *manifest* effects. Beginning in the Symbolic register, we would thus inquire into the way the text in question operates with the master signifiers of the ego ideal. First, does the Symbolic Other gratify or frustrate the audience's passive narcissistic desire for recognition? What form does this particular recognition (or lack of it) take: Does it address the ideal ego, either affirming or denying that the audience actually embodies the master signifiers of its ego ideal, or does it address the ego ideal itself, either affirming or denying the privileged status of the audience's master signifiers? In the case of gratification, are the audience's master signifiers simply confirmed and reinforced, or are some used to undermine or promote others? In particular, what fantasies are recognized and valorized by the Symbolic Other: are these fantasies congruent with or opposed to the audience's fantasies? Similarly, what images, governing Imaginary-order identity and desire, are recognized and validated by the Symbolic Other, and what images are rejected by this Other, implicitly or explicitly?

In the Imaginary register, we would need to examine both the cultural artifact and the audience response for evidence of Imaginary-order desires (including identification) of the various sorts we have discussed. On the side of the artifact, we would look for elements that could affect the audience's body ego in some way. Such elements would include images of the human body, spatial images that situate the human body in certain ways, and other images that have some bearing (positive or negative) on one's sense of bodily integrity and well-being. Representations of parade, prestige, mirroring, and other narcissistic gratifications, as well as instances of competition, rivalry, and aggression or violence would also be included. The basic question we would ask is: What desires are evoked by the imagery of the discourse? We would thus need to investigate what effects the representations of bodies and of space, and the imagery in general of the discourse (i.e., signifiers appealing to the audience's senses), have on the audience's Imaginary,

Symbolic, and Real identifications. That is, does the imagery reinforce or oppose the audience's Imaginary identifications and sense of well-being or vulnerability supported at the level of the ideal ego or body ego, the audience's ultimate values or ideals (S1), and the audience's specific fantasies?

Concerning the register of the Real, we would identify instances of the object a, particularly the surplus enjoyment that exceeds and is excluded by the System (S2) and its dominant ideals and values (S1). We would then inquire whether the a functions for the audience as an anaclitic or a narcissistic object and whether the audience assumes an active or passive position with regard to the a, that is, whether the audience assumes the position of desiring subject ($) or the position of the a, cause of the Other's desire.

In addition, we would need to assess how the Other's lack is dealt with: Is it ignored (repressed, denied), or is it acknowledged? If it is acknowledged, is this acknowledgement sustained by all the other elements of the artifact, or is it denied by some of them?

After we have answered these questions, we should note the degree of resonance or dissonance among the contents of these three orders of interpellation. This will allow us to determine the resultant vector of interpellative force produced by the complementarity and/or opposition among various instances of desire (including identification) operating in all three registers.

Such a procedure is in many ways analogous to an analyst's interventions in a patient's discourse, which, as we have seen, involves mapping the analysand's identifications, uncovering the analysand's fundamental fantasy, and working through these two processes repeatedly in many different situations and contexts. Operating in this way from the position of an analyst with regard to culture means analyzing the various, mutually disjoint and even contradictory discourses of a culture in order to reveal both the collective master signifiers and the a, unconscious jouissance, cause of desire, which operates in fantasy behind the facade of the master signifiers and the entire signifying apparatus.

What must be done, essentially, is to reveal to subjects that what they are asking for (and perhaps think they are getting) in their values, ideals, conscious wishes, and identifications is not the only expression or even the most truthful embodiment of what they really desire or find gratification in. By exposing the Real, which the system of signifiers, and particularly the master signifiers, fail to grasp, the discourse of the Analyst interpellates those subjects who have responded in the particular way that one is examining to an activation of their alienated condition, their nonidentity with their master signifiers, and thus creates an impetus for them to produce new master signifiers.

Ethics and Efficacy of Cultural Criticism

A strictly psychoanalytic mode of cultural criticism, then, would reveal the desires (including identifications) operating in a particular type of response to a particular discourse. Like the discourse of the Analyst in individual psychoanalytic treatment, such a procedure would promote change without offering advice or suggestion to the analysands, that is, without demanding that the analysands change (attitudes, behavior, ideals, or values) in any particular way. Any change that might occur would result from the use that the analysands made of the insights attained concerning their own conflicting desires. Such a procedure, I would maintain, is simultaneously more powerful and more ethical than other current modes of cultural criticism.

It is more powerful in that, as experience demonstrates and as Lacan's account of psychological change explains, merely asserting a new system of knowledge or belief (the discourse of the University, which promotes S2) or insisting on new ideals or values (the discourse of the Master, asserting S1) or lamenting or protesting the current state of affairs (the discourse of the Hysteric, asserting $) often has little effect. As we have seen, most cultural criticism has operated in one of the first two modes, and even criticism that escapes the impasses of the discourses of the Master and the University usually remains hystericized and thus enthralled to either a master signifier or a fantasy (object *a*) imposed by the Other. Only psychoanalytic criticism makes possible the exposure of the most powerful forces exerted on group psychology by discourse: the forces of drives, desire, and jouissance attached to fantasy. And only Lacan's model, so far as I know, has made it possible to articulate rigorously how an analysand/audience's fantasy and unconscious desires can be revealed and allowed to emerge in a way that constitutes an *internal* challenge to the audience's master signifiers (S1) and knowledge or belief (S2).

The internal nature of this challenge not only makes the challenge more forceful, it also constitutes a different ethical position. Like Marxist and deconstructive analyses, one moment of such a critique involves summoning and exposing the S2, the S1, and the $—the $ being identified by Marxism as the alienated subject and by deconstruction as the aporias of S1 and S2. But a Lacanian analysis of the sort I have outlined involves two crucial differences. First, psychoanalytic deconstruction of S1 and S2 results from the emergence of the subject's desire rather than from a general logical or social contradiction. And second, and even more importantly, having exposed the contradictory and/or illusory nature of the central values (S1) of a discourse, and the alienation or split ($) embodied in them, a psychoanalytic critique searches for new values along a different path to truth than the ones followed by Marxism, deconstruction, or any other current critical method. Rather than promoting certain a priori and universal truths (S1) or knowledge (S2) about social justice, human nature, or historical necessity (i.e., master signifiers of Marxism) or declaring undecidability to be the last word, or unlimited semiosis or the abyss of aporia the final reference point (master signifiers produced by the insistent skepticism of deconstruction), the mode of analysis I am proposing refers the audience to its own desire—embodied in the fantasies imbricated in its own response—as the basis upon which the audience could establish new master signifiers. Such a procedure allows the audience to relinquish master signifiers without involuntarily abandoning their fantasies. Marxism and deconstruction, in contrast, attempt to take away or demolish the master signifiers without taking subjects' fantasies or other desires into account. As a result, such modes of criticism encounter insurmountable resistance from a subject, or they provide new master signifiers that have no guarantee of not being every bit as alienating as the original ones. The psychoanalytic path outlined here thus has the potential to be less violent and authoritarian than Marxism or deconstruction, in addition to being more effective in undermining oppressive structures and promoting collective psychological and (thereby) social change.

It remains now to put this critical apparatus and strategy into practice to see how effective they are in exposing the psychological grounds and the social ramifications of specific instances of interpellation. It should be emphasized that any change produced by such a mode of cultural criticism would, like the change promoted by psychoanalytic treatment, occur only after working through these identifications and fantasies in numerous diverse texts and discourses. And like psychoanalytic change, this change cannot be charted precisely or even guaranteed ahead of time by the analyst.

PART II

PRACTICE

CHAPTER THREE

PORNOGRAPHY

The Social Effects of Pornography

Pornography is an obvious test case for the sort of cultural criticism I am proposing. Of all discourses, it is probably the most blatant in its exposure and manipulation of an audience's desire, and this manipulation, moreover, is also thought by many to have profound social effects, the most significant being the degradation of women to the status of mere sexual objects for heterosexual men. As Jacquelyn Zita puts it, "The pornographic apparatus is a social practice which imposes certain codes on the bodies of women, and can result in texts and images which produce effects in battered, raped or murdered women" (39–40).

Pornography thus confronts a cultural critic with three fundamental questions: Does pornography actually promote such effects? If it does, how does it do so? And what is the most effective way to counteract these effects? The following analysis suggests, first, that pornography for heterosexual men (which will be the focus of my analysis) does indeed promote such effects, although it in all likelihood also produces some positive effects for certain people; second, that the way in which these effects are produced is somewhat different than has been assumed; and third, that the most effective manner of undermining these effects is not, as current practice tends to assume, to denounce the chauvinistic and destructive attitudes of heterosexual men but rather to psychoanalyze their response to pornography.

The prevailing explanation of how pornography produces degradation of women focuses on the behavior that is portrayed in pornography: actual men, it is argued, behave as they do because they imitate the represented behavior of male characters in pornography—behavior that men have already embraced as the result of other cultural conditioning—and then coerce women into adopting the complementary roles that are likewise represented in pornography. According to this view, pornography teaches men to be active and assertive, and women to be passive and submissive, by representing men and women behaving in these respective ways. Zita's version of this account runs as follows:

> Within the pornographic apparatus, and on the deepest sexual level, what it means to be "female" and what it means to be "male" *are dependent on what gets done to whom* within the codic determinations of pornographic sex. The pornographic construction of "male" requires domination and ability to penetrate, usually excited through the use of force. The pornographic construction of "female" requires submission and provision of sites for penetration, whether orifices or the skin itself. (30; emphasis added)

Susanne Kappeler presents a similar assessment, seeing the major effect of pornography—and, indeed, of all representation—as deriving from the positioning of men in the role of the active subject and women in the role of the passive object. "What feminist analysis identifies as the pornographic structure of representation," Kappeler contends, is "not the presence of a variable quality of 'sex', but the systematic objectification of women in the interest of the exclusive subjectification of men" (103). "The objectification of women," she states, "is a result of the subjectification of man. He is a pure subject in relation to an object, which means that he is not engaging in exchange or communication with that objectified person who, by definition, cannot take the role of a subject" (50).

Central Features of Pornography

Contrary to this account, however, examination of the central motifs of pornography suggests that the effects of pornography derive not so much from the representation of certain *actions*—"what gets done to whom," as Zita puts it—as from the representation of the Other's desire in relation to these actions. For what pornography for heterosexual men (historically the primary audience) in fact presents is not simply women as objects for male subjects, but rather a multifaceted array of desire in which the desire of the Other (in various forms) is central, and in which both men and women figure as both subjects and objects.[1] More specifically, the arousal of desire and the production of jouissance for heterosexual men is achieved through a number of very particular presentations of the desire of the Other:

I. The desire represented in this pornography is predominantly anaclitic desire, or the desire for sexual jouissance, rather than narcissistic desire, that is, love or the desire to be loved. Anaclitic desire is isolated from narcissistic desire, or love, with love being excluded from the field of signification.

II. This desire of the Other for sexual jouissance is presented in all three registers, and involves the Other as both subject and object.
   A. In the register of the Real, the Other sex (Woman) is presented as being:
      1. An object for masculine desire, and
      2. A subject *desiring* to be the object of masculine desire.
   B. In the Imaginary register, the desire of the Other is presented in the form of:
      1. The image of a woman's body functioning as a sexual object, and
      2. The image of the desiring male protagonist, functioning as either alter ego or rival.
   C. In the Symbolic register the Other (Society, Nature, God) is presented as desiring particular forms of jouissance and as

[1]The role of the desire of the Other in pornography has for the most part been either overlooked or misunderstood in most analyses to date. Blindness to the role played by the desire of the Other extends even to those scenes in pornography where this desire is most obvious. Thus Linda Williams, for example, declares that in hard-core pornographic films "the money shot [i.e., the shot of the man ejaculating onto the woman] fails to represent the satisfaction of desire as involving a desire for, or of, the other [i.e., the woman]" (113). In fact, precisely the opposite is often true: for example, when the woman eagerly laps up the ejaculate, what is being represented is her desire. Kappeler similarly overlooks the desire of the Other (see 90–91), and when she does acknowledge the presence of female desire in pornography, she reduces its role to that of being a challenge and threat to the man (138).

sanctioning these forms by legitimizing (sexual) identity and giving recognition.

III. The phallus is presented as the privileged signifier of both masculine and feminine identity and desire.[2]

Most of these functions can be found in two recent accounts of two different pornographic media and genres.[3] In the first, on Victorian pornographic fiction, Peter Webb describes a novel entitled *Raped on the Railway* as "a very average example" of this genre:

> The author states his position at the outset: "To get a strong-bodied wench, in the prime of health, down on her back, and triumph over her virtue, in spite of all her struggles, is to my mind the height of delightful existence, the sum of all human ambition." He then relates the story of Robert Brandon whom we meet at Euston Station as he boards the Glasgow train. Seeing a lady whose face is concealed behind a veil, he takes a seat in her compartment, and manages to keep other passengers from joining them. Once the journey has begun he loses no time in making sexual advances towards the unknown lady. She refuses even to show her face, and so he snatches at the veil and finds her to be extremely beautiful. She then threatens him with a revolver but collapses in a faint as the train comes to a sudden halt. He immediately lifts her skirt and petticoats and reveals her sexual charms: "uttering an exclamation of joy, he tore open his trousers, and there sprang out, ready for the fray, his huge member rearing aloft at the end of the big straight hard column of muscle the round red gland which had hunted love through so many soft, damp velvety caverns, and though exhausted by the chase, was ever ready to begin again after a short rest. At that moment the lady opened her eyes, and the first thing she caught sight of was the big machine prepared to impale her."

[2]In focusing on these functions, I do not mean to suggest that they are the only factors in pornography that affect heterosexual men, or that all heterosexual men respond in the same way to these factors, identifying and desiring always and exclusively in the ways that I describe. Rather, my claim is that these functions are the most significant, since they can explain the most basic and common responses of heterosexual men to pornography.

[3]As a foundation for this inquiry, I am taking the accounts that several recent studies provide of the predominant features characterizing pornography. Basing the analysis on the accounts of others rather than on my own reading of pornography guards against the danger of my distorting the phenomenon in order to make it fit the theory I am employing. And my reliance on several accounts rather than a single one provides further controls—for medium (film versus print), historical period (contemporary versus Victorian), and gender of observer (female versus male).

A vigorous battle ensues, the outcome of which is never in doubt: "as she arched up her buttocks that she might better be able to twist sideways and get rid of the intruder, Brandon gave a powerful downward lunge, and as the head of his tool was already within her lips the double force sent two thirds of his big column into her vulva. She knew then that he had won the game, and woman-like burst into a flood of tears." After he has completed the rape, Brandon proceeds to apologize, blaming his behaviour on her extraordinary beauty. The lady is flattered and forgives him, realizing that she has quite enjoyed the experience. (94)

Webb's description of this particular work, together with his accounts of other Victorian pornographic novels, allows us to identify five common motifs of this genre, each of which embodies one of the factors listed above, identified in brackets:

1. The act of rape [II.B.2]
2. The woman's subsequent enjoyment of the act [II.A.2]
3. The deification of the man's penis (by the woman) [III],
4. The description of the woman's vagina (and other body parts) as objects of the man's desire [II.B.1], and
5. Whipping (of either the man or the woman) [I].

Zita, in her recent article on contemporary pornographic films, identifies six "codes that are commonly found in the pornographic construction of 'woman'" (34), each of which also embodies one of the factors identified above:

1. Sex without reproduction [I]
2. Sex as dangerous [I]
3. Sex as defined by phallic options, specifically women being defined as a function of their relationships with men [III],
4. Sex as willed by the woman [II.A.2],
5. Sex as a violation of the woman [I and II.C]
6. "Woman" as sex [II.A.1] (34).

The Desire of the Other

The Real Other

As this preliminary sketch suggests, the crucial factor in the pornographic arousal of desire and production of jouissance for heterosexual men is the presentation of the desire of the Other in its various anaclitic modes. In the first place, the desire of the woman, the Real Other who is the object of heterosexual male desire, is crucial for arousing heterosexual male desire. The importance of the desire of this Other is demonstrated by the tendency of men to fantasize it when they can't actually find it. Some of the more obvious and outrageous instances of this fantasy are to be found in the clichés with which some men respond to rape ("She was asking for it") and to a woman's rejection of a man's sexual advances ("You know you really want it"), as well as in the notion some men have that if lesbians have sex with a "real man" they will become heterosexual.

This fabrication of the desire of the woman is one of the major means by which pornography arouses active anaclitic desire in heterosexual men and provides satisfaction for them. Zita describes the ubiquity of this message in pornography:

> That every woman desires penetration, sexual force, violation, transgression, and the fear and danger that comes with the romantic anarchy of sexual desire, becomes the one and only secret about women that pornography finds worthy of constant exposure. . . . Woman is always constructed as desiring what is done to her. Where questions of will, desire or consent might exist, these are erased by the biological occurrence of orgasm construed as *the will of sex*. (32, 35; emphasis in original)

Linda Williams makes much the same observation in relation to hard-core pornographic films:

> Hard core desires assurance that it is witnessing not the voluntary performance of feminine pleasure, but its involuntary confession. . . . The animating male fantasy of hard-core cinema might therefore be described as the (impossible) attempt to capture visually this frenzy of the visible in a female body whose orgasmic excitement can never be objectively measured. It is not surprising, then, that so much early hard-core fantasy revolves around situations in which the woman's sexual pleasure is elicited involuntarily, often against her will, in scenarios of rape or ravishment. (50)

Zita's and Williams's observations are corroborated by Anthony Crabbe's contention, in his discussion of feature-length sex films such as *Emmanuelle* and *Deep Throat*, that many elements of such films are designed to address "the [male] viewer's wish for his desires to be reciprocated" (65), including such things as the woman's begging to be fucked, her moaning during the act, and her licking up the man's semen. Gary Day's description of hard-core "loops" (short films) reveals the same feature: "The typical scenario of the hard-core loop is of a woman who either initiates sex or is easily persuaded into it because 'it's what she really wants', and it ends with her licking the semen that the man has ejaculated over her" (95). This "money shot," as it is called, is described by Williams as "the most prevalent device of the . . . hard-core film's attempt to capture an involuntary confession of pleasure [on the part of the woman]" (95).[4] This device is pursued further in *Deep Throat*, where, Crabbe observes, "with the help of a horny doctor, [the heroine] discovers that she enjoys oral sex best of all because her clitoris is in her throat" (54). The narrative device of this fantasy clitoris, Crabbe comments, "helps the viewer to believe that fellatio is *mutually* rewarding and not, as is often argued, an exploitative form of male masturbation" (56).

This need of the heterosexual male viewer's to find the desire of Woman, the Other Sex, complementary to his own desire extends beyond the female characters in the film to the actresses themselves. "[The] issue of whether the actress enjoyed her role," Crabbe reports, "is of the first importance for the confirmed viewer" (58). Hence, the celebrity system in recent hard-core porn, which produces such reassurance in the form of interviews with the actresses. "The interviews," according to Crabbe, "provide reassurance that the actresses concerned are not prostitutes, and so actually *enjoy* their work" (57; emphasis in original).

The desire of the Other Sex—desiring Man—is thus a central feature of pornography. It is powerfully present in Victorian pornography, where the woman's desire is signified most obviously and notoriously by her subsequent enjoyment of being raped, an instance of, in Zita's words, "the biological occurrence of orgasm [being] construed as *the will of sex*" (35).[5] It is also present wherever a woman is represented as

---

[4]Williams denies, however, that this money shot has anything to do with the desire of the other (113). I will address this point in greater detail later.

[5]See also Williams (65). The rape, moreover—which is simply the most extreme instance of the code of "sex as violation" described by Zita—functions, as we shall see, in several additional ways to signify the desire of the Other.

being actively seductive. This feature is ubiquitous, for example, in the photographs of magazines like *Playboy*, where the relative (if not total) undress of the women, together with their come-hither gazes, signifies that their desire is to be the object of male desire.[6]

The Imaginary Other

The desire of the Other also operates in several ways in the Imaginary order—the register of the audience's response to the image of the human body. As Lacan notes, "The primary imaginary relation provides the fundamental framework for all possible erotism. It is a condition to which the object of Eros as such must be submitted" (I 174). More specifically, as we discussed in Chapter 1, an image of the human gestalt can arouse sexual desire in the subject. "The libidinal drive," Lacan declares, "is centred on the function of the image" (I 122). "The mechanical throwing into gear of the sexual instinct is . . . essentially crystallised in a relation of images" (I 121–22). This function is obvious in pornography, forming the core of pornographic films and of publications like *Playboy* and playing a central role in much verbal description as well.

In addition to thus functioning as the *object* of male desire, the Imaginary other can also function as the *subject* of desire, through being the object of the audience's identification. This form of the desire of the Imaginary other—the desiring body of the male protagonist as alter ego of the (male) audience—is present whenever a heterosexual male protagonist is represented as desiring. Here again, rape is a powerful instance, for in presenting an image of the desire of the male body as monolithic (only one thing can satisfy it) and irrepressible (nothing can stop it), the rape provides the male audience with an Imaginary other in whom they can recognize and consolidate their own sexual

---

[6]Such desire can also be seen to operate even in a woman's opposition to a man's sexual desire. At first it might seem that a woman's opposition would work against male desire, insofar as what the man desires is for the woman to desire him. But the woman's opposition can actually work to stoke male desire, for opposition, too, is a form of intense desire—albeit in negative form—with the man and his desire as its object. This negative desire can be highly arousing, as can easily be seen in many other fictional and actual instances of women opposing the advances of a man. This type of desire of the other—desire as resistance—is present to a degree whenever the man must persuade the woman to have sex with him. (Desire of this sort operates partially in the Imaginary register, where aggression, rivalry, and competition are significant components of desire.)

desire—such Imaginary identification being, as Lacan notes, a fundamental way in which desire comes to be constituted in the first place.

The Symbolic Other

Images, whether pictorial or verbal, thus play a central role in pornography's arousal of desire. However, in human subjectivity, as we have seen, images are ultimately governed by the signifier: recall the deflation of desire experienced by the heterosexual man who ogles a shapely woman in a bar only to be told that "she" is really "a man." Thus although an image of the female body may be a necessary factor in the production of heterosexual male desire, it is not by itself sufficient to produce such desire. In order for the *image* of woman to produce male heterosexual desire, that image must be coupled with the *signifier* "woman," because "woman" is the object of heterosexual male desire in the Symbolic order.

This operation of the signifier in pornography (and elsewhere as well) involves the desire of the Symbolic Other in several ways. First, it involves the male subject's passive narcissistic desire—the desire to be loved, recognized, valued by the Symbolic Other (e.g., Nature, Society, or God). In pornography this desire of the Symbolic Other is largely implicit, for instance, in the Symbolic Other's approbation of pornography, implied by the mere fact that the porn industry is allowed to exist, as well as in the explicit or tacit endorsement offered by various voices of authority (e.g., narrators and characters) concerning the desires and actions of the pornography consumer.

This passive narcissistic desire for recognition and approval by the Symbolic Other entails an active narcissistic desire, the desire to identify with and come to embody those signifiers that are valorized by this Other and that thus carry with them the Other's recognition. As we have seen, subjects desire to embody not only the master signifier itself (e.g., "man") but also any other signifier bearing a metonymic or metaphoric relation to the operative signifier—that is, any signifier that functions as a synonym, attribute, or even associate of the master signifier (e.g., "strong," "virile," or "big").

Moreover, in coming to embody certain signifiers, subjects also assume certain specific desires, since some of these signifiers preferred by the Symbolic Other govern desire itself. Such desire is central to the operation of pornography, which offers numerous instances of desires with which the male audience can identify, as well as numerous objects for such desires. It is in the offering of such signifiers—signifiers of women's bodies and of male desire—that pornography exercises its most powerful interpellation in the Symbolic register of desire. This desire of the Symbolic Other for "woman" also manifests itself in other ways in pornography, including the representation of rape. Insofar as prohibition against rape was instituted less out of concern for *women's* rights than out of concern for *men's* supposed rights to women as property (i.e., objects of desire), the very category of rape serves to signal that any given woman is the property of the Symbolic Other (Society, God, or Nature) and, hence, an object that the Symbolic Other values and desires.

This form of the desire of the Symbolic Other is also engaged by any other instance in which sex is portrayed as transgressing the Law, which, strictly speaking, would mean any instance of sex that is not between husband and wife. This would include virtually all instances of sex in pornography. As Day observes, "Sex [in hard-core loops] is presented as perverse and forbidden. . . . The forbidden character of sex in these loops emerges in the way that intercourse takes place among people between whom it would not normally or conventionally take place. Thus the bride has sex with everyone except her husband; there are numerous adulteries and even examples of incest" (95).[7] Such representations evoke narcissistic desire in several ways. First, they mark women as objects desired by the Symbolic Other and thus make them more desirable to men, insofar as a man's desire for "woman" marks him as a man. Second, such representations elicit a certain competition and even aggressivity on the part of heterosexual men, whose desire is blocked by the Symbolic Other. And third, in triumphing over the Symbolic Other's prohibition, masculine subjects experience a momentary and partial overcoming of the castration produced by their accession to the Symbolic order.

The Phallic Signifier

This transcendence of Symbolic-order castration receives more powerful and overt support in pornography from the operation of the

[7]Day continues: "To do what is forbidden is an expression of power, the individual defying the right of the community to determine what is and is not acceptable behaviour

phallus, a signifier that is central not only to masculine identity and desire but also to the construction of "woman" as the object of that desire. Pornography manipulates this phallic signifier in a number of fundamental and quite specific ways in both film and literature to produce and fortify desire in the heterosexual male audience.

It is in the representation of rape, again, that the function of the phallic signifier in pornography can be seen most clearly. First, it is around the penis as signifier that the desire of the Symbolic Other (Society) is constructed, since it defines rape as penetration by the penis. Second, in the act of rape the man's desire is concentrated in and signified by his penis: not only does the man have no concern for the woman as a person, he also has no concern for other physical enjoyments for himself besides that centered on his penis. Third, the desire of the woman victim is also focused on the man's penis—she wishes above all not to be penetrated by it (or precisely to be penetrated by it, in some pornographic representations of rape). And finally, and most significantly, the woman's enjoyment of rape in pornography is represented as the result of the marvelous nature of the male organ. This fact is made quite explicit in a passage from a novel called *The Lustful Turk*, cited by Webb, in which Emily, who has been raped by the Turk, writes to her friend Silvia:

> I was lost to everything but the wonderful instrument that was sheathed within me. I call it wonderful, and I think not improperly; for wonderful must that thing be that in the midst of the most poignant grief can so rapidly dissolve our senses with the softest sensations, spite of inclination, so quickly cause us to forget our early impressions, our first affections, and in the most forlorn and wretched moment of our existence make us taste such voluptuous delight and lustful pleasure. . . . You, Silvia, who are yet I believe an inexperienced maid, can have no conception of the seductive powers of this wonderful instrument of nature—this terror of virgins, but delight of women. . . . I was soon taught that it was the uncontrolled master-key of my feelings. (Webb 99)

This representation of a woman's deification of the male organ shows clearly how male heterosexual desire constructs the desire of its

---

for him or her" (95). My point is that the more important function of the forbidden nature of sex is to signal the Symbolic Other's desire.

Other through a phallic metaphor. This phallic metaphor, moreover, is present even when a woman is not represented as overtly desiring a man's penis. For from the perspective of male heterosexual desire, the mere possession of a vagina becomes a signifier of woman's desire for the penis. Focusing on the vagina's capacity to accommodate the male organ, male heterosexual desire engages in a process of metonymic slippage from organ to desire: that is, since the female *organ* physically accommodates and complements the *male organ* as a sheath does a knife (to borrow the metaphor used by Emily in the passage just quoted), the desire embodied in those organs must (so the logic goes) be similarly complementary: if the man wants to thrust his penis into a woman, she must want to receive it. In this way, metonymic slippage from organ to desire ushers in the phallic metaphor that overwrites the vagina as lack of, and hence desire for, the penis.

This function of the vagina as the signifier that Lacan calls "minus phi," lack-of-phallus, is demonstrated by the fact that the real, physical qualities of the vagina are in and of themselves neither necessary nor sufficient to arouse male desire. That they are not by themselves *sufficient* is demonstrated by the fact that for most men, a vagina, to be arousing, must at least be signified as a human vagina rather than that of the female of another species. That the unique physical qualities of the vagina are not in themselves absolutely *necessary* for the arousal of male heterosexual desire can be seen by the fact that although just any hole won't do, holes other than the vagina will often do if they are governed by the signifier "woman." Many heterosexual men, that is, find the mouth and the anus to be attractive harbors for their male organ when these ports are possessed by a woman, but not when they are possessed by a man. Even if another man's mouth or anus desires the penis of a heterosexual man, in most cases neither these physical attributes nor the desire of this other will produce desire in the heterosexual man, for the simple reason that they are governed by the wrong signifier. These facts demonstrate once again that sexual desire and jouissance are not just a matter of organs and orifices, or of images; they are also fundamentally a matter of signifiers. It is the vagina's status as the signifier minus phi that makes it and the person possessing it an object of desire for the heterosexual male. By signifying women as lacking/desiring this organ-signifier which he experiences himself as possessing, the heterosexual man is able to fully possess the phallus, which allows him both to find women desirable and to satisfy both his active anaclitic and his passive narcissistic desire in the Symbolic order.[8]

The Exclusion of Love

In addition to fabricating the desire of the Other and constructing a privileged position for the phallic signifier around which masculine identity and desire are built up, pornography also performs one additional, corollary signifying function that is crucial to the arousal of heterosexual male desire—namely, the exclusion of love from the field of signification. Love (active narcissistic desire) and (active anaclitic) desire are incompatible at a fundamental level. "Desire in its pure state," Lacan explains, "culminates in the sacrifice, strictly speaking, of everything that is the object of love in one's human tenderness" (XI 275). This is the case because love and desire aim at two different things in their objects, and conversely, the objects of desire and love, respectively, respond to two different dimensions of the desiring or loving subject. Love (active narcissistic desire), which, Lacan says, is always the demand to *be loved* (passive narcissistic desire), aims at the subject as such, the subject insofar as it is subjected to the law of the signifier, the Symbolic order. Insofar as a man *loves* a woman, she exists for him as embodying that which complements and reinforces his subjecthood, his identity, his sense of being somebody: his ego and ego ideal. In loving, what we seek is the reinforcement and enhancement by the other person of the very center of the particularity of our subjecthood.

In contrast with love, in active anaclitic desire one focuses on that aspect of the other that can function as a means for one's jouissance. Similarly, in passive anaclitic desire, one seeks the other's recognition not of what one *is* as subject, but of what one *has* that is beyond what one is as subject—something in oneself but more than oneself, as Lacan puts it. Here active and passive anaclitic desire converge. What a heterosexual man desires, as we have seen, is not just the woman's

[8]As Zita notes, "Since the penis is central to a sense of ego and manhood, it is only natural that anything that causes a pleasurable and powerful erection is to be privileged" (38).

body, but the woman's desire. Hence, insofar as a man *desires* a woman, she does not exist for him as an object he is capable of loving; rather, she exists as desiring, lacking, and thus as signifying minus phi, precisely the phallic desire that finds itself in her. Conversely, when a man is loved by a woman rather than desired by her, his own desire is not aroused. Strictly speaking, his active anaclitic desire is aroused only in relation to a woman's desire for that part of himself where his active anaclitic desire—his want-of-being that is also an excess of being—is centered: his phallus.

In pornography, the exclusion of love is thus crucial to the production of (anaclitic) desire, because love interferes with the inscription of a woman as minus phi, operating to inscribe woman not as wanting the phallus but as possessing what will fulfill a man in his subjecthood, as possessing a subjectivity that can accord recognition to other subjects. As I have suggested, pornography works in a number of ways to exclude love. The rape and whipping motifs are perhaps the most notable. In rape, the man clearly cares nothing for the woman's subjectivity as such. His desire is solely for that part of her that signifies his own phallic desire to him. The case is similar in whipping. Whether it is the man or the woman who is doing the whipping, the crucial factor is the same: it is not the other as subject that is the object of the whipping but rather the other's desire or jouissance. Whipping signifies here, for the male audience, "She does not love me," and "I do not love her." Whipping excludes love from the field of signification and thus, like rape, leaves the field free for (anaclitic) desire.

Rape and whipping, however, are only two of the more extreme ways of representing—and thus producing in the audience—the exclusion of love. When they are absent, the function is performed quite ably by other means, such as emphasizing the anonymity of sex, representing animosity between the partners, or portraying their sexual passion as so intense as to exclude everything else. The first two motifs noted by Zita (see above) also function to exclude love: (1) the exclusion of reproduction (since reproduction, if it does not necessarily involve love, nonetheless introduces a factor beyond both anaclitic desire and jouissance) and (2) the representation of sex as danger, which emphasizes that what is at stake is not the well-being of the subject but rather the pursuit of an object that promises to provide limitless jouissance.

Psychological and Social Effects of Pornography

The Desire of the Other

Given this account of the ways in which pornography arouses desire and produces jouissance for heterosexual men, we can now draw a number of conclusions concerning the effects of pornography on this audience's psychic economy and consequently on society as a whole. One effect of pornography may well be positive. There is anecdotal evidence, for instance, that pornography, in intensifying the sexual desire of men, improves—and in some cases even enables—their sexual relations with women.[9] For some men (and hence some couples) pornography may exercise a salutary effect on jouissance, desire, and even identity. Pornography may make greater jouissance possible for these men by counteracting an overwhelming prohibition against masturbation and/or genital intercourse, for example, that had been the dominant message of these men's Symbolic Others concerning phallic jouissance.

But pornography can also have a negative effect on sexual relations, as a result of encouraging its audience to deny the fact that there is no sexual rapport, or exact fit, between men and women. This results from the fact that pornography represents the desire of the Real, Imaginary, and Symbolic Other Sex in such a way as to allow men to experience their own desire and the Other Sex's desire as complementary natural forces that exist in a preestablished harmony transcending the artificiality and contingency attendant upon law, culture, and the Symbolic order: all women, men are assured, ultimately desire to have done to them exactly what men desire to do to them. By reinforcing the masculine conviction that such complementarity is the natural order of things, pornography encourages men to seek and demand women whose desire is simply a mirror image of their own—a wish that can exist unconsciously even in men whose consciousness has been raised by feminism.

Such an expectation produces disappointment or resentment in men and alienation and suffering in women in two ways. First, women whose desire does not conform to men's phallic desire are often psychologically, socially, or even physically abused by men who demand

[9] I am grateful to Diana Rabinovich for calling my attention to this point.

that women's desire be complementary to masculine phallic desire. Second, women who, in response to the interpellations of the dominant male culture, have in fact developed a desire that is in conformity with masculine phallic desire, are castrated a second time, as it were, beyond the castration to which every subject (masculine and feminine) is subjected: certain parts of their being (bodily and otherwise) are effectively cut off, rendered incapable of providing enjoyment and fulfillment—jouissance/*jouis-sens*.

The Phallic Signifier

Pornography's reinforcement of the phallic signifier, like its representation of the desire of the Other, would seem to promote both positive and negative effects. On the positive side, the reinforcement and consolidation of phallic desire may help some men achieve a more accommodating, less repressive attitude toward their phallic desire and thus toward their desire in general. Moreover, it is conceivable that for some men, pornography's operations with the phallic signifier may help secure one of those *points de capiton*, or anchoring points, that knot together the Real of one's bodily sensation and the Imaginary grasp of one's bodily unity with the signifiers of the Symbolic order that pin down one's identity. The absence of such *points de capiton*, Lacan demonstrated (see III, passim), is an essential feature of psychosis, and for Schreber, at least, the inadequacy of *points de capiton* can be linked to his father's (the Other's) prohibitions against masturbation and Schreber's resultant repression of both images and sensations of his penis.[10] Pornography activates and knots together all three registers—Symbolic, Imaginary, and Real—around the phallic signifier: real penile excitement is aroused and conjoined with images of the penis and/or its "mirror-image," the vagina, as well as with signifiers of the penis as phallus. This conjunction of bodily sensation with body image and signifier repeats the way in which the ego is established in the first place[11] and thus reinforces the male ego and its identity—a function the lack of which entails psychosis.

But the promotion of the phallic signifier also reinforces male castra-

[10]See Maurits Katan, "Schreber's Delusion," pp. 65–66, and "Childhood Memories," pp. 368–69.

[11]For an account of how this occurs, see Lacan's discussion of Melanie Klein's patient Dick, and Rosine Lefort's patient Robert (I 68–88 and 89–106, respectively).

tion, by reiterating the Symbolic order's excision of certain body parts and functions as sources of desire and foci of jouissance. Most significant in this regard is the fact that promotion of the phallic signifier entails repression of desires and jouissances that would detract from the power of phallic desire and jouissance—especially desires and jouissances considered "feminine."

Pornography's subversion of the feminine also occurs in a more subtle manner, analogous to that of strategies of containment on the social level: pornography allows marginal, clandestine expression of nonphallic desires and jouissances, and by thus partially bypassing the repression under which they operate, it partially deprives them of their oppositional force. Pornography, that is, helps men defend against homosexual and "feminine" impulses or fantasies[12] by prompting them to unconsciously indulge these fantasies. Such "feminine" fantasies are surreptitiously indulged by pornography insofar as men assume the position of the desired (i.e., passive) object—a position we have seen to be operative in the desire to be desired by the Other Sex. The existence of these surreptitious "feminine" satisfactions in pornography indicates the widespread (Freud would say universal) presence of such passive, "feminine" fantasies in men, which, however, the phallic insistence of pornography represses, thus reinforcing male castration.

The repression of the feminine entailed by the promotion of the phallic signifier concerns not only the feminine in men but also feminine desire and jouissance in general, which, as many feminists have pointed out, is denied equality in relation to masculine desire and jouissance by being defined and imaged always in relation to the image/signifier of masculine desire, the phallus, rather than in terms of images and signifiers derived from the female body. By thus reducing feminine desire to the desire for masculine phallic desire, pornography ironically promotes the castration of both men and women and further exacerbates the nonrapport between the sexes. In addition, the more the phallus is emphasized as the bearer of identity and desire, the more

[12]Zita also observes the defense against homophobia present in pornography: "Penetration of 'woman' often symbolizes power over another, if not possession of another. While these relations of domination and possession constitute 'the masculine,' it is the presence of real women in the role of "woman" that qualifies the perpetrator as heteromasculine. Clearly, this gender strategy belies a deeper homophobia that fuels the redundancy of phallic transgressions against real women, and heterosexual rage towards 'faggots'" (36).

feminists try to eliminate the phallus, and this attempt threatens to promote new repressions—in men, of phallic desire, and in women, of the desire to be the object of phallic desire. And what is repressed, we know, eventually returns.

The Exclusion of Love

Finally, pornography works to suppress love in general, including the only kind of love that, according to Lacan, can coexist with desire: a love that exists beyond the law, a love of difference and otherness, which psychoanalytic treatment makes possible. As we saw in Chapter 2, psychoanalytic treatment, by mapping the subject's relations with the unsymbolized portion of the subject's being (the object *a*), is in a sense an extended training of the subject to recognize, then tolerate, and finally accommodate a radical otherness that is nonetheless part of the core of one's own being.[13] This accommodation of otherness—of alien jouissance—which culminates in the emergence in the ego ideal of new signifiers bearing one's identity, makes subjects more capable of accepting and nurturing otherness not only in themselves but also in other subjects.[14] (Such nurturing, in fact, is precisely the role of the psychoanalyst, which is why Lacan suggests that the outcome of every successful psychoanalysis is in a sense the emergence of the analysand as analyst.)

It is precisely this type of love—a love that accommodates otherness without alienating the subject from itself—that is desperately needed on both sides of the sexual (non)equation, and pornography moves in the opposite direction, reducing otherness (the female subject) to a version of the same (phallic desire). Pornography, although it may produce alteration of some secondary identifications (e.g., of the order of the superego)—an effect, as we have noted, that can be salutary for some men—works precisely to preclude any of the alterations of fundamental identifications of the order that psychoanalysis addresses. In this way, pornography functions quite clearly as a powerful and massive tool working in support of the forces of patriarchy that not only

---

[13]For an account of this radical otherness and its participation in one's most intimate being, see Jacques-Alain Miller, "*Extimité*."

[14]These new signifiers to a degree escape the network of the Symbolic order (the Law) and thus constitute an embrace of otherness, a love of what is beyond the signifiers constituting one's previous ego ideal and the identity and desire constructed upon it.

limit the desire and jouissance of women and men but also prevent the problematic relation between the sexes from attaining any amelioration of a fundamental nature—that is, at the level of identification and desire.

Implications for Strategies of Change

These conclusions corroborate the claims of many feminists that pornography produces suffering by reinforcing sexist attitudes among men, including the valorization of phallic aggression and narcissism, and general insensitivity to women's actual or potential desires and jouissances. But the analysis provided here of how these effects are produced, that is, of what psychological functions these effects are based on, suggests a substantially different strategy for coping with these negative effects than the strategies advocated by most feminists (e.g., censuring and/or censoring pornography).

The most promising approach for undermining the destructive effects of pornography, I would argue, is the analytic strategy rather than the polemical response that has dominated discussion of pornography to date. The analytic strategy—the path pursued in the preceding pages—by mapping identifications and revealing repressed desires, promotes the kind of love endorsed by both the practice and the ethics of psychoanalysis, a love that Lacan describes as a desire for absolute difference. As explained above, what the analyst desires is not for the patient to become a clone of the analyst, or even someone the analyst approves of but rather to come to recognize and express his or her own singular desire. The transformation that the analyst desires to promote in the patient comes not as a result of the analyst's suggesting alternative values, desires, or modes of behavior, or even from criticizing or pointing out contradictions in the patient's actions, desires, or ideals, but rather from helping the patient come to recognize his or her hitherto unconscious desire and integrate it in some fashion into life.

Such a position, Lacan maintained, is not only the sole ethically tenable position for an analyst, it is also the only truly effective one for a revolutionary. As we saw in Chapter 2, Lacan declared to students in the aftermath of May 1968 that the only sure way to promote true revolution is to occupy the position of the analyst rather than assuming—as do most revolutionaries, including feminist revolutionaries—the position of the hysteric, who demands a new master signifier and the codes (legal and moral) that maintain it in place, and thus winds up instituting a new order of oppression and repression.

Pursuing the Lacanian revolutionary strategy (which has been the aim of the present chapter) involves getting heterosexual men to look more closely at their own ideals, desires, and jouissances[15] and work through them, rather than demanding or even directly suggesting that these men change their desires. This strategy, by opening heterosexual men up to heretofore alien modes of desire and jouissance within themselves, also promises to make these men less anxious when they confront such modes in others, including women. Since the strategy of psychoanalysis is less direct than demanding a change in masculine desire and its phallic signifier, it might therefore seem more risky. The results of such a strategy, in any case, cannot be guaranteed with certainty, any more than the outcome of any given analytic case can be predicted by the analyst. But the potential change promoted by this strategy is substantial: by operating precisely with the forces that construct the desiring heterosexual masculine body, the psychoanalytic approach to pornography offers the possibility not just of suppressing, repressing, or deconstructing that body, but of reconstructing it, producing a heterosexual masculine subjectivity that is not only capable of greater jouissance itself but that is also less destructive in relation to feminine subjects.

[15]See Williams, p. 276, for a similar suggestion.

CHAPTER FOUR
———————————

ANTIABORTIONIST
DISCOURSE

Another contemporary discourse of considerable power and social significance is that of antiabortionists. The conflict over abortion has been one of the most hotly contested and divisive social debates of recent years, and antiabortionists, who have been particularly fervent, and in some cases violent, in advancing their cause, owe much of their success to the passionate commitment that their discourse has been able to arouse in a large number of people. Surprisingly little has been written about this discourse, however, and the only comprehensive treatment it has received, a thoughtful and illuminating book by Celeste Condit, leaves largely unanswered the question of how this discourse has been able to elicit such passionate support for the crusade against abortion—a question that holds considerable interest not only for those who are pro-choice but for anyone who is concerned about the patriarchism that antiabortionist discourse embodies and promotes. For like pornography, antiabortionist discourse serves as a powerful weapon for patriarchy, functioning to deprive women of the right to control their own bodies—not only by denying that they have a right to choose abortion but also by focusing almost entirely on the fetus and ignoring women's bodies and subjectivities.[1] In order to contest this patriarchal thrust of antiabortionist discourse, the key is to understand and demonstrate how it operates on the identifications and desire of those who embrace it. Exposing the identifications and other

———————————
[1]For pointing out the significance of this fact for my argument, I am grateful to Jennifer Berkshire, Eve Moore, and Paul Smith.

forms of desire at play is, as I have been arguing, the psychoanalytic—
and ultimately the most effective and ethical—method of bringing
these forces under criticism and thereby subjecting them to potential
alteration.

In investigating the sources of the interpellative power of antiabortionist discourse, we can begin from the recognition that if this discourse has aroused in so many people such an intense opposition to
abortion, it must have succeeded in making abortion extremely threatening to these people in one sense or another. Our investigation into
the interpellative power of antiabortionist discourse can thus concentrate on searching the discourse for elements in each of the three
registers—Symbolic, Imaginary, and Real—that are threatening to
one's sense of identity or well-being—that is, one's narcissism.

Threats to Master Signifiers and Symbolic-Order Identity

Perhaps the most obvious threat is the challenge that abortion is
presented as posing to certain systems of values or beliefs. As a number
of commentators have noted, what is at stake in antiabortionist discourse is not simply the issue of abortion but an entire moral code
(Luker 174, 183), and beyond that a fundamental worldview (Luker
158) or philosophy of existence (Merton 30). This threat to the moral
code is articulated in the argument that forms the cornerstone of the
antiabortionist position: the contention that a fetus is alive and that
abortion is therefore murder and should be illegal. As Andrew Merton
puts it,

> the movement accuses anyone who condones legal abortion of, at the
> very least, standing by and doing nothing while millions of innocent
> human beings are slaughtered. The logic goes this way: a) zygotes/embryos/
> fetuses are human beings in the fullest sense of the term, and therefore
> deserving protection; b) abortion kills zygotes/embryos/fetuses; therefore
> c) abortion is murder, and d) anyone who condones abortion condones
> murder. (7)

Anyone who practices abortion is thus placed by antiabortionist discourse in the positon of an outlaw, someone excluded not from the na-

tion's law but from God's law or Nature's law. The result is to deny such subjects the Symbolic Other's love (passive narcissistic gratification).

"Life"

This denial of recognition or validation of one's identity by the Symbolic Other is also presented as being promoted indirectly by abortion, through the threat that abortion poses to a number of master signifiers forming part of the core of one's Symbolic-order sense of identity located in the ego ideal. The threat here can be one of two sorts. Either the value of the master signifier itself is felt to be attacked, which constitutes a threat to the ego ideal, or the possession of the master signifier for human subjects is felt to be challenged by abortion, thus threatening the ideal ego of subjects.

The most prominent master signifier that antiabortionist discourse operates on is "life." As Condit observes, "Throughout the abortion controversy, the major constitutive value grounding the anti-abortion position was Life" (59). One of the major accomplishments of anti-abortionist discourse has been to establish metonymic relations between "fetus" and "life." "From the late sixties onward," Condit informs us,

> the major rhetorical effort of the pro-Life movement was . . . expended in constructing and amplifying the verbal linkages between the terms *fetus* and *Life*. The concrete term *fetus* and the abstract value of Life were woven together primarily through a frequent recitation of the claim that the authority of "science" had discovered that the fetus was a human being from the time of conception. (61)

These metonymic connections are also produced through metaphor: the term "unborn baby" is substituted for "fetus," bringing with it metonymic relations with "life."

Insofar as antiabortionist discourse convinces its audience, through such operations of metaphor and metonymy, that the fetus is an instance of human life, it succeeds in positioning abortion, which destroys the fetus, as a threat to "life." This threat is often voiced quite explicitly, as in the frequent refrain that abortion undermines "the sanctity of human life." In Ronald Reagan's short book on abortion, for instance, phrases like "the sacred value of human life" and "the sanctity of human life" occur repeatedly as designations of the ultimate value that abortion threatens to destroy. The threat that abortion thus represents to one's identity is made quite explicit when Reagan declares, "We will never recognize the value of our own lives until we affirm the value of the lives of others" (38), and warns that diminishing one category of human life diminishes the value of all life (18).

Abortion, in short, is perceived by antiabortionists as threatening because it is seen as compromising the status of the master signifier "life," which antiabortionists wish to make function as a transcendental signifier. Reagan's book ends with precisely such an attempt to establish "life" as an absolutely stable and unambiguous signifier, insisting on the "transcendent right to life of all human beings, the right without which no other rights have any meaning," and warning that if we fail to preserve the absoluteness of this value, the "preservation of America as a free land is in danger" (38). Abortion is thus positioned as a threat to one's national identity as well as to one's species identity, both prominent elements of one's ego ideal.

"Personhood"

Closely related in function to the master signifier "life" is another master signifier, "personhood" (or synonymous terms), which antiabortionists insist on attaching to the fetus and even the zygote. As Merton observes, "grounds for debating the personhood of the fetus— let alone the zygote—are many and varied. Yet, a powerful movement has grown up around the certainty of zygote as person. Most right-to-life literature presents this notion as fact—as something so obvious it need not be explored" (6)—precisely, as we have seen, what defines a master signifier. The value and sanctity of this signifier, like that of "life," goes without saying, and anything that threatens the aura or privileged status of this signifier is tenaciously resisted. This insistence on the personhood of the fetus in effect produces a metaphoric substitution ("personhood" for "thinghood") that brings with it closer metonymic ties with signifiers carrying the antiabortionists' sense of their own identity.

Abortion clearly threatens the status of "personhood," in the same way that it threatens the status of "life." As Kristin Luker explains, abortion "seems to strip the rights of personhood from 'persons' who have always enjoyed them. If the rights of personhood can be so easily taken away from babies (embryos), who among us will be next?" (156). Thus, Luker concludes,

> To argue that embryos are entitled to all the rights of personhood, despite their condition of dependency, because they possess the entry card of forty-six human chromosomes is to emphatically assert that personhood *is a 'natural,' inborn, inherited right, rather than a social, contingent, and assigned right.* . . . If genetic humanness equals personhood, . . . one's destiny is therefore inborn and hence immutable. (157, 208; Luker's emphasis)

The master signifier "personhood" establishes an identity beyond the reach of castration—that is, not subject to the contingency of the Symbolic order or the vagaries of the Real. Abortion represents a profound double threat to this signification: those proposing to allow abortion either (1) deny that the fetus is a person, in which case "personhood" retains its aura but its natural, innate, and necessary linkage to the human organism is denied, and it becomes a contingent quality, of which one might be deprived, or (2) they accord personhood to the fetus, in which case the linkage between "personhood" and every human organism remains intact, but the value of "personhood" is severely compromised, deprived of its ontological aura, since personhood is not felt to be valuable enough for Society to preserve by prohibiting abortion. In the first case, the ego ideal remains intact, but one's ideal ego is severely damaged, while in the second case the ego ideal itself is threatened.

"Natural"

Another major area in which abortion is presented as posing a threat to Symbolic-order identity is that of sexual identity. As Luker has noted, one frequently encounters the argument that

> abortion is wrong because it fosters and supports a world view that deemphasizes (and therefore downgrades) the traditional roles of men and women. Because these roles have been satisfying ones for pro-life people and because they believe this emotional and social division of labor is both "appropriate and *natural*," the act of abortion is wrong

because it plays havoc with this arrangement of the world. (162; emphasis added)

The operative master signifier here is "natural." Abortion is seen as threatening because it is itself not a "natural" act, and, more importantly, because it opposes the "natural" consequence of sex: procreation.[2] Many antiabortion activists believe that sex should lead to procreation; they refuse contraceptives because they feel it is wrong to "stop the consequences of a *natural* act" (Luker 163–66; emphasis added).

Abortion is the most obvious—and in their minds, the most egregious—instance of interfering with the natural consequences of sex: i.e., procreation and therefore parenthood. "Natural" clearly functions here as a master signifier. Most antiabortionists (and many other people as well) assume that what is "natural" is good, right, real, and so on. As one erstwhile antiabortionist put it, "I thought pregnancy was a natural part of marriage, and I believed so much in the word *natural*" (Luker 169).[3] For all those with such a belief, abortion represents a fundamental threat to either their ego ideal or their ideal ego, for if an "unnatural" act like abortion is allowed, then either "natural"

[2]As Merton observes, "There is considerable evidence . . . that right-to-lifers are appalled by what they see as the rampant sexuality of today's society, and they view the outlawing of abortion as a means of restoring a more repressive sexual climate" (8). One convincing piece of evidence is a survey of antiabortionists conducted by an institute of progressive Catholics called the Quixote Center. "If 'pro-life' is an accurate description of the anti-abortion movement," the group reasoned, "then views favorable to a 'Human Life Amendment' should correlate positively and strongly with other pro-life stands: opposition to the death penalty, a concern for racial equality (because inequality has led to violence against Black people), and something less than total reliance on the U.S. military for security" (quoted in Merton 189). But, Merton reports, "when the Center polled 2,718 Catholics who favored the human life amendment, it found 'a moderate negative association' with this pro-life index. In a subsequent set of questions, those favoring the human life amendment were asked about their views on sex and marriage, as well as birth control, remarriage after divorce, and priestly celibacy. The study . . . showed that 'views on an anti-abortion amendment were much more strongly associated with views about sex and marriage than with opinions on "pro-life" issues.' [The group concluded:] 'These findings call into serious question the claim of the anti-abortion movement to the title "pro-life." They indicate that the movement derives its most fundamental motivations less from a reverence for human life than from a concern for sexual morality'" (Merton 190).

[3]This sanctity of the "natural" is also integrally involved in the issue of the personhood of the fetus. As we have seen, the insistence that the fetus is a person is a way of asserting "that personhood is a *natural* . . . right" (Luker 157; emphasis added).

is not a paramount value (in which case the ego ideal is eroded) or this quality is not as easily possessed as was assumed (which undermines the ideal ego).

"Motherhood"

Another important, and related, master signifier in antiabortionist discourse is "motherhood." As Luker notes, the abortion debate is, among other things, "a referendum on the place and meaning of motherhood" (193). For the majority of antiabortionists, motherhood is the primary signifier of feminine sexual identity: "Most pro-life activists believe that motherhood—the raising of children and families—is the most fulfilling role that a woman can have" (Luker 160; see 201). To refer to motherhood as a fulfilling role, however, does not adequately describe the impact of abortion. For here the threat is to the status of the master signifier as master signifier. And a threat to one's master signifier, as we have seen, is a threat to one's ego ideal and hence one's sense of self. Abortion represents such a threat because it, in Luker's words, "strips the veil of sanctity from motherhood" (205), by tacitly embracing the position that bearing children is not the only, or even necessarily the most important, element of a woman's existence—that feminine identity does not necessarily equal motherhood. This creates tremendous anxiety for those people, men as well as women, whose own sexual identity is tied to an assumed sanctity of motherhood specifically or to reproduction more generally.

The ultimate source of the sanctity of "motherhood" lies in its role as the signifier that most readily compensates for the fact that, as Lacan observed, there is no fixed formula for what it means to be a woman in relation to a man, or what it means to be a man in relation to a woman. Moreover, since women have been denied by the patriarchal Symbolic order a signifier of their sexual identity commensurate with the phallus, "motherhood" comes to serve as that signifier for many women, who, somewhat excluded from the identity-conferring (patriarchal) law—that is, the (patriarchal) Symbolic order, in which the Symbolic phallus has primacy—find an obvious, tangible support for their sexual identity in the production of children. Fatherhood can also fill this function for a man, to a lesser extent, insofar as he happens to feel disenfranchised, excluded by the Law.

We can see more clearly how being a parent can operate in this way if we recall that "feminine subjects" (not all of whom are women), are, in Lacan's view, "not-all" submitted to the castration of the phallic order, and are thus more subject to experiencing anxiety about their identity—a sense that they are nothing, nobody. As a result, to overcome this fundamental division, what a feminine subject wants is for something to come to the place of the lacking signifier (André 263). For such subjects, having a baby, in making them a "mother" or a "father," may provide the most substantial sense of identity they have, offering powerful gratification of their passive narcissistic Symbolic-order desire.

Such gratification is particularly strong for women, as a result of collective representations of motherhood—the mere ubiquity of such representations being already in itself an indication of the Societal Other's love for mothers, which is then reinforced by the positive light in which motherhood is usually represented. Western cultures are full of such representations. Moreover, in some of these representations one aspect or another of the Symbolic Other itself is often personified and portrayed as viewing motherhood with approbation and love. One of the interpellatively most forceful instances of such a representation is found in Christianity, especially Catholicism, where several different instances of the Symbolic Other are portrayed as loving motherhood: the Cosmic Other, God, is personified as the Father (the second embodiment of the Symbolic Other for the child), whom loving daughters desire to please—a father who gives the Law (the Societal Other), which all loving daughters try to live in accordance with, and whose avatar, the Son, is born of the Virgin Mother (an embodiment of the primary instance of the Symbolic Other), from whom the devout seek succor and whom devout women seek to emulate. The Catholic discourse of motherhood thus involves a narrative in which numerous instances of the Symbolic Other (father, mother, Society, the cosmos, God) play active roles in promoting motherhood, which is itself portrayed as bringing ultimate meaning and fulfillment—passive narcissistic gratification.

Abortion, in being positioned by antiabortionist discourse as a threat to "motherhood" and "fatherhood," as well as "life," "personhood," and the "natural," threatens at its roots the Symbolic-order identity of many people. The opposition to abortion is thus partly motivated by the impulse to protect both the sanctity and the possession of certain master signifiers that are integral to one's identity and that antiabortionist discourse has positioned as threatened by abortion.

Images and the Threat to the Body Ego

But master signifiers do not carry the entire interpellative burden; part of the force of the antiabortionist discourse derives from something other than master signifiers. As we have seen, one's sense of self ultimately resides not solely in moral codes or knowledge (S2) or even in master signifiers (S1), but also in one's body ego, the stability of which is dependent in part upon external images of the human body.

The inference that such images of bodily impairment and even actual dismemberment are central to the interpellative force of antiabortionist discourse is corroborated by two things. First, antiabortionists' fervor is often greatest when the issue of aborting a physically handicapped fetus is discussed. Luker reports that for the majority of antiabortionists interviewed by her group, "the abortions they found most offensive were those of 'damaged embryos'" (207). Second, antiabortionists' own testimony indicates that the most convincing element of their argument for themselves as well as for their opponents is the pictures they have assembled—"hundreds of pictures of bloody, battered, and dismembered fetuses" (Merton 76). Condit agrees that such images have clearly played a crucial role in antiabortionist discourse: "The pictures—a baby-like fetus, a smiling fetus, a fetus that sucks its thumb. Butchered fetuses—bloody mounds of human tissue, hacked arms, mangled legs, crushed skulls. Without these compelling and brutal photographs the American abortion controversy probably would not continue" (79).

We can distinguish two moments in the response to such images, corresponding to the two types of images described by Condit. The first moment is that of Imaginary identification with the fetus. This identification is elicited by our recognizing in pictures of the fetus a human form like our own. Antiabortionist discourse goes to great lengths to prompt such recognition; as Condit notes, "Pro-Life rhetoric works hard to obscure the differences between me and these developing incomplete human forms" (91). In addition to insisting verbally on such similarity, antiabortionist discourse also manipulates photographs of fetuses to emphasize the fetus's human form, cropping the photos so as to exclude nonhuman features of the image, such as the placenta and umbilical cord (Condit 82).[4]

One result of this use of images, as Condit notes, is to persuade people that the fetus is a human being.[5] But the most important function of such images is not, as Condit seems to assume, their role in supporting the minor premise ("a fetus is a person") in the fundamental syllogism of the antiabortionist argument.[6] Rather, the crucial function of these images is to produce a corporeal, Imaginary-order identification of audience with fetus. For it is on the basis of such an identification that the audience can be interpellated into a visceral opposition to abortion, by being confronted with images of the second type, those of mutilated and dismembered fetuses, which many people experience as threatening at the level of their own body egos. One such photo shows a "purple torso of a fetus . . . displayed against a white background. Arms are still attached to the fetus. The two detached legs and the head are placed alongside the torso. Another photo shows two

---

[4]One of the most striking techniques is the synecdochic use of a photograph of the feet of a fetus, which look like tiny baby's feet. Condit explains how this image operates: "This image was most persuasive because of its synecdochic structure. An accurate, full picture of a young fetus includes features not associated with adult human beings—the placenta and the umbilical cord and, in a six-week fetus, even a 'tail.' With these and its ungainly face and head, off-balance and poorly formed, a young fetus looks like a wretched creature, bloody and undernourished. Such 'negatives' and 'variances' weigh heavily against the 'A is B' formulation. Fetal feet, however, are very close to baby feet in shape. The identity of the part is crucial. Our visual logic 'recognizes' such feet as 'small human feet' and we synecdochically expand the unseen picture to see a full 'small human.' Thus, the synecdoche tightened the identity between fetus and adult by eliminating all those components that reveal the differences between the two, focusing on one single, stunning similarity." (88–89)

[5]Condit writes: "The consensus seems to be that in Michigan a major change in public opinion was eventually brought about by these visual materials, which portrayed the fetus not as a 'blob of tissue' but, in the later stages of gestation, as a 'baby.' Thousands of picture packets were distributed, and television ads as well as billboards focused on the human-like features of the physical appearance of the fetus. Most Americans had had no idea what a fetus looked like at any stage of development. Once they saw the late-stage fetus, it was more plausible to characterize the fetus as a human person and much more difficult to dismiss the relevance of Life. . . . Thus, visual display and supporting scientific argument worked together to characterize the fetus as a human being." (61).

[6]Condit concludes that "in the broad popular realm concrete images [have been] the most potent factors in *determining the ultimate public vocabulary* adopted for the practice of abortion" (73; emphasis added), and explains that the "persuasive power [of such images] derived ultimately from the *real material substance of unborn human beings* as well as from the rhetors' skill with tropes" (94; emphasis added). These

tiny, detached arms and two legs against a pulpy red background" (Merton 11).

When actual pictures of dismemberment are not present, they are often painted with words. Ronald Reagan paints such a picture in his reference to "the abortionist who reassembles the arms and legs of a tiny baby to make sure all its parts have been torn from its mother's body" (22). Merton describes "a brochure written by a Baptist preacher from Texas that [gives] a graphic description of abortion—cutting up the baby, crushing its head" (100). At the very least, there is the evocation in antiabortionist discourse of the image of a tiny human being suffering terrible pain. One antiabortionist fundraising letter notes that over four thousand fetuses are aborted each day, "and," it declares, *"each one will suffer horrible pain* before their little hearts stop beating" (166; emphasis in original).

The assault on the audience's body ego is perhaps most fully developed in a cartoon book entitled "Who Killed Junior?" (Merton 137), where the dismemberment is depicted graphically, and the audience's identification is promoted by the personification of the fetus. Merton describes the book as follows:

> In a simplistic manner, the drawings traced the growth of a fertilized egg in the womb. By the sixth week Junior is a fully formed baby, standing up and smiling; by the eleventh week he is running in place and has a

---

comments indicate that Condit sees the primary impact of the images as being their reinforcement of logical claims that can be, and have been, advanced independently of the images. In the present case, she assumes that images are useful to the antiabortionist argument because they support the argument that the fetus is an instance of "life." This view is made even more explicit in Condit's general explanation of "the role of visual images in public argument," where she states: "Images may either replace narratives or summarize narratives visually (the pro-Life images did the former, the pro-Choice images, the latter). Like narratives, visual images provide concrete enactments of abstract values and thereby allow a different kind of understanding of the meaning and impact of an ideographic claim about public life. They help "envision" the material impacts of abstract policy commitments. Images therefore provide a useful form of grounding for the acceptance of an argument. They, like any other form of argument, however, are subject to analysis of the accuracy of the claims they make.

"Visual forms of persuasion present special problems of analysis. Visual images seduce our attention and demand our assent in a peculiar and gripping fashion. Many audiences are leery of verbal constructions, which only "represent" reality, but because we humans tend to trust our own senses, we take what *we* see to be true. Therefore, our trust in what we see gives visual images particular rhetorical potency" (81). Images, in Condit's explanation, function basically as supporting evidence for abstract arguments.

decent command of colloquial English; he is thinking, "Time for me to get going soon." At three months, Junior has his hand cupped to his ear, listening in alarm. The caption says, "His mother and her doctor are already discussing how to kill him." Then follow four panels in which the basic methods of abortion are listed. In the first, Junior screams as a vacuum cleaner sucks him out of the womb (the vacuum suction method). In the second Junior screams as a knife slices him to pieces (dilation and curettage). In the third, Junior screams as a hand plucks him from the womb (hysterotomy). And in the fourth, Junior screams as a hypodermic needle injects saline into the womb (salting out). The next panel shows a fully formed baby with a knife through it, and says, "If you are a teenage girl—you need to know abortion means killing a Human Being. It is not like a Tonsil Operation." (137)

Through such representations of abortion, many people come to experience the assault on the fetus as a threat to their own integrity at the level of the body ego. The feelings of dismay, disgust, and even horror that many people experience when they are confronted with the thought and/or image of the destruction of the fetus result from the fact that images of dismemberment assault them at the bodily core of their identity. In the image of a fetus being aborted, these people thus encounter a deep sense of their own radical lack, a sense grounded in the earliest mnemic traces laid down by their own infant body's experience of chaos and dismemberment, which, Lacan maintains, constitutes the ultimate (Imaginary) referent of one's notion of death.

Desire in the Real: Fantasy and the Object a

In addition to making use of powerful interpellative forces of master signifiers and images of dismemberment, antiabortionist discourse also relies heavily on desire and identification in the order of the Real. The fetus, that is, is represented in such a way that it functions as the object a for the audience—in two ways. First, it serves for many people as the object of inestimable value, the possession of which, they believe, will make their life complete (active narcissistic desire, or love). And second, it functions as an object of identification for many people, responding to their desire to be the object of inestimable value that completes the life of the Other (passive narcissistic desire, or being loved).

A baby, according to Lacan, often functions as the object *a* for a mother. In fact, a baby—and a fortiori a fetus—would seem in many ways made to order for filling that role. Lacan, we recall, describes the object *a* as an *hommelette* ("little man"), which he pictures as "a phantom of an infinitely more primary form of life" (Ecrits 845). The object *a*, moreover—which is a representative or equivalent of "the libido, qua pure life instinct, . . . immortal life, irrepressible life" (XI 198), and which is what gets left out when the subject assumes a sexual identity in the Symbolic order—is embodied by certain parts of the body that are detachable and that have some relation to lack of being (XI 103), such as feces, urine, voice, gaze, breast, phoneme, and the void.

Concerning the criterion of simultaneous connection with and detachability from the body, a fetus is part of the mother's body, yet from the moment of conception it is quite easily detachable from this body, and as the pregnancy progresses, the fetus becomes more and more independent until, at the moment of parturition, it becomes physically separate. As concerns the irrepressible life or immortality represented by the object *a*, here too the fetus as potential child fills the role: not only mothers, but many fathers as well, experience through their children a sense of immortality.

This function is most obvious in the Christian representation of the baby Jesus, who is presented precisely as the bearer of immortality, the restorer of that fullness of being that was lost with the assumption of sexual identity (in the accession to knowledge in the Garden of Eden). This baby of the Virgin Mother—who is herself represented, as Kristeva points out, as escaping from the limitations of sex and death—is clearly that which promises to fill the void, and to redeem all those subjects who will acknowledge their subjection to him. The fact that this particular representation of mother and baby has mobilized such a massive and powerful collective fascination through the ages suggests that the child of the Virgin Mother is not merely a special case but rather functions as a paradigm of the significance that a baby has for many other mothers—and fathers, too.

A final factor that makes the fetus a powerful embodiment of the being that all subjects have lost is its status as a living entity that resists subsumption by the Law. It is precisely the ambiguous status of the fetus with regard to the legal code (Is it human? Is it a person? Does it have legal rights?) that makes it such a fitting representative of the Real that is lost to all subjects who have acceded to the Law of the Symbolic order. That this exclusion from the Law (i.e., the Symbolic order) plays an important role in establishing the significance of the fetus for antiabortionists is corroborated by the fact that many antiabortionists feel the need to invoke "the laws of nature" or "God's law" in an attempt to come to grips with sexuality and procreation.

That what is at issue in this invocation of the Law is essentially the establishment and preservation of a sense of identity is evident in the fact that it is precisely a lack of such identity under the law that characterizes both those *for* whom the law is usually evoked—the fetus, the legal and Symbolic status of which is extremely ambiguous, and feminine subjects, who are not-all subjected to the Law—and those *by* whom the law is usually evoked in this case, those whose position with regard to the social order is somewhat marginal (see Luker 157). Some measure of the interpellative power exercised by the fetus as a result of this ambiguous status in relation to the Law can be gauged from the fact that unambiguously human victims—victims who have more fully acceded to the Law—generally arouse much less sympathy, even when their suffering is much more intense, extensive, and unquestionable than that of the fetus. Witness the absence of similarly massive and passionate crusades to protect the victims of disease, starvation, torture, wife abuse, and child abuse.

Hence one of the deepest causes of passionate opposition to abortion is the fantasy evoked by antiabortionist discourse, and the life that self-styled pro-life advocates want so passionately to preserve is in the final analysis that part of their own life or being that is lacking. Abortion, by tacitly denying the inestimable value of the fetus, threatens to undermine the fantasy of many people that they do indeed possess (or have the possibility to possess) something that transcends the limitations and contingencies of the Symbolic order: the object *a*. In fighting to protect the fetus, then, antiabortionists are fighting for their own "libido, *qua* pure life instinct, that is to say, immortal life, or irrepressible life" (XI 198), that was lost when they assumed a Symbolic-order identity and thus sacrificed part of their being to the Law.

The fetus has the same function in the inverse fantasy in which the subject identifies with the fetus as object *a*, cause of the Other's desire. Here, what is at stake is the Other's love: if a fetus is not of inestimable value for the Other (God, Society, or Nature), then one's own ontological status is felt to be radically undermined. This is made abundantly clear by the observations of some of the antiabortion activists themselves, who speak quite openly about their identification with the fetus. Merton describes the testimony of one activist addressing an antiabortionist convention: "'Once upon a time,' he said, 'I was a nubbin, so big. . . .' He was holding his thumb approximately an eighth of an inch away from the end of his little finger. 'Where the thumbnail lands is where the nubbin stops. . . . If that nubbin had been killed, I would not be talking . . . today'" (184). Luker quotes the testimony of another opponent of abortion, who recalled seeing as a child a picture of

> a cross-section of a clay jar that they'd found in an excavation, and inside was a little kid with his skull cracked. And the caption saying that the Canaanites had practiced the sacrifice of the first-born male child. I'm a first-born male child. . . . It was something that hit a nerve. . . . A few years later, apparently, when I first came across the concept of abortion, it was just this immediate, personal identification. [I thought] that's like what happened to the little boy in the jar, and that's what could have happened to me. (132)

Both of these testimonies reveal the same fear: the fear of not being loved or valued by the Other. Abortion poses such a threat because if even a single fetus is not valuable to the Other, that means that no fetus is of value simply as a fetus, which, in turn, renders one's own value radically contingent and suspect. As Lacan observes, we all begin life as the object a of the Other's love, and at bottom we are still in this position; the denial of the Other's love at the level of the Real can thus be more devastating than anything else. It is this force as much as anything else that accounts for the fact that a fetus, for many antiabortionists, is of inestimable value, and to protect it, they will risk financial loss, social ostracism, and even imprisonment.

For many antiabortionists, then, the fetus functions as the embodiment of both the object a and master signifiers constituting the ego ideal, and this combination, as Lacan noted, is what produces fanaticism. Add to these factors the Imaginary-order threat that antiabortionist discourse represents abortion as constituting for the body ego, and one has a formidable array of psychological forces marshaled in opposition to abortion. The powerful forces in antiabortionist discourse evoking vulnerability in the Imaginary and the Real explain the relative ineffectiveness of pro-choice discourse in countering antiabortionist discourse.

Psychological and Social Effects

This understanding of how interpellation operates in the Symbolic, Imaginary, and Real registers of the antiabortionist audience puts us in a position to infer the more general psychological and social effects, beyond opposition to abortion, that are likely to be promoted by this discourse. One important general effect is likely to be a reinforcement of fundamentalism among antiabortionists—their insistence on holding certain signifiers (values and ideals) sacrosanct, erecting them into transcendental signifiers.

This ossification of S1 produces a similar rigidity in S2, the system of knowledge and beliefs that is ordered by master signifiers. Such fundamentalism (S1) and dogmatism (S2) lend support to a general conservative, even reactionary agenda, which insists on certain master signifiers ("family," "country," or "God") and on certain readings of these singifiers as well (e.g., the "family" must be based on a monogamous heterosexual relationship, devotion to "country" must express itself as opposition to countries opposed to ours in economic or military conflict; and "God" must be anthropomorphic, omnipotent, omniscient, benevolent, and so on.). In addition, fundamentalism (S1) and dogmatism (S2) combine with fantasy in antiabortionist discourse to promote repression of psychological or social realities that demonstrate the lack of a transcendental signifier or that manifest the excluded Real, both of which undermine the stability of master signifiers and the sense of security erected upon them. And finally, the intense passive narcissistic threats and gratifications that antiabortionist discourse produces in all three registers function to divest active and anaclitic desire of its force and thus reinforce the subjugation of subjects to the Other.

CHAPTER FIVE

POLITICAL CAMPAIGN RHETORIC

Another form of discourse that can produce quite obvious and fairly immediate psychological and social effects is political campaign rhetoric. What is not so obvious is what sorts of long-term psychological effects might be promoted by such discourses and what kinds of political ramifications these long-term psychological effects might have. Specifically, what types of desires are promoted and what types are repressed by different kinds of political discourse, and what are the psychological and social consequences? We can begin to answer these questions if we consider the discourses of two of the most effective campaign speakers of recent memory, Ronald Reagan and Jesse Jackson, who employed significantly different modes of discourse to elicit massive and fervent support from opposite ends of the political spectrum.

Ronald Reagan

Reagan's speeches were always confident and often smug, condescending, and even cocky; they reassured people that all was well and made them feel good about themselves. Examination of Reagan's acceptance speech at the 1980 Republican National Convention demonstrates how these effects were produced and allows us to infer the long-term psychological effects entailed in the discourse in the collective subjectivity of a large segment of the American public.

Typical of Reagan's discourse, this speech derives much of its force from its insistent imposition of master signifiers (S1), which are often used to ward off feelings of deficiency and lack and provide a sense of security and identity—an instance of passive narcissistic gratification in the Symbolic order. The only lack acknowledged in Reagan's account of the state of our nation is deficiency that we bring on ourselves when we fail to adhere rigorously to our master signifiers:

> *Work* and *family* are at the *center of our lives,* the *foundation of our dignity as a free people.* When we deprive people of what they have earned, or take away their jobs, we destroy their dignity and undermine their families. These are *concepts* that stem from an economic *system* that for more than 200 years has helped us *master* a continent, create a previously undreamed of prosperity for our people, and has fed millions of others around the globe. And that *system* will continue to serve us in the future if our government will stop ignoring the *basic values* on which it was built. (Emphasis added)

One could hardly hope for a better example of the logic of the discourse of the Master: the insistent identification with certain "basic values" or "concepts" as the "foundation" and "center of our lives" constitutes them as master signifiers (S1), which simultaneously repress all lack ($) and fantasy ($ ◇ a) and call for systematic embodiment in the System or Law (S2), which in turn produces the *a*—the surplus jouissance (plus-de-jouir) now repressed and thus no-longer-to-be-enjoyed (plus-de-jouir). Reagan's discourse, as indicated in this passage, presents this loss of jouissance as the result not of the systematic embrace (S2) of master signifiers (S1) but rather as the result of a system that has failed to embrace these master signifiers completely. In Reagan's discourse, loss of jouissance is seen to result from failure to embrace master signifiers absolutely, rather than, as is actually the case, precisely from the embrace of master signifiers. The main thrust of Reagan's speech is to promise the return of lost jouissance through more complete submission to the master signifier.

More specifically, Reagan's discourse produces the signifier "America" as the supreme master signifier, the phallic signifier, which Lacan defines as the signifier of a life that has succeeded in escaping from the limitations imposed on it by the agency of the signifier—that is, a position free of the castration, the deprivation of enjoyment, entailed by the various aspects of the Symbolic order or Law. Reagan establishes this phallic signifier by first evoking, throughout his speech, the specter of national castration, which elicits anxiety or perturbation ($) in many Americans. Reagan then offers a signifier of their collective identity, "America," that provides many Americans with a sense of security and identity and represses the anxiety evoked by the dangers and problems referred to. In terms of discourse structure, Reagan interpellates his audience to the position of the hysteric

$$\frac{\$}{a} \longrightarrow \frac{S1}{S2}$$

and from there immediately puts them in a position of mastery

$$\frac{S1}{\$} \longrightarrow \frac{S2}{a}$$

by offering them a master signifier that represses their sense of lack and provides instead the sense of a stable and substantial identity.

The Imaginary Threat

This dialectic begins early in the speech, where, after referring vaguely to "the nation's problems," Reagan proposes to respond to those problems with a list of master signifiers, proclaiming "a new consensus with all those across the land who share a community of *values* embodied in these *words*: family, work, neighborhood, peace, and freedom" (emphasis added). A few moments later he repeats the dialectic. First he invokes the threat, declaring in a grave tone:

> Never before in our history have Americans been called upon to face three grave *threats to our very existence*, any one of which could *destroy us*. We face a *disintegrating* economy, a *weakened* defense, and an energy policy based on the sharing of *scarcity*. . . . [The Democrats] say that the United States has had its day in the sun, that our nation has passed its zenith, . . . that the future will be one of *sacrifice*. (Emphasis added)

The threat here affects one's narcissistic sense of security not only on the Symbolic level but also in the Imaginary register, where words and phrases like "threats to our very existence," "destroy us," "disinte-

grated," "weakened," and "scarcity" have a subtle but ominous resonance for the body ego that is at the core of our narcissism and sense of
well-being.

Reagan categorically rejects this vision of national castration and
dismemberment: "My fellow citizens, I utterly reject that view. The
American people, the most generous on earth, who created the highest
standard of living, are not going to accept [this]. . . . [T]he American
people deserve better." He first takes up the economic threat, which he
invokes in terms of devourment, disintegration, impotence, and ultimately extinction—all of which subtly threaten the audience's sense of
well-being all the way down to the body ego. "Many . . . people are
out of work," he observes. "Many have seen their savings *eaten away*
by inflation. Many others on fixed incomes, especially the elderly, have
watched *helplessly* as the *cruel* tax of inflation *wasted away* their
purchasing *power*. And today," he adds, "a great many who trusted
Mr. Carter wonder if we can *survive* the Carter policies of national
defense" (emphasis added).

The Symbolic Solution

For the audience to escape from this largely Imaginary-order threat
that he has here evoked, Reagan offers a Symbolic-order narcissistic
solution. He proposes a reduction of government—a lessening of
taxes, regulations, and controls—which, he maintains, will decrease
inflation and increase productivity and prosperity. The primary appeal
of this proposal does not lie in its economic policy per se or in that
policy's promise of prosperity. Rather, it lies in the passive Symbolic-
order narcissistic gratification that the discourse expressing the policy
offers to the audience: in pledging "to bring our government back
under control" and "to restore to the federal government the capacity
to do the people's work *without dominating their lives*," Reagan is
offering the audience the position of the master—i.e., a position in
which the subject seems not to be dominated by the Law. Instead of
being subjected to external restraints and limitations, Reagan's subjects would ultimately be subjected only to themselves—in a perfect
embodiment of the position of the master—the *maître/m'être à moi-
même*, being me to myself. "My view of government," Reagan explains, "places trust not in one person or one party, but in those *values*
that *transcend persons* and parties" (emphasis added). And these tran-

scendental signifiers, he says, reside in the subjects themselves: "The trust is where it belongs—in the people."

Reagan's type of government thus involves "a special kind of compact," which entails "a *voluntary binding together* of *free* people" to "live *under the law*" (emphasis added). Reagan's discourse insists on submission to the law, subordination of the subject to the collective social order. But in presenting submission to the law as a voluntary matter, Reagan's portrayal of government, allows the illusion that living under the restrictions of the law is a contingent rather than a necessary state. And the idea of controlling the government—the notion of restricting the restricting system—allows the illusion that one can escape restricting systems altogether.

This portrayal of American government offers the audience, as Americans, the position of the master, the *maître*, the *m'être à moi-même*—a position in which one is autonomous, self-sufficient, and subjected to no external constraints. In short, it is a position of identity with the phallic signifier. Thus the numerous references to reducing government regulations, controls, and taxes all serve as metaphors or metonyms for freeing Americans from the Law altogether. And it is from this discursive function, rather than from their status as actual principles of an economic policy and its promise of prosperity, that these references derive the greatest portion of their psychological force and thereby their political power.

Reagan reinforces this subject position of the master in his subsequent comments, where he observes: "The descendants of [the Pilgrims] pledged their lives, their fortunes, and their sacred honor to found this nation. Some forfeited their fortunes and their lives; none sacrificed *honor*" (emphasis added). Here we have, as clearly as we could wish, a staging of what Lacan calls the *vel* (Latin for "or") of alienation, which all speaking beings are always confronted with: like a traveler accosted by a highwayman who declares, "Your money or your life," speaking beings are forced to make a choice between their meaning and their being. This vel of alienation, as Lacan calls it, "is not an arbitrary invention, nor is it a matter of how one sees things. It is a part of language itself" (XI 212). "The vel of alienation is defined by a choice whose properties depend on [the fact that] there is . . . one element that, whatever the choice operating may be, has as its consequence a neither one, nor the other. The choice, then, is a matter of knowing whether one wishes to preserve one of the parts, the other

disappearing in any case" (211). In the choice offered by the highwayman, if we choose the money, Lacan observes, we lose both our life and
our money. On the other hand, if we choose life, we have "life without
the money, namely, a life deprived of something" (212). Similarly,
when subjects are faced with the possibility of entering into language
and assuming a meaning and identity by embracing a master signifier,
if they choose being, jouissance, they lose their meaning and sense of
identity (the sense of *m'être à moi-même*), and if they choose meaning
and identity, they lose being and thus meaning as well, since meaning is
based upon being. Either way, something essential is lost.

Reagan's staging of the vel, however, ignores this consequence, and
forcefully interpellates his audience into a choice of meaning and identity over being and jouissance—that is, honor over life. To have one's
"sacred honor" is to be in the position of *m'être à moi-même*, being
true to oneself, to the master signifier one has identified with, and this
gives a sense of ultimate meaning to one's life. Such meaning, in Reagan's discourse, is more valuable than life itself, as he himself makes
clear one sentence later when he asks, "Isn't it once again time to
renew our compact of freedom, to pledge to each other all that is best
in our lives, all that gives *meaning* to them—for the sake of this, our
beloved and blessed land?" (emphasis added).

Here, having identified with the phallic signifier he has offered them,
Reagan's supporters have assumed a position of self-sufficiency—of
m'être à moi-même—that allows them to contemplate with equanimity the very threat that minutes earlier had been used to push them
toward the master and phallic signifiers: the prospect of sacrifice. Earlier, in response to the notion that "the future will be one of sacrifice,"
we recall that Reagan had declared, "I utterly reject that view." Now,
just minutes later, after having begun to produce "America" as the
phallic signifier, he once again invokes transcendental signifiers and
urges that his audience *sacrifice* for them: "Together," he admonishes,
"let us make a new beginning. Let us make a commitment to care for
the needy; to teach our children the virtues handed down to us by our
families; to have the courage to *defend those values and virtues* and the
willingness to *sacrifice for them*" (emphasis added). This is what maintaining honor, the position of the master, means: sacrificing one's
being and jouissance for one's meaning and sense of identity—a sacrifice which, however, is nothing other than castration, which is why, as
Lacan says, the master is castrated.

Thus by offering his audience the (illusory) phallic signifier, Reagan is able surreptitiously to get them to accept the very condition—castration and the vel of alienation—that the phallic signifier offers to save them from. This is hegemony with a vengence, and the human results of this rhetorical act are not hard to discover: we need only recall those people—many blue-collar workers, for instance—who wound up sacrificing economically as a result of their mass identification with Reagan's phallic signifier.

The dialectic of castration and the phallic signifier is repeated later in Reagan's speech, when he discusses defense. Here, after invoking numerous examples of the Soviet threat and of American humiliation in foreign affairs, Reagan launches into a rhapsodic characterization of "America" that frees this signifier from the laws not only of government but also of history and of language, the Symbolic order itself—a release that is tantamount to the very definition of the phallic signifier. "It is *impossible to capture in words*," Reagan says, "the splendor of this vast continent which God has granted as our portion of His creation. *There are no words to express* the extraordinary strength and character of this breed of people we call Americans" (emphasis added). He quotes Tom Paine's "We have it in our power to begin the world over again," and ends his speech by calling America "this island of freedom" that "a Divine Providence placed . . . here as a refuge for all those people in the world who yearn to breathe free." Here the passive narcissistic Symbolic-order gratification provided by master signifiers is expressly linked to the Other's love, which, as we have seen, underwrites all narcissistic gratification. This supposed beneficence of the Symbolic Other, moreover, serves to cover over the lack that characterizes this Other—that is, the failure to provide a signifier that is truly transcendental and absolute.

The Supplement from the Real

Embrace of the Symbolic Other and its master signifiers, as well as the denial of the Other's lack, are further promoted by means of the object *a*, which is presented not as irretrievably lost but rather as recuperable through the systematic embrace of master signifiers laid out in Reagan's discourse. The object *a* is discernible in a number of places in Reagan's speech, including his discussion of the energy problem, where he evokes the shortage of energy and then promises to fill this lack with the object *a* constituted by those natural resources that have been unnecessarily excluded by the law:

> Large amounts of oil and natural gas lie beneath our land and off our shores, untouched because the [Carter] administration seems to believe the American people would rather see more regulation, more taxes, and more controls than more energy. Coal offers *great potential*. So does nuclear energy produced under rigorous safety standards. It could supply electricity for thousands of industries and millions of jobs and homes. It must not be thwarted by a tiny minority opposed to economic growth which often finds friendly ears in regulatory agencies for its obstructionist campaigns. Our problems are both acute and chronic, yet all we hear from those in positions of leadership are the same tired proposals for more government tinkering, more meddling, and more control—all of which led us to this sorry state in the first place.

Here, once again, lack is presented as not a necessary but a contingent, even voluntary condition: our "sorry state" derives not from our destiny as speaking beings but rather from "government tinkering, . . . meddling, and . . . control." Moreover, oil, coal, natural gas, and nuclear energy are each offered as the precious substance—the object *a*—that has been excluded by the System (here incarnated as the Carter administration) and that would make life fully meaningful and enjoyable if it could only be acquired. Moreover, it can be acquired: all that is needed is for Reagan to be elected president.

There are even more significant instances of the object *a* in Reagan's discourse, however, embodied in the man himself: his voice and his gaze. Lacan noted in 1964 the significance of the voice and the gaze in the mass media (XI 274), and Reagan is widely agreed to have derived much of his success from his effective use of the most powerful mass medium, television. In his speech, his sometimes determined and always reassuring (and even soothing) vocal intonations and his self-assured, often resolute, but never unfriendly gaze function as instances of the object *a* that are continuously present for the audience as that which promises to fill whatever desire may be aroused—and to plug up any hole that might appear in the Other. Reagan's voice invokes the primordial voice: the soothing tones of the mother's saying that dissolved all lack for the infant and the reassuring certitude of the father's pronouncement in which there was no sign of deficiency. Reagan's gaze, likewise, provides his supporters with the reassurance they felt as infants when they were watched over and caressed by the eyes of their parents. His voice and his gaze thus implicitly but continuously emit the same message that his comments about oil, coal, natural gas, and nuclear energy explicitly articulate: that he can procure the lost jouissance, the object *a*, for America if only he is given control of the System. This promise arouses great active anaclitic desire in the Real register of his supporters' subjective economies, and it establishes electing Reagan as the way to gratify that desire and possess the object *a* that will provide limitless jouissance.

Reagan's discourse thus operates in all three registers to deny radical lack. And the effect of such discourse goes far beyond persuading millions of people to vote for Reagan. The discourse also validates and even promotes numerous other denials of inescapable lack in specific systems, with the result that human suffering is exacerbated and the system is itself rendered even more deficient. Events promoted by such discourse would include such actions as Ed Meese's infamous denial that there is any real hunger in the United States, which undercut the already meager efforts to ameliorate this problem; James Watt's promotion of increased consumption of natural resources, which served to hasten the day when these resources will be severely lacking; and the entire policy of supply-side economics, which dramatically increased the number of people living below the poverty line. Reagan's master discourse, in short, in interpellating its audience to embrace a master and his master signifiers, promulgates a general repression of lack, and this repressed lack returns in the already disenfranchised or in future generations.

Jesse Jackson

Jesse Jackson's discourse seems quite different from Reagan's—most notably in the fact that whereas Reagan's discourse moves quickly to repress lack and overtly offer a phallic signifier and an object *a*, Jackson's discourse focuses on the lack. Jackson spoke much more from the position of the alienated, lacking, desiring subject and less from the position of the self-assured, self-contented phallic signifier or even master signifier. Although, like Reagan, he offered reassurance, he also challenged people and made them yearn for a better world—for others if not for themselves. Thus while the effect of Reagan's discourse derives largely from the passive narcissistic gratification it provided for its audience, Jackson's discourse seems to derive its impact more from *evoking* passive narcissistic desire than from gratifying it. In terms of discourse structure, while Reagan's discourse is predominantly a discourse of the Master eliciting identification with the S1, Jackson's would seem to be primarily a discourse of the Hysteric prompting the audience to identify with the $.

Imaginary-Order Lack

Much of the force of Jackson's discourse, in fact, comes precisely from exposing the lack that the ego ideal and fantasy attempt to cover, and embodying this lack and operating with it. In his 1988 speech to the Democratic National Convention, Jackson opened with a graphic evocation of this lack, when he observed:

> Many were lost in the struggle for the right to vote: Jimmy Lee Jackson, a young student, gave his life; . . . a white mother from Detroit, called 'nigger lover,' and brains blown out at point-blank range; Andrew Goodman, Michael Schwerner, and James Chaney, two Jews and a Black, found a common grave, bodies riddled with bullets in Mississippi; the four darling little girls in a church in Birmingham, Alabama: they died that we might have a right to live.

The images of mutilation in this utterance bring us face to face with what may be our earliest and most profound experience of lack, our lack of a unified, coordinated body. These "imagos of the fragmented body" (*Selection* 11), as Lacan would call them, recall "all the original distress resulting from [our] intra-organic and relational discordance during the first six months" of our life (19). Even fear of death, Lacan suggests, which we usually assume to be the ultimate instance of lack, "is psychologically subordinate to the narcissistic fear of damage to one's own body" (28). Such Imaginary-order threats to narcissistic security were also present, we recall, in Reagan's speech. But Reagan's discourse limits its acknowledgment of lack to tacit, Imaginary-order evocations, which, moreover, serve only as a basis for offering passive narcissistic Symbolic-order gratification.

Symbolic-Order Lack

Jackson's discourse not only places greater emphasis on Imaginary lack, it also powerfully invokes Symbolic-order lack, as in the following passage from his 1988 convention speech:

> Farmers, you seek fair prices, and you are right—but you cannot stand alone; your patch is not big enough. Workers, you fight for fair wages; you are right—but your patch of labor is not big enough. Women, you seek comparable worth and pay equity; you are right—but your patch is not big enough. Women, mothers, who seek Head Start, and day-care and prenatal care on the front side of life, relevant jail care and welfare on the back side of life, you are right—but your patch is not big enough. Students, you seek scholarships; you are right—but your patch is not big enough. Blacks and Hispanics, when we fight for civil rights, we are right, but our patch is not big enough. Gays and lesbians, when you fight against discrimination and a cure for Aids, you are right, but your patch is not big enough. Conservatives and progressives, when you fight for what you believe, right wing, left wing, hawk, dove, you are right from your point of view, but your point of view is not enough.

Here, recognition (passive Symbolic-order narcissistic gratification) at the level of the ego ideal—being "right"—is available to the audience only at the price of acknowledging their lack. This simultaneous granting of recognition and calling forth of the lack is recapitulated in the litany with which Jackson responds to his naming of each lack: "You are right, but your patch is not big enough." The first clause ("you are right") provides the recognition, and the second clause ("your patch is not big enough") calls forth the subject's acknowledgment of his or her own lack. Other declarations also, through the very granting of recognition, interpellate listeners into an assumption of their lack. The exclamatory assurance at the end of Jackson's speech recognizes a fundamental lack in the subject in the very utterance of reassurance:

> Wherever you are tonight, you can make it. Hold your head high. Stick your chest out. You can make it. It gets dark sometimes, but the morning comes. Don't you surrender. Suffering breeds character, character breeds faith; in the end faith will not disappoint. You must not surrender. You

may or may not get there, but just know that you're qualified and you hold on and hold out. We must never surrender.

This last sentence, moreover, locates the lack not just in the subjects in the audience, the "you," but also in a "we" that includes the entire nation and Jackson himself as subject presumed to know and representative of the Symbolic Other. This manifestation of lack in the Symbolic Other is a crucial element in the power of Jackson's oratory, and it occurs in a number of additional, more direct and intense instances. The most important occurs immediately before the passage just quoted, when Jackson says:

> Why can I challenge you this way?
> "Jesse Jackson, you don't understand my situation. You're on television—you don't understand. I see you with the big people. You don't understand my situation."
> I understand. You see me on TV, but you don't know the me that makes me me. They wonder why does Jesse run, because they see me running for the White House. They don't see the house I'm running from. I have a story. I wasn't always on television. Writers weren't always outside my door. I was born late one afternoon, October 8, Greenville, South Carolina. No writers asked my mother her name. Nobody chose to write down our address. My mother was not supposed to make it. And I was not supposed to make it. You see, I was born of a teenage mother, who was born of a teenage mother. I understand. I know abandonment, and people being mean to you, and saying you're nothing and nobody and can never be anything. I understand. . . . I wasn't born in the hospital. Momma didn't have insurance. I was born in the bed at house. I really do understand. Born in a three-room house—bathroom in the back yard, slop jar by the bed, no hot and cold running water. I understand. Wall paper used for decoration? No: for a windbreaker. I understand.

With these words, the lack in the Other becomes palpable, and it intersects with the lack in the listening subject. That is, the audience answers this lack in the Other with their own lack, and as a result are recognized and validated by the Other in the ground of their being: the lack.

All of this interpellates Jackson's followers away from S1 into the position of $, the hysteric, in contrast to Reagan's discourse, which lures the audience in the opposite direction, into an (illusory) assumption of the identity offered by the master (phallic) signifier. Jackson's focus on lack would thus seem to entail a fundamentally different ethical position than does Reagan's valorization of master signifiers. In fact, one might argue that the most fundamental difference between the discourses of Reagan and Jackson relates to the respective ethical stance promoted by each discourse. Reagan's discourse, like traditional ethics, operates from a position of power and seduces subjects to enter into what Lacan calls the service of goods and thus give up on their desire. Reagan even says at one point in his speech, "We must have the clarity of vision to see the difference between what is essential and what is *merely desirable*" (emphasis added). This is the attitude of power. "The moral of power, of the service of goods," Lacan says, "is: as for desires, you will get to them later. Let them wait" (VII 363). Reagan's offerings of master signifiers, the Symbolic phallus, and the object *a* to his audience are so many attempts to get them to give up on desire by sinking back into the passive narcissistic gratification that his master signifiers continually provide. Jackson's discourse, in contrast, tends to promote the ethics of psychoanalysis, for which "the only thing of which one could be guilty is to have given up on one's desire" (VII 370).

Symbolic-Order Gratification

At the same time, however, the recognition that Jackson offers of his audience's lack provides the same sort of passive narcissistic Symbolicorder gratification that Reagan's master signifiers provided. In fact, Jackson's discourse comes very close to constituting lack itself as a master signifier. This effect derives largely from the fact that Jackson functions for his supporters as the subject presumed to know, the object of the transference and representative of the Other. He represents the Symbolic Other in a number of ways. First, as a minister, he is seen by some to speak with the voice of God, one of the primary cultural embodiments of the Cosmic Other. In addition, as a prominent public figure and an important politician, he also fills the role of the Societal Other. Because of these factors, and because he is a powerful speaker who pronounces judgment and allocates names and attributes, he fills the ultimate role of the Symbolic Other: the witness of speech and guarantor of truth—which is precisely the role that the object of the transference is called upon to assume.

Speaking from this position of the Symbolic Other, Jackson utters statements that provide the fundamental recognition (i.e., passive narcissistic gratification) that we all need (and that most of us receive) in order to go on living: assurance (even if only of the most indirect and tacit kind) by the ultimate authority (whether societal or cosmic) that our individual existence and identity are valuable, that they matter—that the Other loves us. Perhaps the most powerful instance of this passive narcissistic gratification in Jackson's campaign speeches was his leading his audience in the chant, "I am somebody," which responds to the passive narcissistic Symbolic-order desire in the most direct manner possible.

Numerous other instances of passive narcissistic gratification are offered in Jackson's speeches. In his 1988 convention address, for instance, Jackson provided such gratification to numerous people by naming their group identity—workers, farmers, women, Hispanics, and AIDS victims, at one point—and thus providing recognition for precisely that aspect of these subjects' identity that Society has failed to accord full recognition. Such gratification was also abundant when Jackson, at the end of the speech, assured his audience: "You are right," "I understand," "I care," and "I love you." The latter three pronouncements, insofar as they are heard as emanating directly from the Symbolic Other, provide powerful, immediate, and direct passive narcissistic gratification.

Jackson's discourse also provides more subtle and indirect forms of such gratification. In fact, in interpellating his audience to the position of $, Jackson's discourse is providing an incipient narcissistic gratification for those subjects that are "not-all" submitted to the Symbolic order. The chant, "I am somebody," for example, has the effect of drawing into the Symbolic order those who have heretofore found no place in it, or rather who find themselves not-all in it. This position, which Lacan characterizes as the traditionally feminine position, involves being, in Serge André's words, "not-all submitted to the signifying law" (223). "The feminine division," André explains, "is constitutive of another split than that of the subject of the unconscious ($), . . . [a] split between $ and what [one] is as non-subject, non-subjectivizable" (232). What people in this position want is "to be made subjects there where the signifier abandons them" (239). They desire "that something come to the place of this lacking signifier"

(244). The following passionate declaration uttered by Jackson makes this process clear:

> Jesse Jackson is my *third name*. I'm adopted. When I had *no name*, my grandmother gave me *her name*. My name was Jesse Burns till I was twelve. *So I wouldn't have a blank space, she gave me a name*, to hold me over. I understand when *nobody knows your name*. I understand when you *have no name*. . . . Every one of these *funny labels* they put on you, those of you who are watching this broadcast tonight in the projects, on the corners—I understand. Call you outcast, lowdown, you can't make it, you're nothing, you're from nobody, subclass, underclass. When you see Jesse Jackson—*when my name* goes in *nomination, your name* goes in *nomination.*(Emphasis added)

Here, through identification with Jackson as the subject presumed to know, Jackson's audience receives a signifier, a name, validation by the Symbolic order and hence, passive narcissistic Symbol-order gratification of a most basic kind—the sort we first get when we assume an identity in the Symbolic order.

Metaphor and Metonymy

Another indirect form of passive narcissistic Symbolic-order gratification is provided by the sense of social unity produced by Jackson's metaphors and metonymy. One of the most effective ways that metonymy produces this sense of unity in Jackson's speech is through the repetition of certain words and phrases. Perhaps the most obvious instance involves the phrase "common ground," which appears about a dozen times in the first half of Jackson's 1988 convention speech. Every time this phrase is used, the sense of unity grows, increasing its mass and momentum like a snowball rolling down a hill. It is first introduced at the site of a tension between unity and division, between "battlegrounds" and "higher ground":

> We meet tonight at the crossroads, a point of decision. Shall we expand, be inclusive, find unity and power, or suffer division and impotence? . . . Tonight there is a sense of celebration because we are moved, fundamentally moved, from racial *battlegrounds* by law, to economic *common ground; common ground. Common ground!* . . . When we divide we

cannot win. We must find *common ground* as a basis for survival. . . .

We find *common ground* at the plant gate that closes on workers without notice. We find *common ground* at the farm auction where a good farmer loses his or her land to bad loans or diminishing markets. *Common ground* at the schoolyard where teachers cannot get adequate pay, and students cannot get a scholarship, and can't make a loan. *Common ground* at the hospital admitting room, where somebody tonight is dying because they cannot afford to go upstairs to a bed that's empty waiting for someone with insurance to get sick. (Emphasis added)

Linking the phrase "common ground" to each of these groups effectively establishes an identity among them all, and participation in this collective identity constitutes a powerful sense of recognition, or passive narcissistic gratification in the Symbolic order.

Jackson employs metaphor to a similar end. His metaphors produce a sense of social unity, and hence, passive narcissistic gratification, by repressing the conflict (and the resulting fragmentation and weakness) that inevitably arise from the differences inherent in a diverse group of people and by substituting the attributes of harmony, beauty, and strength for the attributes of conflict and division that are normally attached to difference and opposition. One instance of this metaphoric transformation is the name of Jackson's campaign, "The Rainbow Coalition," a metaphor in which the conflicts that exist among the different groups and individuals supporting Jackson are completely repressed. A similar effect is achieved in the metaphor of the quilt employed by Jackson in his 1988 convention speech:

America is not a blanket, woven from one thread, one color, one cloth. When I was a child growing up in Greenville, South Carolina, and grand-momma could not afford a blanket, she didn't complain and we did not freeze. Instead, she took pieces of old cloth—patches—wool, silk, gabar-dine, crokersack—only patches, barely good enough to wipe your shoes with. But they didn't stay that way very long. With sturdy hands and a strong cord, she sewed them together into a quilt, a thing of beauty and power and culture. Now, Democrats, we must build such a quilt.

The way in which Jackson's metaphors repress conflict is even more striking in his descriptions of the relation between his campaign and that of Michael Dukakis and of the relation between liberals and conservatives in the Democratic party. Of Dukakis, Jackson observes: "His foreparents came to America on immigrant ships. My foreparents came to America on slave ships. But whatever the original ships, we are in the same boat tonight." Similarly, concerning the split within the Democratic party between the left wing and the right wing, Jackson declares that it takes two wings to fly, thus turning division and weakness into an image of unity and strength and providing passive narcissistic gratification for his audience. The most powerful metaphoric and metonymic operations in Jackson's discourse thus function to produce a sense of social unity for his audience, a sense that is essentially a passive narcissistic gratification, since union with society implies accord with the societal Other.

The Supplement from the Real

The deepest reassurance offered by Jackson, however, as well as the source of his charisma, comes (as with Reagan) from his embodiment of the object *a*. On the one hand, Jackson's voice and gaze have the opposite function of Reagan's: Jackson's voice, like the primordial cry of utter desolation, and his gaze, like the uncanny experience of being regarded by something not completely evident, serve not to fill the lack but rather to open it and keep it open. On the other hand, however, Jackson functions for his audience as the possessor of, if not limitless, at least unusual jouissance, which serves to promote racist fear in some, but serves in others to reinforce the notion that Jackson has to a degree escaped the Law and its castration and thus approximates the primordial mythical father (described by Freud in *Totem and Taboo*) who escaped castration and experienced limitless jouissance. This sense reinforces Jackson's role as object of transference for his supporters, which, we recall, is accorded to anyone whom we presume to possess precious knowledge of jouissance of which we are deprived.

Jackson's race and the ambiguous status that it and other characteristics of his entail in relation to the Law, the System, allow Jackson to operate for many in a way similar to that of Reagan: as the primordial father who has escaped castration, or at least knows how to escape it. The ambiguous position of Jackson in relation to the Law derives from several factors. First, he is a black and thus partially excluded from the Law, insofar as blacks are still not totally equal under the present system, and they are imagined by many whites to have greater sexual potency or capacity for jouissance. At the same time, however, Jackson occupies a prominent position in the white echelons of power at the heart of the Law. Second, as an illegitimate child, he is outside the Law, but as an ordained minister and a candidate of national stature, he is a paragon of legitimacy. And finally, as a proponent of fundamental social change, he is opposed to the Law in its present social incarnation, but as an advocate of traditional religious values he embraces the most venerable aspects of the Law. Thus one of the deepest, most hidden layers of Jackson's discourse—much of which is conveyed tacitly by his personal identity and history and his unique present subject position—functions for his supporters in the same way Reagan's discourse operated on his followers: as a promise of the S1 and/or the object a that will fill all lacks.

In this way, Jackson's discourse, like Reagan's, functions as what Lacan described as a hypnotic discourse, producing a collective fascination, of the sort elicited by Hitler and Mussolini (XI 272). Lacan explains that collective fascination or mass enthusiasm is produced by a mode of discourse that marshals the different types of identification in a way opposite that of psychoanalysis (273). Rather than maintaining a separation and dialectical tension between Imaginary and Symbolic identifications, on the one hand, and desire in the Real, on the other, as does psychoanalytic treatment, hypnotic discourse collapses the three in relation to a single object/person: the masses identify with the figure at all levels, thus investing him or her with tremendous psychological and therefore political power. Hitler and Mussolini worked this discourse to near perfection in the 1930s and more recently, Reagan and Jackson, it seems, have also operated quite effectively with it, in somewhat different ways and for different groups of people. In each of these cases, the figure in question embodied for his followers not only insignia of their ego ideal but also emblems of their desire in both Real and Imaginary orders (the latter entailing the narcissistic gratifications of parade, prestige, rivalry, and murderous opposition).

Political discourse, then, at least in the cases of Reagan and Jackson, operates primarily through its audience's desire for a master. Although gratification is promised more overtly in Reagan's discourse than in Jackson's, the desire for a master is no less profound in Jackson's audience than in Reagan's. As Lacan observed, the discourse of the Hysteric inevitably seeks a master. It would thus seem that one fundamental result of political discourse, whether the discourse is one of anger and protest or one of celebration and congratulation, may well be to prompt subjects to look to the Other to supply their lost jouissance, whether that Other takes the form of a charismatic political figure, the government, society itself, or God. Beneath the energy and activism promoted in some subjects by political discourse, there lurks a profound passivity, which derives not only from the very real limitations confronting the actions of a single subject but also from the desire to repeat the primordial passive narcissistic gratification of being loved (recognized or desired) by the Other, the supreme authority.

CHAPTER SIX

H E A R T   O F   D A R K N E S S

Ideology in *Heart of Darkness*

The case of *Heart of Darkness* furnishes an instructive example of how a work of "high culture" can operate politically in ways that have been almost totally overlooked by cultural criticism as it is presently practiced—even though the novella has long been viewed in terms of its ideological concerns. Many readers, responding to Marlow's ironic and caustic comments about the Europeans' behavior in Africa, have taken *Heart of Darkness* as a powerful and effective critique of imperialism.[1] In recent years, however, most critics have emphasized not Marlow's criticism of imperialism but the work's own implication in racist and sexist ideologies. Chinua Achebe, for instance, in his well-known attack on *Heart of Darkness*, finds its representation of Africans to be "grossly inadequate" (260), and declares it to be "an offensive and deplorable book, . . . a book which parades in the most vulgar fashion prejudices and insults from which a section of mankind has suffered untold agonies and atrocities in the past and continues to do so in many ways and many places today" (259).

While some critics have defended Conrad against this charge, emphasizing the progressiveness of his views on race in contrast with the attitudes of his contemporaries,[2] most recent commentators who ad-

---

[1]Adena Rosmarin states: "As almost every critic has recognized, the work is obviously—if complexly—critiquing late nineteenth-century imperialism" (151).

[2]Hunt Hawkins, for example, in response to Achebe, contends that "it is overly severe simply to write Conrad off as a racist. His attitude is complex, itself critical of racism,

dress the issue conclude that the way the novel (mis)represents Africans makes it a racist work. Thus Patrick Brantlinger, while acknowledging that the novel is less grossly racist than "hundreds" of others of the time,[3] concludes that Conrad's impressionistic rendering of Marlow's experience causes him to misrepresent Africa,[4] and that "Achebe is therefore right to call Conrad's portrayal of Africa and Africans 'racist'" (371). Reynold Humphries reaches the same conclusion. "Whether it be women, customs, or language itself," he declares, "the methods of representation in Conrad move towards a homogenization of the world of the other through the discourse of the Other in a way that travesties reality" (117).

Like Humphries, other critics have also found abundant evidence of sexism in the way the novella represents women. Peter Hyland, for instance, notes "the inadequacy of Marlow's concept of women" (7), in the form of a discrepancy between Marlow's ideas about women and one's actual experience of women (6), and comments: "The attitudes of Victorian patriarchy structure the response to women and to savages in the same way, by imposing a sentimental and reductive definition upon the object that removes the necessity of actually looking at it" (4). Johanna Smith, similarly, presents a detailed and perceptive analysis of the way in which Marlow's descriptions of women in the novella fix upon certain aspects of the women in order both to ignore other aspects of the women and to disguise Marlow's "complicity in the Company's imperialism" (182).

The common theme in all of these ideology critiques is that there is a

---

and, I believe, ultimately sympathetic to non-European peoples. . . . Perhaps Conrad was not able to break entirely free from the racial biases and epithets of his age. But we should recognize his special status as one of the few writers of his period who struggled with the issue of race, and we should appreciate the remarkable fair-mindedness he achieved" (163, 169).

[3]Brantlinger states: "The fact that there are almost no other works of British fiction written before World War I which are critical of imperialism, and hundreds of imperialist ones which are racist through and through, is a measure of Conrad's achievement" ("Anti-Imperialism" 382–83).

[4]Brantlinger observes that "evil *is* African in Conrad's story; if it is also European, that's because some number of white men in the heart of darkness behave like Africans. Conrad's stress on cannibalism, his identification of African customs with violence, lust, and madness, his metaphors of bestiality, death, and darkness, his suggestion that traveling in Africa is like traveling backward in time to primeval, infantile, but also hellish stages of existence—these features of the story are drawn from the repertoire of Victorian imperialism and racism that painted an entire continent dark" ("Anti-Imperialism" 371).

discrepancy between reality and the novella's representation of that reality. Some critics (Adena Rosmarin, for instance) identify this ideology as Marlow's, while others (such as Hyland)[5] locate it in Conrad and/or Victorian society. But in either case, critics place the work's ideology in the putative intentionality of the producer of the narrative (Marlow, Conrad, or Victorian society) and equate ideology with (mis)representation. Such an approach, as we saw in the Introduction, constitutes a double diversion from the aim of producing a socially significant criticism. First, falling victim to the historicist diversion, it fails to assess the ideological impact of *Heart of Darkness* on readers today, and second, embracing the epistemological bias, it neglects to investigate those elements besides the work's (mis)representations that interpellate contemporary readers in ways that are ideologically significant.

A number of recent feminist critiques have begun to engage these issues. Valerie Sedlak, for example, criticizes the epistemological bias, lamenting the fact that "most of those critics [interested in the portrayal of women in the novella] are concerned with the issue of truth versus illusion in the portrayal of those women" (443). But Sedlak then falls into this bias herself. She observes that "Marlow's preconceived notions about the 'beautiful' world of woman are fallacious," that "his preconceived ideas about women . . . do not coincide with the situations in which these women live" (465). She defines the task of the feminist critic as one of perceiving the truth behind the illusion presented by Marlow: "Our job, then, as Conrad's readers, is to bring all that we are to the narrative context of *Heart of Darkness*, . . . in an attempt to 'see' what Marlow sees and also what Marlow does not see" (450).

In another feminist analysis, Bette London criticizes the historicist diversion of most ideology critiques. As for herself, she avers, "I am not particularly interested in pursuing the particular manifestations of the racism or sexism of author, narrator, or text. . . . What interests me . . . is the way the narrative enacts the construction of cultural identity: the construction of the white male speaking subject as narra-

---

[5]Hyland states that "Marlow's response to the Intended is the result of a particular kind of anti-feminism that pervades the novella and may well reflect Conrad's own inadequate response to the feminine" (4).

tive authority" (239). But London, like Sedlak, ultimately conceives ideology primarily in terms of truth and illusion, as is manifested in her observation that "ideology determines not only what an observer writes, but what a 'first-hand' observer sees" (241). Her point here—that "reality" itself is an ideological construct—remains an epistemological point. Thus although London's discussion does begin to take into account the interpellative power of ideology, it fails to apprehend the full ideological force of Conrad's tale because it focuses primarily on the interpellative force exerted by Marlow on the *Nellie* audience within the tale, rather than on the tale's impact on Conrad's audience, and because it conceives of ideology largely in epistemological terms, omitting ideals, identifications, desire, and jouissance.[6]

Thus despite an abundance of concern with the ideological significance of *Heart of Darkness*, critics have not yet gotten to the heart of the novella's ideological force. To do so, as we saw in the Introduction, it is necessary both to focus on audience response and to take into account all of the interpellative forces operating on the audience in such a way as to produce that response. Only thus can one begin to determine some of the subject positions (or subjective dispositions) and the concomitant political ramifications produced by the combined interpellative forces of the work.

To get to the root of the novella's ideological force, then, we need to begin by identifying common denominators in the actual responses of a significant number of readers. Next we must explain how specific textual elements operated on particular psychological structures in such a way as to produce these common responses. Finally, by explaining the impact of these interpellative forces on the psychic economy, we can extrapolate how such a psychic economy would operate vis-a-vis specific political issues, such as racism, sexism, and homophobia. In pursuing this path, I will argue that a review of criticism reveals that *Heart of Darkness* interpellates many of its "critics" into reinforcing

---

[6]This same deficiency is present in an essay by Nina Straus, who explicitly declares her intention to analyze the effect the text has on readers. "The question of Conrad's intentions for his tale," she observes, "[are] difficult to adjudicate. What can be analyzed, however, is the effect of Conrad's words on various readers: and it is the contention of this essay that these words are understood differently by feminist readers and by mainstream male commentators" (129). Straus's analysis itself, however, is limited by her tendency to assume, with Jauss, that "the impact of a literary work can be described by referring to the 'frame of reference of the reader's expectation'" (124).

the battle lines and ignoring the possibility of compromise between unconscious desires, drives, fantasies, and jouissances, on the one hand, and the ego ideal, on the other. Such an interpellation, which is the inverse of that produced by the discourse of the Analyst in psychoanalytic treatment, cultivates the grounds of racism, sexism, and homophobia.

The Response to *Heart of Darkness*

Perhaps the most striking factor in the critical response to *Heart of Darkness* is the number of critics who have come, through their various interpretations of the work, to advocate resistance, renunciation, and restraint in relation to drives, desires, jouissances, and fantasies. The frequency of this response indicates that significant forces are at work in the novella to interpellate readers to such resistance. Jocelyn Baines, for instance, in her 1960 biography of Conrad, states that "the 'sombre theme' of the story, in part at least, is the conflict between the power of the wilderness to release 'forgotten and brutal instincts' and the capacity of a human being to *resist* this pressure" (226; emphasis added). Another commentator declares that "in his stage of enlightenment [Marlow] teaches what his descent into the imperfections of the human soul has taught him—egoless compassion. Canceling out all personal desire and fear, he has made available to humanity the *gift* of complete *renunciation*" (cited in Crews 509, n. 2; emphasis added).

This priestly solution to the problem of the drives is unmistakable in the conclusion of an actual priest, Walter Ong, who in an essay entitled "Truth in Conrad's Darkness" declares: "In 'The Horror!' Kurtz had faced the *truth* at last," which is that "man . . . is deep and dark and dangerous from within, and more so if a person does not recognize this fact openly" (156; emphasis added). For Ong there is no question of transforming the drives; one must simply recognize "the terror within" and "counter" it. Ong concludes: "Recognition of the truth is at least initial conversion, or change, from which redemption can start. [For] in recognizing the terror within himself, Kurtz had countered it in some measure at least" (156).

This affirmation of salvation through the rejection of alien drives and jouissances finds a more explicit and only slightly more secular form in other articles.[7] Nor is the moral of restraint of drives and renunciation of alien jouissances limited to moral criticism. It also characterizes much psychoanalytic and rhetorical commentary on the novella. John Tessitore, for instance, citing passages from *Civilization and Its Discontents*, finds in the story "the dark *truth* that the cultural claims of the group are *irreconcilable* with the individual's claim to freedom" (39; emphasis added). For Tessitore, a battle between "instinctual freedom" and "slavish suppression" (38) or between "pleasure" and "reality" (36), can lead only to "denouncement" of or "surrender" to (36) one or the other, not to compromise or transformation of either force.

Similarly, rhetorical studies of the story—even those informed by the skepticism of Nietzsche and Derrida—wind up embracing the value of restraint, thus repeating the very rhetorical forces they set out to analyze and reinforcing the interpellative force of Conrad's discourse. John McClure, for instance, in "The Rhetoric of Restraint in *Heart of Darkness*," concludes with a moral in which restraint is once again presented as salutary, only this time displaced from action to speech: "Marlow senses . . . that the forces of this psychological darkness, man's 'unlawful' appetites and dreams, can easily 'capture' man's speech. And he realizes . . . that when these impulses are allowed *unrestrained* expression, the utterances which result only compound the darkness in which men already move" (326; emphasis added). Thus while Kurtz, "surrendering to appetite, . . . sinks deeper into delusion and depravity, until he is beyond return, cut off irrevocably from any social salvation" (320), "Marlow attains the *saving insights*" (323; emphasis added).[8] By thus reengaging the issue of human fate in terms

[7]Jerome Meckier, in an article entitled "The Truth about Marlow," speaks of "Kurtz's bleak but saving vision," which through Marlow's "salvationary" "truth-telling" about Kurtz, "broaden[s] the awareness of his involuntary pupils . . . [and] supplies his listeners with something more reliable to live with" (379). Fred Madden has essentially the same response, only in a more stoic vein: "Conrad is advocating man's *acceptance* of a limited, imperfect, and corruptible existence. . . . Marlow's growth and final realization . . . suggest the necessity of '*restraint*' and compassion as counterforces to man's propensity to exploit others. . . . This '*restraint*' . . . must continue in the *certain knowledge* that it is, at best, merely a gesture against overwhelming forces, and for the reader of *Heart of Darkness* this gesture is all that illuminates Conrad's vision" (517; emphasis added).

[8]Vincent Pecora, in "*Heart of Darkness* and the Phenomenology of Voice," sees clearly the ideological dimension of Marlow's perspective and notes that most readers

of knowledge versus illusion concerning the way things are, critics, like the story itself, repress the possibility that the way things are might be susceptible to change.

This repression of change that results from focusing on epistemological issues achieves its most powerful enactment in Hillis Miller's essay, which connects the struggle between knowledge and ignorance in *Heart of Darkness* with the parabolic and apocalyptic discourses of religion, both of which, Miller explains, are acts of unveiling (210). Miller finds that "the book's claim to give the reader access to the dark truth behind appearance is withdrawn by the terms in which it is proffered" (219), owing to the ironic tone of Marlow's narration. "Irony," he explains, "is truth-telling or a means of truth-telling, of unveiling. At the same time it is a defense against the truth. This doubleness makes it, though it seems so coolly reasonable, another mode of unreason, the unreason of a fundamental undecidability" (222). This irony of Marlow's speech, Miller argues, makes it "another version of that multiple cacophonous and deceitful voice flowing from the heart of darkness" (223).

Such an account of *Heart of Darkness* represses the possibility of arriving at a compromise between the realm of knowledge and the realm of the drives, ignoring the latter realm entirely by transposing the conflict between ideals and knowledge, on the one hand, and drives and fantasy on the other entirely into the realm of a knowledge whose completeness and supremacy make it the most effective repetition yet of that narcissistic closure supposedly attained in Kurtz's "supreme moment of complete knowledge." This fetishization of knowing climaxes in Miller's concluding enraptured plunge into aporia:

> The final fold in this folding in of complicities in these ambiguous acts of unveiling is my own complicity as demystifying commentator. . . . My

---

have shared Marlow's bias: "Marlow *needs* the moral victory and the sign of Kurtz's indefatigable presence that he perceives in Kurtz's last words, just as his culture needs such final moral affirmations—a need that, as the history of our criticism of this story would show, has been recapitulated in interpretation after interpretation" (1008). But in identifying this ideological bias of Marlow and the novella's commentators, Pecora himself repeats a deeper ideological strain of the story: the valorization of knowing and the repression of both the drives and the possibility of change. Observing that "it is a belief in the illusory presence signified by Kurtz's voice that finally sustains Marlow," Pecora declares: "What Marlow has not been forced to do is look behind the illusion of this 'gift of speech'" (1009).

commentary unveils a lack of decisive unveiling in *Heart of Darkness*. . . . By unveiling the lack of unveiling in *Heart of Darkness*, I have become another witness in my turn, as much guilty as any other in the line of witnesses of covering over while claiming to illuminate. My *Aufklärung* too has been of the continuing impenetrability of Conrad's *Heart of Darkness*. (223–24)

Miller's discourse, in which knowledge knows itself as both knowing and ignorant of itself, is, in Lacanian terms, an obsessional dialect of the hysterical discourse to which *Heart of Darkness* interpellates its readers: it is a monumental attempt by the ego to consolidate itself in a discourse of mastery, despite Miller's claim that "irony is the one trope that cannot be mastered or used as an instrument of mastery" (223). On the contrary, irony is the ultimate trope of ego-mastery, a favorite obsessional strategy for remaining free of all limitations or encumbrances.[9] Miller's valorizing and highlighting of the ironies of *Heart of Darkness* is a game in which the ego plays hide-and-seek with itself, trying, by repeating to itself its knowledge that knowledge is always incomplete, to repress and/or reduce to the realm of knowledge what always exceeds knowledge—the object *a* and the drives and fantasies with which it is involved.[10] By engaging the ego in a relation to the text that is fraught with undecidability, Miller's ironic perspective allows readers to achieve a tacit final pronouncement of rejection in relation to their own unconscious drives and fantasies precisely while congratulating themselves on their open-minded, undogmatic attitude and their ability to resist closure because of the fact that they

[9]As Johanna Smith notes, irony is a way of removing ourselves from disturbing feelings (195).

[10]A similar response can be found in Charles Eric Reeves's essay, "Conrad's Rhetoric of the Unspeakable." Reeves sees Conrad's novella as presenting "a narrative form which relentlessly insists on subverting or compromising nearly all its central claims" (305), many of which concern the relation between "word and world" (306) or "language and experience" (308). At the end of the story, according to Reeves, "we are made aware of how untenable Marlow's narrative has become: bound in by the dark triumph of a lie and by a truth that would have been too dark—too dark altogether, language is rendered inert, passive, unable to sustain further Marlow's restless voice. . . . This silence brings to *tragic completion* Conrad's drama of narratability" (308). Here too the primary effect of Conrad's text is narcissistic ego gratification, derived from a knowledge of epistemological impass that brings a sense of "tragic completion," a fatalistic resignation which like Miller's position not only denies the possibility of transformation but also completely ignores the drives and fantasies whence transformation might originate.

have refrained from any final pronouncement concerning the manifest content of the text.[11]

The Interpellative Force of *Heart of Darkness*

We thus see that numerous responses of critics employing various approaches and methodologies are characterized by the same basic position: the assumption that unconscious drives, desires, and jouissances are irreconcilably opposed to the critics' basic values and ideals and that the only viable response to this situation is to take refuge in knowledge about the hopelessness of the situation. The question now becomes: how does *Heart of Darkness* manage to prompt this type of response, and what are the possible long-term psychological, social, and political effects of such an interpellation?

Concerning the first part of this question, I will argue that the basic response to *Heart of Darkness* is the result of a threefold interpellative force that the work exercises on its audience. First, the novella constructs the wilderness as a threat to the audience's Imaginary sense of bodily mastery and integrity. Second, the wilderness is evoked as an agent that both harbors and elicits brutal drives and repulsive fantasies and jouissances, instances of the Real that constitute a threat to both Imaginary- and Symbolic-order dimensions of the audience's ego— both their sense of bodily integrity and their ego ideal. Third, *Heart of Darkness* offers knowledge as a means of mastery that allows one to escape from the threats of the Imaginary and the Real orders.

As intimated above, the discourse of *Heart of Darkness*, like the discourse of the Hysteric to which psychoanalytic treatment interpellates the patient, positions the subject between ideals/knowledge and drives/jouissances

$$\frac{\$}{a} \longrightarrow \frac{S1}{S2}$$

where $\$$ is the subject split between (1) its identification with certain master signifiers (values and ideals, or S1) in the systems of knowledge and belief constituted by the Symbolic order or language (S2) and

[11]Such responses on the part of readers are, like Miller's analysis, an obsessional dialect of hysterical discourse, in which the subject gives the $\$$ of self-division as its official address while actually continuing to reside in the S1—which is present in signifiers like "undecidability"—and in S2, which is present as a savoir faire of ironizing

reinforced by Imaginary-order identification and (2) its subjection to the unsymbolized portion of being (*a*), which mobilizes unconscious fantasies and forbidden drives and jouissances. In interpellating many readers to such a position, *Heart of Darkness* parallels an essential moment of the process of psychoanalytic treatment: the struggle between, on the one hand, the subject's assumed identity, based on the ego ideal and its values, and on the other hand, the unconscious drives and fantasies that push for a jouissance forbidden by or excluded from the ego ideal and its narcissistic satisfactions.

But while *Heart of Darkness* and the discourse of the Analyst both interpellate subjects to assume their self-division, Conrad's discourse is diametrically opposed to the discourse of the Analyst when it comes to the response elicited from the subject in this split. As we saw in Chapter 2, the discourse of the Analyst attempts to bring these two opposing forces, S1-S2 and *a*, together in a way that will effect a modification of both forces: the subject acknowledges and works through the *a* until a new master signifier is formed, that is, until the ego ideal is altered in a way that is more accommodating of the previously repressed and excluded portion of being. Conrad's discourse, on the other hand, promotes no such transformation; instead, it exerts all its interpellative power in the opposite direction, toward establishing in readers the sense of an unbridgeable gulf between these two forces, with the resultant feeling that they must choose one force, the ego ideal and its narcissistic closure, and reject the other. The choice offered readers is between a position of acting out (Kurtz's response in the jungle) and a position of refuge in knowledge (even if illusory), with the concomitant repression, suppression, and/or denunciation of alien desires, fantasies, drives, and jouissances (Marlow's response all along, and, apparently, Kurtz's final response). Readers are coerced to choose between, in Marlow's terms, restraint and lack of restraint, with no option of compromise or transformation of either drives or ideals. And many readers, as we have seen, succumb to this coercion.

Interpellation to Bodily Vulnerability

The basic forces that interpellate readers to choose in favor of consolidation of the ego ideal (S1) and the system of knowledge and belief

---

and deconstructing and as knowledge of the lack of firm knowledge—a knowledge that constitutes in advance a transcendence not only of the illusory imperialistic ideals but of any other illusion that might arise besides.

(S2) in the Symbolic order, and against the drives (*a*), are thus, first, the novella's emphasis on the security and sense of meaning, being, and identity produced by ideals and knowledge/belief, and, second, the threat to the sense of meaning, being, and identity posed by other forces. Throughout the novella, various features operate to reinforce both the locus of security and the locus of threat and thus push readers more and more into the realm of ideals and knowledge (S1-S2).

The threat exists on both a moral and a corporeal level, and the source of the threat is both the external world and the internal world of the body. The external threat to bodily integrity is imposed on readers most forcibly by the variegated images of dismemberment, which, through the identificatory force they exert, serve to deny readers a sense of bodily mastery and integrity and the more general feeling of well-being dependent upon that sense. The most obvious instance of such dismemberment is the literal deterioration of human bodies in the wilderness, both before and after death—for example, the deterioration of the natives at the first station who have withdrawn to die:

> Black shapes crouched, lay, sat between the trees, leaning against the trunks, clinging to the earth, half coming out, half effaced within the dim light, in all the attitudes of pain, abandonment, and despair. . . . They were dying slowly. . . . [T]hey were nothing earthly now—nothing but black shadows of disease and starvation, lying confusedly in the greenish gloom. . . . [T]hey sickened, became inefficient, and were then allowed to crawl away and rest. These moribund shapes were free as air—and nearly as thin. . . . One, with his chin propped on his knees, stared at nothing, in an intolerable and appalling manner: his brother phantom rested its forehead, as if overcome with a great weariness; and all about others were scattered in every pose of contorted collapse, as in some picture of a massacre or a pestilence. (31–32)

Marlow's reaction to this scene of almost total lack of bodily unity and mastery serves as a prompt for the response of readers: "I stood horror-struck," Marlow reports (32), echoing the famous words that he later reports Kurtz to have spoken in response (apparently) to the other, interior threat.

Kurtz's emaciated appearance is also a powerful instance of this Imaginary-order interpellation: "His covering had fallen off, and his body emerged from it pitiful and appalling as from a winding-sheet. I could see the cage of his ribs all astir, the bones of his arm waving. It was as though an animated image of death carved out of old ivory had been shaking its hand" (75). Other instances of decomposing bodies, such as that of Captain Fresleven with grass growing through his ribs (23) and that of the African with a bullet hole in his forehead (34), reinforce readers' sense of bodily vulnerability.

Nor is this effect limited to the images of human bodies. Images of broken-down buildings and machinery produce a similar result, if more subtle, serving in effect as metaphors for the human body. Such is the effect of Marlow's observations upon landing at the first station, where the connection between broken machines and dead bodies is made explicit: "I came upon a boiler wallowing in the grass, then found a path leading up the hill. It turned aside for the boulders, and also for an undersized railway truck lying there on its back with its wheels in the air. One was off. The thing looked as dead as the carcass of some animal. I came upon more pieces of decaying machinery, a stack of rusty rails" (29).

Descriptions of landscape also function, in the manner discussed in Chapter 1, to deny a sense of bodily mastery to readers. Such a subject position is evoked by Marlow's early description of the hostile and alien appearance England must have had for the first Roman who arrived there:

> Imagine him here—the very end of the world, a sea the colour of lead, a sky the colour of smoke, a kind of ship about as rigid as a concertina— and going up this river. . . . Sandbanks, marshes, forests, savages— precious little to eat fit for a civilised man, nothing but Thames water to drink. No Falernian wine here, no going ashore. Here and there a military camp lost in a wilderness, like a needle in a bundle of hay—cold, fog, tempests, disease, exile, and death—death skulking in the air, in the water, in the bush. They must have been dying like flies here. (20)

Marlow's descriptions of the African wilderness similarly undermine the readers' sense of bodily mastery: "The great wall of vegetation, an exuberant and entangled mass of trunks, branches, leaves, boughs, festoons, motionless in the moonlight, was like a rioting invasion of soundless life, a rolling wave of plants, piled up, crested, ready to topple over the creek, to sweep every little man of us out of his little existence" (44–45). "You lost your way on that river as you would in a desert," Marlow reports, "and butted all day long against shoals, trying to find the channel, till you thought yourself bewitched and cut off for ever from everything you had known once" (48).

Interpellation to Cognitive Vulnerability

In this last passage, the threat is mental as well as physical: the wilderness cuts one off from the systems of knowledge that support one's sense of identity. This incommensurability between the wilderness and European knowledge is experienced numerous times—by the audience as well as by Marlow. It is encountered, for example, at the beginning of Marlow's trip, when he meets with the folly of European savoir faire in its attempt to subdue Africa. One instance of this folly is seen in the image of the French man-of-war firing on the African coast: "There she was, incomprehensible, firing into a continent. Pop, would go one of the six-inch guns; a small flame would dart and vanish, a little white smoke would disappear, a tiny projectile would give a feeble screech—and nothing happened. Nothing could happen. There was a touch of insanity in the proceeding" (28).

Another instance is found in the effort to construct a railway: "A heavy and dull detonation shook the ground, a puff of smoke came out of the cliff, and that was all. No change appeared on the face of the rock. They were building a railway. The cliff was not in the way or anything; but this objectless blasting was all the work going on" (29–30). The savoir faire produces reassurance merely because it is enacted, not because it produces any significant effects in its objects—an irony epitomized in the vignette of one of the men fighting the fire of the storage shed, which was already irretrievably lost to the flames: "The stout man with moustaches came tearing down to the river, a tin pail in his hand, assured me that everybody was 'behaving splendidly, splendidly' dipped about a quart of water and tore back again. I noticed there was a hole in the bottom of his pail" (38).

Later, readers encounter another instance of incommensurability between knowledge and the Real, this time in the failure of the company to provide food for the cannibals who had been hired for six months: "They had been engaged for six months . . . , and of course, as long as there was a piece of paper written over in accordance with some farcical law or other made down the river, it didn't enter anybody's head to trouble how they would live" (55–56). Marlow's sense of the incommensurability between European knowledge and African Real reaches its height when the Russian foolishly extols Kurtz's ability to make him see. Marlow describes his own reaction: "I looked around, and I don't know why, but I assure you that never, never before did this land, this river, this jungle, the very arch of this blazing sky, appear to me so hopeless and so dark, so impenetrable to human thought" (71).

Interpellation to Moral Vulnerability: The Object a

But the threat of the wilderness is not just external. Marlow's description of his encounter with the wilderness indicates that he experiences it as the embodiment of his own lost vitality and immortality (such loss being precisely what the object *a* represents, in Lacan's formulation) and that this experience provokes an uneasiness which causes Marlow to repress this object *a* and flee to the security of the "reality" constructed by the ego and ego ideal (S1) and the system of knowledge/belief (S2) that sustain the ego. Conrad's account of Marlow's response to this lost vitality, or alien jouissance, blazes a trail for readers toward repression. First Marlow describes the sense of irrepressible life: "Going up the river was like travelling back to the earliest beginnings of the world, when vegetation rioted on the earth and the big trees were kings" (48). Next, the sense of the heterogeneity between this force and the habitual sense of reality constructed by the ego: "You lost your way . . . [and] thought yourself bewitched and cut off for ever from everything you had known once—somewhere—far away—in another existence perhaps" (48) Then, the breaking through of this ego-alien force in the feeling of being watched: "And this stillness of life did not in the least resemble a peace. It was the stillness of an implacable force brooding over an inscrutable intention. It looked at you with a vengeful aspect. . . . I felt often its mysterious stillness watching me at my monkey tricks just as it watches you fellows" (49). And finally, the repression of this force by the "reality" constituted through the systems of knowledge/belief (S2): "I got used to it afterwards; I did not see it any more; I had no time. . . . When you have to attend to [watching for hidden snags, sunken stones, etc.], to the mere incidents of the surface, the reality—the reality, I tell you—fades. The inner truth is hidden—luckily, luckily" (49). Here, through Marlow's testimony, repression—the hiding of "the inner truth"—is offered to readers as a positive relief.

This convergence and connection in the audience of external and internal threat is facilitated by being described explicitly, when Marlow, at the beginning of the novella, muses further on the experience he imagines the first Roman settler to have undergone:

> Land in a swamp, march through the woods, and in some inland post feel the savagery, the utter savagery, had closed round him—all that mysterious life of the wilderness that stirs in the forest, in the jungles, in the hearts of wild men. There's no initiation either into such mysteries. He has to live in the midst of the incomprehensible, which is also detestable. And it has a fascination, too, that goes to work upon him. The fascination of the abomination—you know. Imagine the growing regrets, the longing to escape, the powerless disgust, the surrender, the hate. (20)

The "fascination of the abomination"—the simultaneous feelings of attraction and repulsion for the alien jouissances (the "mysterious life of the wilderness that stirs . . . in the hearts of wild men")—is elicited in the novella's readers by their simultaneous attraction and aversion to Kurtz. On the one hand, readers experience a continuous identificatory attraction to Kurtz insofar as he functions for them (as for Marlow) as the subject presumed to know—presumed, here, to know how to achieve unlimited jouissance, free of castration. For much of the story, Kurtz occupies for readers, as for Marlow, the position of the mythical father of Freud's primal horde, the one exception to the rule that all subjects are subjected to Symbolic castration, the restriction of jouissance. But on the other hand, readers are positioned in aversion to Kurtz's drives, because of the opposition of the drives to the law and the Symbolic order, and also because of the destruction these drives produce in Kurtz.

This double response is further evoked in readers by the presentation of two particular forms of the object *a*, the voice and the gaze. The voice is one of the central forces of the story—in both Kurtz and Marlow, but particularly in Kurtz, the passion and conviction of whose voice serves as the object *a* that promises fulfillment by filling the deficiencies of Symbolic-order identity. The power and mystery of Kurtz's voice are constructed for readers through, for instance, the account of Marlow's first encounter with Kurtz: "The volume of the tone he emitted without effort," Marlow marvels, "almost without the trouble of moving his lips, amazed me. A voice! A voice! It was grave, profound, vibrating, while the man did not seem capable of a whisper" (76).

Later, Marlow (and through him, the audience) experiences the inverse of this voice: its power to express desire and evoke a sense of profound lack. "'I was on the threshold of great things,' [Kurtz] pleaded, in a voice of longing, with a wistfulness of tone that made my blood run cold" (81–82). Even when Kurtz is near death, his voice has the capacity to project an aura of power that simultaneously veils and emphasizes the profound emptiness and nonbeing at his heart: "Kurtz discoursed. A voice! A voice! It rang deep to the very last. It survived his strength to hide in the magnificent folds of eloquence the barren darkness of his heart" (84). Kurtz's voice has such a powerful effect on those who hear it that when Kurtz dies, it seems to have been the very core of his being. "The voice was gone," Marlow says. "What else had been there?" (86). Kurtz's voice thus embodies, on the one hand, ultimate potency, and, on the other hand, fundamental lack, and these two aspects function, respectively to evoke in readers the senses that Kurtz's heart of darkness is both very fulfilling and quite threatening and destructive.

Even more significant than the voice in offering readers the fantasy of ultimate fulfillment while also posing a threat is the gaze, another instance of the object *a* that manifests itself throughout the story. The gaze, like the voice, is powerfully present in Marlow's first encounter with Kurtz, where, like one aspect of his voice, Kurtz's gaze gives Marlow the sense that Kurtz has escaped castration and achieved total fulfillment, absolute jouissance. "I was struck by the fire of his eyes," Marlow recalls, "and the composed languor of his expression. . . . This shadow looked satiated and calm, as though for the moment it had had its fill of all the emotions" (76). A similar sense of unbounded vitality and jouissance is present in the gaze of Kurtz's African consort: "She stood looking at us without a stir, and like the wilderness itself, with an air of brooding over an inscrutable purpose. . . . She looked at us all as if her life had depended upon the unswerving steadiness of her glance" (77). Moreover, the gaze here seems present in the wilderness itself: "the immense wilderness, the colossal body of the fecund and mysterious life seemed to look at her, pensive, as though it had been looking at the image of its own tenebrous and passionate soul" (76).

The threatening nature of the wilderness and its arousal of drives toward alien jouissance is driven home to readers by its destruction of Kurtz. Marlow makes this quite explicit for his audience. "The wilderness had found him out early," Marlow declares. "I think it had whispered to him things about himself which he did not know, things of which he had no conception till he took counsel with this great solitude" (73). "Both the diabolical love and the unearthly hate of the mysteries it had penetrated," Marlow reports, "fought for the possession of that soul satiated with primitive emotions" (84). Readers are drawn further into this conflict when Marlow confronts the escaped Kurtz and encounters the seduction of the drives and their alien jouissances, "the heavy, mute spell of the wilderness . . . that seemed to draw [Kurtz] to its pitiless breast by the awakening of forgotten and brutal instincts, by the memory of gratified and monstrous passions" (82).

Through Marlow, readers immediately apprehend such drives as impermissible, requiring rejection: "This alone, I was convinced, had driven him out to the edge of the forest, to the bush, towards the gleam of fires, the throb of drums, the drone of weird incantations; this alone had beguiled his unlawful soul beyond the bounds of permitted aspirations" (82). Here the conflicting forces at work within Kurtz and Marlow (and in readers as well) are clearly identified as ideals and drives: on the one hand the "permitted aspirations," those recognized and validated by the Symbolic Other (Nature, God, Society), and, on the other hand, the "unlawful soul" and its "brutal instincts" and "monstrous passions" that "drive" the subject away from the Law of the Symbolic order.

The wilderness, then, functions for many readers (through Marlow and Kurtz) as a kind of cornucopia of instances of the object *a*, offering fantasies of restoration of the fullness of life that was lost with the assumption of sexual identity. "The silence of the land," Marlow reports, "went home to one's very heart—its mystery, its greatness, the amazing reality of its concealed life" (40–41). But like the other instances of the object *a*, this representative of "irrepressible life" is for most readers not only fascinating and seductive but threatening as well, for it embodies the possibility of imminent destruction of the Symbolic order and its master signifers, upon which one's identity is based.

This threat is elicited, for instance, in the following description of the wilderness (quoted earlier as an instance of Imaginary-order threat): "The great wall of vegetation, an exuberant and entangled mass of trunks, branches, leaves, boughs, festoons, motionless in the moonlight, was like a rioting invasion of soundless life, a rolling wave of plants, piled up, crested, ready to topple over the creek, to sweep every little man of us out of his little existence" (44–45). The psychological threat constituted by this "rioting invasion of soundless life" is that it is "incomprehensible": it threatens to destroy the categories of the Symbolic order, in which one's identity and sense of reality are constructed. Once again, readers are nudged further toward this sense by Marlow's comments on the matter:

> The steamer toiled along slowly on the edge of a black and incomprehensible frenzy. The prehistoric man was cursing us, praying to us, welcoming us—who could tell? We were cut off from the comprehension of our surroundings; we glided past like phantoms, wondering and secretly appalled, as sane men would be before an enthusiastic outbreak in a madhouse. We could not understand." (50)

Interpellation to Knowledge/Belief (S2)

The inability to understand experienced by Marlow is also a common experience among the novella's readers. As we have seen, Hillis Miller emphasizes the incompleteness of the novella's unveiling. Other critics make similar observations, Rosmarin commenting, for instance, on the reader's "experience of finding himself left hanging, of having to reread repeatedly, of anticipating what never comes or, if it does come, comes not in the expected way" (165). This frustration, together with the threat to bodily integrity, increases readers' desire for understanding—"the instinct for knowledge," as Freud terms it, being in service of the "instinct for mastery." The audience's desire for knowledge is reinforced by identification with Marlow, and his valorization of knowledge leads the audience to establish knowledge (S2), in effect, as a master signifier (S1)—a response that is probably all the more pronounced in professional readers (academicians) for whom knowledge already functions as a master signifier.

Marlow's embrace of knowledge, identified with by readers, is clear. In response to the psychological as well as the physical aspect of the

threat posed by the wilderness, Marlow and many of the other Europeans seek to reinforce their position within knowledge—either abstract knowledge or savoir faire. Perhaps the clearest instance of such
refuge is found in Marlow's immersion in the copy of *Towson's Inquiry*
that he finds in the abandoned hut. "The simple old sailor, with his
talk of chains and purchases," Marlow says, "made me forget the
jungle, and the pilgrims, in a delicious sensation of having come upon
something unmistakenly real" (53). When he must return to the boat,
he tells us that "to leave off reading was like tearing myself away from
the shelter of an old and solid friendship" (53), thus testifying to the
security that he has found in the knowledge/belief (S2) constituted by
the Symbolic order.

Marlow also finds psychological security in the savoir faire embodied in the work of repairing the steamer: "I don't like work—no man
does—but I like what is in the work—the chance to find yourself.
Your own reality" (44). The chief accountant and the manager of the
Central Station are similarly presented as surviving by reproducing
and proliferating the knowledge system (S2), in which their sense of
themselves is inscribed. This psychological accomplishment is explicitly noted by Marlow, who says of the accountant, "I respected the
fellow. . . . [I]n the great demoralization of the land he kept up his
appearance. That's backbone. His starched collars and got-up shirt-
fronts were achievements of character" (326). About the manager of
the Central Station, Marlow observes that his only virtue was that "he
could keep the routine [S2] going—that's all" (36). The value of this
virtue is indicated to readers by the fact that it by itself allows the
manager to survive and prevail.

Through Marlow, then, readers are led to experience the system of
knowledge as salutary, and as ultimately the only refuge humans have
against internal and external forces of life that have been conflated for
readers into a single force that exceeds and thus threatens a subject's
identity. The most significant instance of salvation through knowledge
is the salvation Marlow attributes to Kurtz's dying words, and the
redemption that Marlow himself experiences through his conviction
that such knowledge is possible. "Droll thing life is," Marlow mutters,
"that mysterious arrangement of merciless logic for a futile purpose.
The most you can hope from it is some *knowledge* of yourself" (86;
emphasis added). Reader-critics, as we have seen, have found similar
refuge in knowledge, whether it be a knowledge about Kurtz and

Marlow, a knowledge about the human condition, or, as in the case of Miller and others, the meta-knowledge that all knowledge is ultimately incomplete.[12]

Marlow's desire for knowledge is most powerfully stimulated by the journey to Kurtz, where readers' identification with Marlow operates powerfully in the service of the repression of drives and the consolidation of the ego ideal. That Marlow's journey is a quest for ultimate ideals and values which Marlow looks for Kurtz to supply is indicated most clearly by Marlow's reaction when, at the end of his journey up the river, fearing that Kurtz is dead, he feels "a sense of extreme disappointment." "I couldn't have been more disgusted," he tells his audience, "if I had travelled all this way for the sole purpose of talking with Mr. Kurtz. Talking with . . . I flung one shoe overboard, and became aware that that was exactly what I had been looking forward to—a talk with Kurtz. I made the strange discovery that I had never imagined him as doing, you know, but as discoursing" (62). As Marlow's subsequent comments indicate, what he hopes for from Kurtz's discoursing is some knowledge of the missing jouissance/*jouis-sens* that would make life meaningful and worth living: "My sorrow," he continues, "had a startling extravagance of emotion. . . . I couldn't have felt more of lonely desolation somehow," he says, "had I been robbed of a belief or had missed my destiny in life" (63).

What Marlow desires from this subject presumed to know he, and apparently many readers as well, receive (for a time, at least) from Kurtz's report for the International Society for the Suppression of Savage Customs:

He began with the argument that we whites, from the point of development we had arrived at, "must necessarily appear to them [savages] in the nature of supernatural beings—we approach them with the might as of a deity," and so on, and so on. "By the simple exercise of our will we can exert a power for good practically unbounded," etc. etc. From that point he soared and took me with him. The peroration was magnificent,

---

[12]In this embrace of knowledge, commentators are simply repeating one of the central concerns of the story itself. As Daniel Schwarz observes, "Both the epistemological quest for a context or perspective with which to interpret the experience and the semiological quest to discover the signs and symbols which make the experience intelligible are central to the tale" (63). The result of critics' pursuit of this knowledge is the repression of a more important issue—the question of whether this known and articulated state of affairs might be altered.

though difficult to remember, you know. It gave me the notion of an exotic Immensity ruled by an august Benevolence. It made me tingle with enthusiasm. (65)

Marlow's desire and testimony (and also the Russian's) serve to evoke in most readers a similar desire for a final pronouncement from Kurtz, the subject who from the beginning functions for Marlow, and thus also for readers who identify with Marlow's desire for recognition, as the subject presumed to know: the representative of the Other and, hence, the object of transference. Marlow himself also functions in this way for those readers who presume Marlow to know not only what happened on his journey but also what happened in his own and in Kurtz's interior journeys. Marlow, in short, functions for many readers as the subject presumed to know not only the nature of the interior forces he describes, but also the best means of dealing with those forces.

The repression of drives to which readers are thus interpellated in multiple ways through Marlow's valorization of knowledge is powerfully reinforced by Marlow's more direct and explicit rejection of drives and fantasy and his embrace of knowledge/belief. In one instance, reflecting on the fact of his own attraction to the savage expression of drives, Marlow declares that a true man

> must meet that [other] truth with his own true stuff—with his own inborn strength. Principles? Principles won't do. Acquisitions, clothes, pretty rags—rags that would fly off at the first good shake. No; you want a *deliberate belief*. An appeal to me in this fiendish row—is there? Very well; I hear; I admit, but I have a voice, too, and for good or evil mine is the speech that cannot be silenced. (51)

Here Marlow opposes the "speech" and "deliberate belief" of the Symbolic order to the "fiendish row" of the drives, denying the contingency (and thus the malleability) of "deliberate belief" in asserting it to be one's "true stuff" and "inborn," the core of one's identity as a true man.

Marlow again makes both his opposition to his unconscious drives and fantasy and his reliance on the Symbolic Other quite clear when he describes his experience of the absence of this Other in an external form—a description which, moreover, serves subtly to reinforce his own value to readers as precisely such a subject presumed to know. "How can you imagine," he asks, "what particular region of the first ages a man's untrammelled feet may take him into by the way of solitude—utter solitude without a policeman—by the way of silence— utter silence, where no warning voice of a kind neighbor can be heard whispering of public opinion? These little things make all the great difference" (64).

In the absence of such an external embodiment of the Other in the form of a subject presumed to know, one must rely on the internalized presence of this Other, which Marlow describes as "your own innate strength." "When [the warning voice and public opinion] are gone," he says, "you must fall back upon your own innate strength, upon your own capacity for faithfulness.... And there, don't you see? your strength comes in, the faith in your ability for the digging of unostentatious holes to bury the stuff in [i.e., repress it]—your power of devotion, not to yourself, but to an obscure, back-breaking business [S2]" (64–65). Here Marlow insists that fulfillment is to be found only through full embrace of the Symbolic order. His insistence on immersing himself in the Symbolic order and thus burying the onerous bestial material that threatens his sense of reality and his sense of who he is interpellates those readers who have identified with him and/or embraced him as a subject presumed to know to take the same course.

Reservations that readers might have about such a repressive solution are decommissioned in several ways. Skepticism about the validity of Marlow's pronouncements is undermined by his role as the only source readers have of the knowledge of the central events of the story and also by his professed fierce allegiance to the truth—an allegiance that is established for readers most overtly by Marlow's aversion to lies. "You know I hate, detest, and can't bear a lie," Marlow says, "not because I am straighter than the rest of us, but simply because it appals me. There is a taint of death, a flavour of mortality in lies—which is exactly what I hate and detest in the world—what I want to forget" (41).

This aversion to lies not only reinforces Marlow's credibility (through the fact that he tells us the truth about his own lie, which is abhorrent to him); the aversion also serves to displace readers' sense of the loss of vitality entailed by embrace of the Symbolic order and thus make this embrace unobjectionable. That is, Marlow associates death not with the Symbolic in general but only with a specific use of the

Symbolic, the lie, thus directing all objection (readers' as well as his own) toward that specific usage of the Symbolic and away from the Symbolic order per se. In actuality, rather than being inimical to the Symbolic order, the lie is more like a synecdoche for it, epitomizing the way in which the Symbolic blinds us and cuts us off from the Real. Thus, in characterizing the lie as the purveyor of death, Marlow establishes it as a kind of phobic object for readers: as in actual phobias, subjects focus all their aversion and anxiety on this (Symbolic) phenomenon as a way of rendering the rest of the (Symbolic) world relatively innocuous.

The interpellation of the audience to embrace the Symbolic order in opposition to their own unconscious drives and fantasies culminates in an instance of what Leavis called Conrad's "adjectival insistence"— that is, Conrad's tendency to characterize the subjectively experienced *quality* of certain actions and experiences without identifying precisely what those events *are*. The effect of this technique is to elicit projections from readers. And since what people project often involves unconscious impulses of their own which they don't want to accept, the indefinite actions in Conrad's novella become the repository of that part of themselves that readers already tend to be in fundamental opposition to. As Achebe puts it concerning the portrayal of Africa in this novella, "Africa is to Europe as the picture is to Dorian Gray—a carrier onto whom the master unloads his physical and moral deformities so that he may go forward, erect and immaculate" (261).

One element that seems particularly effective in prompting such a projective response is the account of Kurtz's final pronouncement. Marlow describes his fascination as he watched the changing expressions on Kurtz's face during his last moments of life, and asks: "Did he live his life again in every detail of desire, temptation, and surrender during that supreme moment of complete knowledge? He cried in a whisper at some image, at some vision—he cried out twice, a cry that was no more than a breath: "The horror! The horror!" (85). This passage exerts a multiple interpellative force upon readers. First, it establishes "complete knowledge" as the fundamental mode of self-relation and self-fulfillment, thus placing the system of knowledge/beliefs in ascendancy in relation to the drives, which are themselves reduced to being the *object* of knowledge, rather than the motivating *agent*. Second, the passage presents the object of this "complete knowledge" as evoking a sense of horror.

The first result is accomplished by means of the logically specious technique of the complex question. Like the frequently cited example, "When did you stop beating your wife," Marlow's query is actually a series of questions. The question readers are *explicitly* asked to ponder—"Did he live his life again in every detail . . . during that supreme moment of complete knowledge?"—interpellates readers to assume a positive response to a previous *implicit* question, "Did he in fact achieve 'a supreme moment of complete knowledge,'" which itself harbors additional begged questions: can knowledge be complete, and if so, can it constitute a "supreme moment"? In focusing on the *explicit* question, readers accord tacit affirmative responses to the *implicit*, begged questions. Moreover, even if readers do identify one of the implicit questions and challenge its affirmative response, they engage the issue of Kurtz's psychological state and possible transformation as essentially a question of Kurtz's knowledge (S2), and of its relation to his final pronouncement (S1). This valorization of knowledge (S2) and of making final pronouncements (which are based on ultimate ideals, S1) is reinforced by Marlow's own benedictory pronouncements on Kurtz's final utterance:

> He was a remarkable man. After all, this was the expression of some sort of belief. . . . He had summed up. . . . I was within a hair's-breadth of the last opportunity for pronouncement, and I found with humiliation that probably I would have nothing to say. This is the reason why I affirm that Kurtz was a remarkable man. He had something to say. He said it. . . . It was an affirmation, a moral victory. . . . That is why I have remained loyal to Kurtz to the last. . . . (86–87)

Conrad's presentation of Kurtz's final utterance not only reinforces readers' embrace of this issue in terms of knowledge and pronouncement (S2 and S1), it also further summons readers to an attitude of opposition to their own fundamental fantasies and deepest unconscious drives. The production of this opposition starts from the fact that readers aren't told the content of the image that evokes the characterization of "horror." As a result, they have to supply that content themselves, and since Marlow presents Kurtz's cry in the context of Kurtz's "desire, temptation, and surrender," many readers involuntarily search for the object of "the horror" among their own most disturbing impulses. And what they come up with—whether it be cannibalism or another kind of aggression or genital or pregenital libidinal gratification of a heterosexual or a homosexual nature—are usually impulses they themselves have deeply repressed, to the extent that they can't imagine even having such urges, much less acting on them. In other words, readers are put in the position of having to find a fantasy to oppose and pronounce judgment on, and such a pronounce- ment precludes their acknowledging this fantasy as their own and working through it.

Thus positioned in extreme opposition to some fundamental fan- tasy, readers are rendered largely incapable of using this fantasy to alter their ego ideal by formulating a new master signifier, an inca- pacity that is rendered almost absolute by calling the fantasy "horror," which invokes preexisting master signifiers to close off the fantasy. Having found impulses which they themselves regard as horrible, read- ers feel they have "understood" this passage and Kurtz. And having achieved this "knowledge" and rendered the moral pronouncement with Kurtz, they need have no more to do with their own internal "horror." Other readers avoid the problem entirely, by searching for the object of Kurtz's vision in European civilization or the imperialism of the nineteenth century. In either case, the passage culminates the interpellation of readers away from any acknowledgment of their own fundamental fantasy other than a moral and/or aesthetic condemna- tion of the fantasy as projected onto an external figure, which closes off any real possibility for the engagement and transformation of either the fantasy or the ideals and knowledge opposed to it.[13]

We could say, then, that *Heart of Darkness* functions for many readers much like an unsuccessful analysis: it engages them in a trans- ference relationship which it fails to resolve, leaving them hanging between alien drives, fantasies, and jouissances, on the one hand, and the ego ideal and its narcissistic gratifications, on the other. The story does what some forms of psychotherapy do, but precisely what suc- cessful psychoanalysis avoids: it offers to the divided subject prefabri- cated, traditional master signifiers (S1, or values and ideals) and knowledge (S2) about the divided subject ($) and its alien jouissances (*a*), thus providing readers with the opportunity to fortify the *mécon-*

---

[13]Moreover, even if readers *embraced* the fantasy that they imagine Kurtz to be horrified with, they would simply be adopting an oppositional stance that leaves the reigning master signifiers intact and isolated from the fantasy and unconscious drives, which thus remain untransformed.

naissances (misrecognitions) of their ego in relation to the alien jouissances embodied in their own drives and fantasies.

The discourse of the Analyst, in contrast, interpellates the subject, as we have seen, to confront the *a* and the lack, and to produce its own new master signifiers by working through fundamental fantasies and the alien drives they give rise to. Analytic discourse thus produces a decidedly different subject position, which results neither in narcissistic consolidation of the ego nor in acting out the fundamental fantasy but in working through the fantasy, which can produce both an alteration of central values and ideals and a transformation of desire and jouissance—both of which are essential elements of all significant political as well as psychological change.

Political Ramifications

The possible political ramifications of the psychological position to which readers are interpellated by the discourse of *Heart of Darkness* are not hard to see. Insofar as the novella promotes *méconnaissance* of and opposition to the alien jouissances of one's fundamental fantasy and unconscious drives, it also promotes reactionary politics of all sorts, including racism, sexism, and homophobia. It has this effect because the most basic cause of these prejudices is fear of alien jouissance. Jacques-Alain Miller explains how this fear operates in relation to racism:

> In racism . . . [none] of the generous and universal discourses on the theme of "we are all fellow-beings" have had any effectiveness. . . . Why? Because racism calls into play a hatred which goes precisely toward what grounds the Other's alterity, in other words its jouissance. . . . [Racism] is not simply a matter of an imaginary aggressivity which, itself, is directed at fellow-beings. *Racism is founded on what one imagines about the Other's jouissance; it is hatred* of the particular way, *of the Other's own way of experiencing jouissance.* We may well think that racism exists because our Islamic neighbor is too noisy when he has parties; [but] . . . what is really at stake is that he takes his jouissance in a way different from ours. . . . Racist stories are always about the way in which the Other obtains a *"plus-de-jouir"*: either he does not work or he does not work enough, or he is useless or a little too useful, but whatever the

case may be, he is always endowed with a part of jouissance that he does not deserve. *Thus true intolerance is the intolerance of the Other's jouissance.* ("*Extimité*" 125–26; emphasis added)

It is the interpellation of its audience to such intolerance of alien jouissance and not the unflattering two-dimensional representations per se of women and Africans that constitutes the most powerful, most fundamental, and most dangerous element of the racism and sexism of *Heart of Darkness*. Horror of one's own unconscious drives and desires for modes of jouissance that are alien to one's ego ideal translates into hatred of other people when those same alien modes of jouissance are perceived or imagined in them. Rather than *causing* racism and sexism, misrepresentations of Africans and women are themselves the *result* of the ego's aversion to alien jouissance.

The fear of feminine jouissance, moreover, operates in many men as a support not only for sexism, but also for homophobia, which, in addition, is fueled by men's own unconscious homosexual impulses. Not surprisingly, it is women who have been most sensitive to the submerged homosexual elements of Conrad's novella. Bette London, for instance, observes that Marlow's dependency on Kurtz's authority puts Marlow in a feminine position and that Marlow's exclusion of women from his world is a reaction against his own feminine position.[14] Moreover, London contends, Marlow's narrative interpellates his audience on the *Nellie* into a similar position:

[14]"Women's expulsion from [Marlow's] world of dark truths," London argues, "does not so much protect women's position as preserve masculine constructs; for women's absence constitutes a condition of narrative coherence—the foundation of masculine authority" (238). Marlow's "performance of masculine authority," London continues, "puts into question what the narrative conceals: Marlow's identification with the position of the feminine or Other in the events his narrative records" (243). Thus "Marlow's narrative would seem to track the acquisition of feminine identity, for it puts Marlow in the feminine place—literally, the place of Kurtz's Intended" (244). "Marlow's account of his climactic meeting with Kurtz," London asserts, "can be seen to set the stage for such a reading. For in it Marlow registers a masculine protest against his enforced dependency—against his (feminine) relational position to Kurtz's absolute authority. The scene encapsulates Marlow's reconstructed role: to wait on Kurtz. Invoking his own audience, Marlow protests his position of powerlessness and passivity: 'And, don't you see, the terror of the position was not in being knocked on the head—though I had a very lively sense of that danger too—but in this, that I had to deal with a being to whom I could not appeal in the name of anything high or low. I had, even like the niggers, to invoke him—himself—his own exalted and incredible degradation.' The real terror of this situation, as Marlow presents it, thus turns out to be *Marlow's* loss of his sexual and racial identity" (245).

The performance puts his audience in Marlow's former place: the place of the feminine—to watch and to wait, to hang on "the man's" words. . . . Badgering his audience, as he does periodically, Marlow assaults their indifference, subjecting them to violent verbal harangues. And . . . he does so by implicitly projecting them as female, or at least challenging their masculinity. (245)[15]

Although London is talking primarily about the effect of Marlow's tale upon the *Nellie* audience, her observations can be extended to Conrad's larger audience—especially contemporary masculine critics, who have had little to say about the feminine/homosexual aspects either of Marlow's position or their own. It is precisely the feminine and homosexual implications, I would argue, that are the most threatening aspects of the unconscious, alien jouissances against which most masculine critics are interpellated by the novella.

We can get a sense of how the novella appeals to such alien jouissance from Nina Straus's account of the feminine and homosexual aspects of the position of Marlow, with whom, as we have seen, many readers identify in fundamental ways. "It is clear," Straus observes, "that Marlow's identification with Kurtz is of a violently passionate kind. . . . There are glimpses in the text's imagery of Marlow's wish to be swallowed by Kurtz, to 'join' him in death, and finally to be 'rush[ed]' and invaded by the wilderness which Kurtz embodies" (132–32). Marlow's representation of women, Straus argues, is a defense against homosexual love: "in *Heart of Darkness* women are used to deny, distort, and censor men's passionate love for one another. Projecting his own love onto the form of the Intended, Marlow is able

---

[15]London elaborates as follows: "Marlow's most prolonged tussle with his audience works through . . . manipulations of positions of identity. . . . Describing his own response to Kurtz's presumed death, Marlow collapses in upon himself savage unrestraint and feminine susceptibility; he admits to 'a startling extravagance of emotion, even such as I had noticed in the howling sorrow of these savages in the bush.' As in earlier instances, however, Marlow's admission launches a counter-attack, an attack facilitated by the audience response he is able to extract: 'Why do you sigh in this beastly way, somebody? Absurd? Well, absurd. Good Lord! mustn't a man ever—Here, give me some tobacco.' Marlow's peremptory demand shifts the narrative ground to the gruff world of masculine community. Having secured a position there, he takes on his audience's objection, making it the mark of *their* lack—their inadequacy: 'You can't understand. How could you?' . . . Marlow's reconstruction of the domain of masculinity positions his audience in woman's place: excluded from knowledge, truth, and adventure" (245–48).

to conceal from himself the dark complexity of his own love—a love
that strikes him with horror—for Kurtz" (134). What works for Marlow works for readers who have identified with Marlow (which most
readers do to some degree, and some readers do to a great degree).
Straus hints at this in noting a parallel between Marlow's relation to
Kurtz and male critics' relation to Marlow:

> Marlow's relation to Kurtz as his commentator is a paradigm of the
> relation of the male critic's relation to the Strong Poet. That a homo-
> centric loyalty exists (a loyalty to the sexist nightmare of one's choice) is
> not surprising, for it confirms the relations of love between men who are
> each other's "narcissistic objects"; or to put it another way, whose enter-
> prise as readers and critics (hearers-speakers) affirms the greatness of the
> one and the possessive attempt to appropriate that greatness by the oth-
> er. . . . The guarding of secret knowledge is thus the undisclosed theme of
> *Heart of Darkness* which a woman reader can discover. (134)

This parallel, I would argue, gives us a glimpse of what is for most
heterosexual men simultaneously the most alien and most intimate
form of jouissance: male homosexual jouissance, which, as Freud indicates, is unconsciously present in all men in the form of the "negative
Oedipus complex." "Everyone," Freud asserts, "even the most normal
person, is capable of making a homosexual object-choice, and has
done so at some time in his life, and either still adheres to it in his
unconscious or else protects himself against it by vigorous counter-
attitudes" (*SE* 11:99, n. 2).[16] The knowing that typifies critics of *Heart
of Darkness* (and critics in general) might thus be seen as a symptom of
the repression of this alien jouissance: it is a compromise formation
that allows male (and male-identified female) critics to experience a
sublimated form of homosexual jouissance while simultaneously reinforcing the repression of their own male homosexual desire. The interpellative forces of *Heart of Darkness* are tailor-made to reinforce such
a response, through the same means by which they cultivate the
grounds of racism and sexism: through promoting in readers a horror
of alien jouissance.

[16]Freud explains: "By studying sexual excitations other than those that are manifestly
displayed, [psychoanalysis] has found that all human beings are capable of making a
homosexual object-choice and have in fact made one in their unconscious" (*SE* 7: 145,
n. 1).

The horror of alien jouissance promoted by a discourse like that of *Heart of Darkness* thus has profound negative social consequences. The most fundamental political ramification of this horror is the tendency to reject alien forms of the object *a* and its jouissances wherever they might appear, not only in other racial or sexual identities but also at the center of social problems—a response that is all too evident in the "Just say No" response that has been advocated for everything from the drug problem to teenage pregnancy, AIDS, and any other activity where alien drives and jouissances threaten the laws and ideals of the Symbolic order.

The ideological significance of *Heart of Darkness* is thus both more profound and more wide-ranging than ideological critiques of the novella have contended, for that significance derives from the totality of interpellative forces that the work exerts on readers and not solely from the work's (mis)representation of various oppressed groups. Any attempt to "help those in the present work towards the construction of a new future in which work is no longer used to control 'the Other' within, but instead directed toward liberating ourselves to help improve the lives of others truly different from us" ("*Heart of Darkness*" 254), as Brook Thomas formulates the aim of ideology critique, must expose (and prompt readers to work through) the desires engaged by these more fundamental and powerful interpellative forces, rather than just identifying and correcting the work's misrepresentations.

CHAPTER SEVEN

"TO AUTUMN"

Audience Response and Ideology in "To Autumn"

While readers have always found *Heart of Darkness* disturbing and enmeshed in ideological issues, most readers of Keats's "To Autumn" have felt the poem to be free of ideological concerns. The poem is often said to be an objective description of reality, completely divorced from mystification, wish fulfillment, or tendentiousness of any kind. The consensus has been that the poem simply describes a natural scene, in which death figures prominently, and that this description somehow brings readers to an acceptance of their own mortality, an acceptance which, moreover, they experience as deeply fulfilling.[1] In fact, few short Romantic poems have received more positive response than Keats's "To Autumn." Among contemporary critics, Christopher Ricks pronounces it "the greatest of Keats's odes" (208), Geoffrey Hartman finds it to be without defect (133), and Harold Bloom declares it to be a "perfect poem" (*Keats* 9), or at least "as close to perfection as any shorter poem in English" (*Visionary* 432). Such superlatives indicate quite clearly that these readers find the poem deeply gratifying; for some readers, at least, the poem seems to satisfy the very core of their desire, offering, in Walter Jackson Bate's experience,

---

[1]In Richard Macksey's view, the poem "calmly accepts emptiness and death" (300); for Anne Mellor the poem is permeated by "a willed acceptance of the contradictions of human experience, of the chaotic infinity of nature, and of human mortality" (107); and for Harold Bloom the poem offers "an image of natural death as an imaginative finality, a human consummation to be wished, though not devoutly" (*Visionary* 434–35).

"what the heart really wants" (*John Keats* 581),[2] or, in Anne Mellor's response, the feeling, "We have had enough" (107).

But how, one might ask, can a poem that simply "accepts" what is given[3]—a poem that "demands nothing, claims nothing, insists on nothing, contains nothing to dispute about, praises no one, attacks no one, [and] never once reflects upon itself" (Pearce (11)—how can such a poem produce an acceptance of death which, moreover, is experienced as a deep fulfillment? The answer, of course, is that it cannot, and in recent years several critics, beginning with Hartman, have observed that the poem's apparent disinterestedness and objectivity are, in fact, illusory and "that ['To Autumn'] is an ideological poem" (124).

One aspect of the poem's ideology has been indicated by Donald Pearce, who notes that Keats is being quite selective in the poem—for example, no one is shown doing any work—and that "under even the simplest natural description there is bound to lie some metaphysical bedrock—something in virtue of which certain attitudes toward a scene (hence certain values) are celebrated and others excluded (or even, by implication, opposed)" (4). Jerome McGann, declaring that "the poem is not impersonal, [that] it is tendentious and ideological in quite specific ways" (1023), observes:

> The poem's special effect is to remove the fearful aspects of these themes [of living and dying, maturing and decaying, staying and leaving] to make us receive what might otherwise be threatening ideas . . . by so manipulating the mythological and artistic mediations that the reader agrees to look at autumn, and to contemplate change and death, under certain precise and explicitly fictional guises. (1019)

Despite their recognition of various ideological elements, however, these critics do not pursue the deeper ramifications of the poem's ideological force. In fact, they tend to repress their own acknowledgement of the ideological nature of the poem. Thus Hartman, while recognizing that "the poem starts on enchanted ground and never leaves it"—that "it hovers between the factual and the fantastic" with no turn from illusion to disillusion (128–29)—nevertheless praises the poem in ways that function to deny this insight and assert the poem's objectivity, such as when he characterizes the poem as "the

[2]Bloom (*Keats* 9) agrees.
[3]See also Blackstone (357), Bush (178), and Bloom (*Visionary* 435; *Keats* 9).

most negative capable of all of Keats's great poems" (133) and declares, "This, at last is true impersonality" (146). Pearce similarly notes the metaphysics implicit in every description but also speaks unironically of the "disinterested loving perception" (19) promised by the poem, which, he maintains, "demands nothing, claims nothing, insists on nothing, contains nothing to dispute about," and so on (11).

A major reason for this oblivion of the ideological lies in the fact that these critics, much like the ideological critics of *Heart of Darkness*, implicitly identify ideology with a discrepancy between description and fact, between representation and the actual events of history. This view of ideology, and the results of this view for criticism, find their clearest articulation in McGann's statement that

> the poem's autumn is an historically specified fiction dialectically called into being by John Keats as an active response to, and alteration of, the events which marked the late summer and early fall of a particular year in a particular place. Keats's poem is an attempt to 'escape' the period which provides the poem with its context, and to offer its readers the same opportunity of refreshment. (1023)

Here, and in earlier comments, McGann tacitly identifies ideology with what "the reader *agrees* to look at"—what is "*explicitly*" and "*recognizably* fictional," and is "*self-consciously* embraced" as such by readers (1019, emphasis added). This, however, is to ignore the most powerful and fundamental locus of the ideological: those elements of experience one doesn't think to question, or even see oneself as assenting to, because they seem self-evident, objective, and natural.

The fundamental problem, then, with the ideological analyses of the poem to date is that even when critics have recognized "To Autumn" as ideological, they have failed to apprehend the true locus of ideology. Contrary to their assumption, ideology, as we observed in the Introduction, cannot be located in the distortion or elision per se of certain facts or events. It must be sought, rather, in the effects that such distortion and elision, and other factors as well, produce in human subjects. Assessing the ideological force of a poem therefore requires more than simply noting where its "objectivity" ends and tendentiousness begins (assuming such a distinction could be made); it requires registering the combined, cumulative effect of all aspects of the poem that function to alter readers' perceptions, thoughts, values, ideals, or desires and that thus produce readers as certain kinds of subjects.

The Ideological Force of "To Autumn"

The ultimate ideological significance of "To Autumn," I will argue, derives from the poem's mobilizing various desires in a way that repositions readers in relation to death in the Symbolic order and engages various aspects of the death drive in relation to readers' fundamental fantasies. The repositioning of death in the Symbolic order is attested to by the comments of several critics. David Perkins observes that in the poem death "is recognized as something inwoven in the course of things, the condition and price of all fulfillment" (294). Michael Cooke speaks of "the poem's incorporation of death into its own positive life" and declares that "far from conceding to the death drift he purports to describe, the poet is penetrating the life that lies concealed in death" (172). Macksey offers the fullest articulation of this point, in his claim that the poem

> calmly accepts emptiness and death—accepts them as defining human life rather than as enigmas standing in lamentable opposition to the absolute that was the earlier goal [in "Ode on a Grecian Urn"]. . . . Now . . . death and absence, instead of being vacancies to transcend, are indispensible to an apprehension of that absoluteness of nature the open mortal self can experience: a calm acceptance of them makes possible one's authentic existence. (300, 306)

While we can endorse the explanation that readers' feelings of fulfillment and acquiescence to death are produced by the poem's interweaving of death in life, we cannot accept this interweaving as simply a fact that "lies concealed" (Cooke), and is now "recognized" (Perkins), "apprehended," and "accepted" (Macksey). Recalling that ideology is precisely that which seems "natural" and given for experience, we must investigate further how death is inscribed by the poem in such a way as to cause readers not only to accept it but to be unaware that the "death" they are accepting is "fictional" (McGann)—a product of textual weavings rather than "something inwoven in the course of things" (Perkins), "beyond any language" (Macksey 301). For death does not exist for us as a simple given. Perhaps more than any other phenomenon, death is a signified produced by the action of signifiers. As Lacan observes, "Without a signifier, no one would ever know anything about [this] state of being" (*Selection* 199). It is only by virtue of our "symbiosis with the symbolic," Lacan says, "that we reconstitute [ourselves] as subject to death" (196).

Although we have indirect access to real death through our empathy with dead or dying humans (and other creatures), we never experience our own death as real; as long as we are alive and experiencing at all, we can apprehend our own death only as an Imaginary and Symbolic phenomenon (see I 223). Thus the normal aversion that we feel to death is an effect of the Symbolic and Imaginary orders rather than a simple response to death as Real—an aversion deriving from the normal Symbolic equation of death with nonbeing and the normal Imaginary association of death with dismemberment. As Lacan puts it, the fear of death is for the most part "psychologically subordinate to the narcissistic fear of damage to one's own body" (*Selection* 28).

Being has a similar status. Being is what subjects want to have, and nonbeing is what they want to avoid. And the fundamental concern of "To Autumn" is (using Macksey's terms) with "being" and "non-being" (300). But what specifically counts as being is not absolutely given and self-evident. As Lacan observes, "The notion of being, as soon as we try to grasp it, proves itself to be as ungraspable as that of speech. Because being, the very verb itself, only exists in the register of speech. Speech introduces the hollow of being into the texture of the real. . . . Before speech, nothing either is or isn't" (I 228–29). Hence, Lacan concludes, "This to be or not to be is an entirely verbal story" (I 233): what we take for being, and therefore try to acquire and preserve, is determined by the Symbolic order that we have internalized—that is, our Symbolic Other.

That the equation between death and non-being (and the corollary opposition between death and being) is a Symbolic construct rather than a given of the Real is demonstrated by the fact that in certain rare instances people break free of this equation. As Hegel noted, in the battle to death for recognition, the combatants identify their true being with something other than life as such. This is true of any person who gives or risks his or her life for any reason at all. Such behavior manifests a disjunction between life and being, and death and nonbeing, pairs of signifiers that are normally regarded as intimately allied. And this disjunction is precisely what gives rise to one sense of the death drive, according to Lacan: the death drive is, in one of its aspects, an effect of the fact that humans desire *being*, which never completely coincides with life and at times is even in opposition to life (see I 171 and 326). It is this disjunction and the death drive that results from it that "To Autumn" activates—in a way that has apparently remained invisible and (partly for that reason) extremely effective for a large number of the poem's readers.

One reason for the invisibility of the linguistic repositioning of death in relation to being is that "death" and "being" as such are not explicitly present in the poem: the only appearance of these signifiers occurs when they are employed metaphorically. Thus the only overt repositioning within the Symbolic Other occurs with signifiers that are metonyms and metaphors of life and death, or being and nonbeing, with the central terms themselves remaining offstage. But since the position of each of these central terms is always a function of its relation with other terms, any repositioning of these related terms automatically produces a repositioning of the central term as well.

Metaphor works in the poem to evoke certain attributes of death and repress others, which amounts to loosening or cutting some ties with certain signifiers in the Symbolic order and reinforcing or producing others. Metonymy works more directly, by inserting death or its metaphoric or metonymic avatars in signifying chains that constitute explicit links with new signifiers. More specifically, the metaphoric and metonymic repositionings in "To Autumn" produce a systematic severance of the signifiers of death from signifiers of nonbeing and images of dismemberment, and a systematic linking of signifiers of death to signifiers of being, images of bodily mastery and well-being, and fantasies of drive gratification. As a result of this multiple operation of desire in the Symbolic, Imaginary, and Real orders, many readers are left at the end of the poem with an intense sense of their own being and feeling of well-being in the face of death. Hence the manipulation of metonyms and metaphors of life, death, being, and nonbeing repositions these central terms, and this repositioning, which is powered by various desires operating in the Imaginary and the Real, as well as in the Symbolic order, produces many readers as a different kind of subject.

To make this production visible will be at once to expose the true ideological force of the poem and to return a measure of freedom to the poem's readers. But in exposing the grounds of the beauty and pleasure we experience upon reading the poem, this analysis will also deprive our experience of its innocence and perhaps diminish its intensity. Insofar as it does this, the analysis may be expected to evoke a certain resistance, an urge to renounce an activity that murders to dissect, and to put our faith instead in what is proved on our pulses. To accede to this urge, however, would be precisely to beg the question; it would be capitulating to the poem's ideology before having understood its significance.

Stanza I

Passive Narcissistic Gratification

One of the most powerful ideological elements of the poem may well be the imagery of the first stanza, where readers' feelings of fulfillment are quite likely at their purest and most intense:

> Season of mists and mellow *fruitfulness*,
>   Close *bosom*-friend of the maturing sun;
> Conspiring with him how to load and bless
>   With *fruit* the vines that round the thatch-eves run;
> To bend with *apples* the moss'd cottage-trees,
>   And *fill* all *fruit* with *ripeness* to the *core*;
>   To *swell* the *gourd*, and *plump* the hazel shells
>   With a *sweet kernel*; to set budding more,
> And still more, later flowers for the bees,
> Until they think warm days will never cease,
>   For summer has *o'er-brimm'd* their *clammy cells*.
>   (ll. 1–11; emphasis added)

These are powerful images, and they provide readers with a fundamental sense of union with otherness, a sense based on the earliest experiences of the infant, including the mirror stage, in which what is external is experienced as being in harmony and accord with what is internal to the subject. This experience of mirroring or reciprocity between the ego and the image of the Imaginary and the Symbolic Other provides a powerful gratification of passive narcissistic desire.

Here such gratification is provided by the numerous images of mirroring, interpresence, and union, both within the natural world and between the human and the natural orders.

First, there is the personification of Autumn. Various commentators have attested to the power of this figuration—Blackstone, for instance, calling it "the greatest personification in English poetry" (356). In giving Autumn a human form, this personification evokes in many readers a resonance of the earliest mirroring experiences, which provided their first grasp of identity as well as the basis for their sense of self-worth. Moreover, the personification also establishes Autumn as a powerful instance of the Symbolic Other, as indicated by the comments of various critics. Ford, for instance, perceives Autumn as a mother figure and earth goddess (59), and Vendler senses in the two figures of Autumn and the sun the aura of earth goddess and sky god (248–49). The benevolent presence of this Symbolic Other presiding over this scene provides substantial passive narcissistic gratification for the audience.

Stanza I provides further gratification of this sort by offering specific images of mirroring and union within nature for readers to identify with. These include the generous and intimate interaction of Autumn and the sun with each other—close bosom-friends who conspire together—as well as the interaction of Autumn and the sun with the vines, trees, nuts, and fruits, and with the flowers, which are themselves of integral significance to the bees, whom they are "for."

This mirroring union is enacted among signifiers as well as signifieds, a fact expressed in Vendler's observation that

> there is scarcely a word in the poem not straitly bound to other words, hardly a chink not filled. The syntax, too, being organized by the double parallelism of enumeration and concatenation, exists in a network full of reduncancy—not a syntactic form but echoes and is echoed by, another phrase. Where there is X, there will be Y; nothing, it seems, is to go lonely or unpartnered, syntactically speaking. (171)

A major effect of these multiple instances of mirroring and union is the repression of all lack, separation, and finitude—that is, all nonbeing—at the level of the Imaginary order. Such mirroring and the corresponding repression occur even more forcefully in the representations of connections between the human and the natural world. This can be seen most clearly in the description of the emblem of human habitation, the cottage (see Pison 42). Here the human element, the cottage, is not named directly and explicitly, an act that would evoke the cottage's distinction and separation from the natural world. Rather, the cottage is presented metonymically, in the locutions "thatch-eves" and "cottage-trees." The first produces a signified that is equally and indistinguishably natural ("thatch") and human ("eves"); here the very substance of the human structure whose function is to separate and protect the human from the natural is itself natural. Moreover, the signifier of this structure ("thatch-eves") functions syntactically as little more than the support for the proliferating fruitfulness of nature in the form of the "vines that round the thatch-eves run." In a similar manner, the compound "cottage-trees" blurs the human/natural distinction even further by presenting the human structure (in its only mention in the poem) as an attribute of "trees." Semantically, then, the human and the natural are drawn closer together in the code constituting the Symbolic Other by the intertwining of their metonyms, and this alteration of the Other both evokes images of union and positions readers in identification with these images. The result is what Ricks calls a "tacit humanizing blush" that pervades the entire poem, and answers to the the "need to be at one with the universe"—the ultimate in passive narcissistic gratification (210).[4]

Fantasy and the Real

Readers' confrontation with death is also made more palatable, and even attractive, through the evocation of various fantasies and the drives associated with them. These include active anaclitic fantasies of possessing the object *a*, as well as passive narcissistic fantasies of being the object *a* of the Other's love. The most obvious anaclitic fantasies are those of oral gratification, whose primordial object is the breast, which provides a global experience of physical pleasure and existential well-being in which oral, esophageal, and ventral sensations predominate. In the first stanza, such fantasies are engaged by images of "fruitfulness," "bosom," "fruit," "apples," "ripeness," "gourd," "sweet kernel," and the "o'er-brimm'd . . . clammy cells" of honey, which all function as objects for unconscious oral fantasies that continue to

[4]See also Vendler (266), Bush (178), Nemoianu (28), and Fitzgerald (955).

inform adult feeling, perception, and desire. In addition, verbs like "fill," "swell," and "plump" serve not only to characterize the object of oral fantasy but signify the subjective state of oral/alimentary satiation as well. One can even detect a breastlike object in the signified produced by these signifiers: Reuben Brower notes "the weighing, cupping sensations which we feel distinctly in hand and lips as we read these expressions" (39).

The breast is evoked not only by the signifieds of the stanza but by the materiality of its signifiers as well, in the physical movements that are produced in pronouncing the words (even subvocally). The numerous (twenty-one) occurrences of bilabial consonants (*b*, *p*, and *m*)[5]— which Annabel Patterson has dubbed "plump labials and bosomy *m*'s" (453)—produce oral movements associated with sucking, while the liquid *l*'s (fifteen in this stanza) produce a motion involved in swallowing, and the preponderantly long vowels (see Bate, *Stylistic* 183) reproduce sounds uttered by the soothing mother and by the infant itself when satiated by the breast. Here we have an instance of phonemes functioning as the object *a*.

Though not as obviously as the oral fantasies, anal fantasies are also evoked here, in the images of filling, swelling, and o'er-brimming. Vendler's description of the audience's reaction to these images, though functioning in service of a different point, articulates this fantasy nicely:

> Many of Keats's verbs representing the actions of autumn are verbs having, if allowed to progress, a natural terminus: loading ends in overloading, bending ends in breaking, filling ends in overflowing, swelling ends in bursting, plumping ends in splitting. . . . Strained as we are by his verbs of loading, bending, filling, swelling, and plumping, we need to be relieved by one action brought to its natural end, and Keats gives it to us: summer has 'o'er-brimm'd' the honeycombs. (247–48)

The feeling of fulfillment produced by these oral and anal fantasies is not limited to the particular bodily zone in question but rather constitutes a more general fulfillment in the form of a subtle, tacit assurance offered the audience that finitude, or lack of being—the lack that underlies and motivates all desire, according to Lacan—has been overcome through the possession of the object *a*. This sense of well-

[5]See Bate, *Stylistic* 182–83.

being and full being culminates in a scopic fantasy evoked by the personification of Autumn (and the sun), in which the audience is put in the position of being the object *a* of the Other's gaze. We have already noted the power of the personification of Autumn, which positions it as the audience's (m)Other. What is evoked in the account of an intimate pair of omnipotent figures "conspiring . . . how to load and bless" the humble human sphere is nothing less than the primal passive narcissistic gratification of being the sole concern, the sole object of the love and attention of the parental Other, the object-cause of the Other's desire that will fill the Other's lack.

The first stanza's evocation of these various fantasies and images that lie at the root of our sense of being and fulfillment provides the foundation without which the poem's central ideological effect—readers' acceptance of death and finitude—would not be possible. For only when one is sustained by a sense of full being, by a jouissance or sense of being that is greater than life, can one contemplate death with equanimity and accept it calmly.

Repositioning Death in the Symbolic Order

Although such contemplation of death is evoked more obviously in the second and third stanzas, the signification of death is nonetheless present in at least three notable instances already in the first stanza. In each case, the very element (word, phrase, or image) that functions as a signifier of death is also made to function simultaneously as a signifier of the absence of death, thus taking the death out of death, that is, removing negativity or loss of being as an attribute of death.

The first signifier of death is "Autumn," which functions in our common Symbolic code as both a metaphor and a metonym of death and dying specifically and loss and nonbeing more generally. It is a metaphor for dying insofar as its position in the course of the year is similar to the position of dying in the course of life, and it is a metonym insofar as it is temporally associated with events of decline, dying, and nonbeing. From the outset, then, the poem's audience is confronted with a topos in which dying is a prominent feature—particularly the various instances of dying in the natural world. But Autumn is also, through its association with harvest, a metonym for culmination and fulfillment—full being, jouissance—and it is this connection, as we have seen, that the first stanza emphasizes, making

Autumn an object of readers' desire by presenting it as the matrix of superabundant life.

Autumn, then, occupies a pivotal, even self-contradictory position in the Symbolic order, embodying jouissance and being through one set of associations, and nonbeing through another. And it is precisely Autumn's embodiment of this fundamental opposition that provides much of the leverage through which the poem repositions death in the code constituting the audience's Symbolic Other. This is a rather abstract point, and its significance may not be evident at first glance, because it involves an effect that occurs for the most part unconsciously. But we can indirectly experience this effect if we note the difference in our response when we substitute for "Autumn" a signifier having solely positive or negative attributes in the register of being, such as "Winter" or "Summer."

The contradiction produced by signifiers that are simultaneously associated with both being and nonbeing is also present in the signifiers of superabundance, the images of ripening. For as Vendler notes, ripeness is continuous with "over-ripeness, bursting of skin, rottenness, and death" (247). The images of ripeness, then, are metonyms (through continuity) of death, and consequently they can evoke—at least for readers like Vendler, who are sensitive to this metonomy—the anxiety usually attendant upon death. But these same images of dehiscence and death—particularly in the one explicit expression of dehiscence, the o'er-brimming of the honey cells—also evoke feelings of jouissance and fulfillment. This is because these images mobilize fantasies not just of anal activity but of the fundamental élan for growth—the force that has been variously described as entelechy (Aristotle), Aufhebung (Hegel), and Selbstüberwindung (Nietzsche), and that Lacan refers to as "vital dehiscence" and finds to be integrally bound up with the death drive (see Selection 21–28).

Vital dehiscence ("dehiscence" denoting literally the bursting or breaking open of a seedpod) is an observable element of psychic structure at least from the onset of the mirror stage, when the child opposes its own actuality and identifies with an external figure that possesses the bodily unity and coordination the child lacks. This is nothing less than an activity of the death drive at the levels of both the Imaginary and the Real: the urge to be something other, to burst the boundaries of its own being, which an entity experiences as limiting and frustrating—to destroy its actual state in becoming something better.

Readers, similarly, in their aspirations for infinity described earlier, and in the identification with which they respond to such representations of vital dehiscence, are being borne along by one instance of the death drive.[6]

Stanza II

Nonetheless, insofar as the first stanza functions to evoke the idea of temporal (and spatial) limits in general, it can produce an anxiety (often unconscious) in readers concerning their own limitations, the ultimate of which is death. The second stanza continues this production of anxiety, which motivates readers to accept the strategies of containment offered by the stanza—strategies (ideologemes, fantasies) that can further reinforce and alter aspects of the audience's subjective economy:

> Who hath not seen thee oft amid thy store?
>   Sometimes whoever seeks abroad may find
> Thee sitting careless on a granary floor,
>   Thy hair soft-lifted by the winnowing wind;
> Or on a half-reap'd furrow sound asleep,
>   Drows'd with the fume of poppies, while thy hook
>   Spares the next swath and all its twined flowers;
> And sometimes like a gleaner thou dost keep
>   Steady thy laden head across a brook;
>   Or by a cyder-press, with patient look,
>   Thou watchest the last oozings hours by hours.
>
> (ll. 12–22)

Dismemberment and Unity in the Imaginary

The anxiety produced by this stanza derives from the presence of certain traditional metaphors and/or metonyms of death. The images

---

[6]The simultaneous acceptance and repression of the negativity of death achieves a subtle culminating enactment when the proliferating infinitives of ripening lead the reader to what appears to be a temporal limit in the word "until": "to set budding more, / And still more, later flowers for the bees, / Until they think warm days will never

of reaping (16, 17), winnowing (15), threshing (alluded to in "granary floor," 14), and pressing (21–22), in particular, refer to the different acts of separation that occur in harvesting—i.e., separation of stalk from roots, of stalks into rows, of grain from chaff, and of juice from apples, respectively—and thus embody the traditional signification of death as a limiting, separating event, rather than an event of union and overcoming finitude. These significations, in addition to reinforcing the common position of death in the Symbolic Other, also evoke images of dismemberment—images of what we might call "mortal dehiscence"—which according to Lacan form the foundation of our imaginary grasp of death (see *Selection* 28).

But the anxiety to which these images give rise is counteracted by the "series of framed pictures" (McGann 1018) of Autumn that we encounter in this stanza. The primary force of these pictures derives from the images they contain of the human body. The images of "sitting careless," being "sound asleep," keeping the head steady, and watching patiently all present the human form in a position of well-being, an attitude without care or strife, a position of restfulness and ease. Such images of repose and contentment embody that composure we have all been trying to attain since, as still fragmented and uncoordinated infants, we anticipatorily identified in the mirror stage with a unified, coordinated image of the human form. Moreover, as noted above, this search for composure that we have been engaged in since the mirror stage involves a turning against our actual being and thus constitutes an instance of the death drive. Our identification with the images of corporeal repose in this stanza thus functions to engage yet another aspect of the death drive. This is especially the case with the image of the sleeping body, sleep being, as Lacan notes somewhere, the most obvious and recurrent emergence of the death drive.

The death drive in readers is also engaged by the assimilation of the human body to the landscape. As Paul Fry notes, the human image

---

cease." "Until," however, marks not an end but a transition into a new space—that of thought—where all limits are overcome: a place where "warm days will never cease" and "clammy cells" are "oer-brimmed." This ending of the first stanza thus functions to deny temporal finitude (death) in the very act of acknowledging it. It acknowledges finitude by positioning the reader outside the bees' illusion, in a perspective that reveals that warm days do, in fact, cease. But in being superior to the perspective of the bees, this position is also superior to the bees' fate of finitude and death. The acknowledgement of the bees' finitude can thus serve the reader primarily as a basis for denying rather than confronting his or her own human finitude.

functions in this stanza as the organizing form of the landscape itself (267): the grain is assimilated to the human hair in line 15 (see Bloom, *Visionary* 433) and, as it lies in the half-reaped furrow, to the image of the entire (sleeping) human body. Readers' Imaginary identification with these images thus entails a subtle but unmistakable merger with an inanimate form, a merger that functions, on the one hand, as a union with an ideal other—a human form that is also the (m)Other— but which, on the other hand, represents a rather advanced point along the itinerary of the death drive, the pursuit of a jouissance that is inimical to, or in excess of, life, described by Freud as a journey back to the earliest (inanimate) state of things.

Unwriting Traditional Metaphors and Metonyms

This confounding of images of death with objects of narcissistic desire positions death as an efflorescence of jouissance and being, and gives the audience a sense of well-being in the face of the more traditional Symbolic positionings of death as nonbeing which are present in the stanza but which are called forth only to be disengaged. This signification of death as nonbeing is embodied in three traditional figures: (1) sleep, a metaphor for death; (2) the hook, a metonym of the Grim Reaper, itself a metaphor for death; and (3) the crossing of the brook, a synecdoche of crossing of the Styx, or Jordan, another metaphor for death.

The traditional images of death alluded to here constitute in and of themselves a first line of displacements and substitutions through which the Symbolic Other that is dominant in our culture represses the very nonbeing and nothingness that this same Symbolic order else-where explicitly establishes as attendant upon death. Sleep, already a comforting metaphor of death in its traditional usage, here works to provide further reassurance: since Autumn is itself a metaphor and metonym of death, the sleep of Autumn signifies at one level something like the death of death. In addition, the syntagmatic positioning of the sleep of Autumn/Death in this stanza makes death much less inexor-able and implacable than it is often felt to be, for it serves to repress the attributes of insistence, impatience, and inexorability that one nor-mally associates with death. This, in fact, is one of the central Symbolic effects of the stanza as a whole: it presents Autumn/Death at one point as entirely disengaged and dormant, and when not asleep, as "careless," "steady," and "patient," engaged in activity that is varied and desultory. Rather than the traditional Grim Reaper who waits for no one, Autumn/Death is here a gentle reaper whose "hook" "spares" rather than cuts off life.

This major reversal of attributes is all the more striking by being made to pivot on the enjambment: when we encounter the subject "hook" at the end of one line, we probably expect to find the verb "cuts" at the beginning of the next. When instead of "cuts" we encounter "spares," we experience a sense of relief and well-being. Even when Autumn/Death does bring an end to things, as in the cider press at the conclusion of the stanza, it produces an ending that doesn't terminate: even the end of the ending—the "last oozings"—lasts and lasts, "hours by hours." Through these repressions and substitutions of its usual attributes, death is separated from its customary connections with nonbeing and is linked to being and jouissance.

Repositioning Readers in Fantasy

The stanza's repositioning of readers in the code constituting their Symbolic Other is reinforced by the evocation of certain scopic fantasies. The feeling of well-being produced by this stanza derives not only from the corporeal imagery that we have spoken of but also from the "availability rather than remoteness" of Autumn (Hartman 143). More specifically, it derives from the *visual* availability of this figure that the previous stanza has located in the position of our (m)Other, the original source of meaning, value, recognition, and jouissance.

The stanza begins with our seeing Autumn in the midst of her plenitude (her "store") and concludes with our seeing her seeing, watching "with patient look." Both moments gratify the active anaclitic aspect of our scopic drive, the desire to see—and thus in a sense possess—the (m)Other. The second moment, moreover, also indirectly gratifies our passive desire to be the object of the (m)Other's benevolent gaze—that is, to have the attention and approval of that ultimate authority and omnipotent power that confers our being upon us and establishes the status of this being in relation to all other values.[7] Here once again we

---

[7]This passive desire is here potentially anaclitic as well as narcissistic, insofar as unsublimated elements of sexual desire are more prominent than the sublimated desire that is love.

have the primal passive narcissistic gratification of being the object-cause of the (m)Other's desire.

Stanza III

With readers' cathexis of Autumn thus secured, the poem is able in the final stanza to admit more manifest consideration of Autumn as a metonym of death and of death as a metonym/metaphor of nonbeing. The third stanza introduces this dimension immediately with an *ubi sunt* theme:

> Where are the songs of Spring? Ay, where are they?
>   Think not of them, thou hast thy music too,—
> While barred clouds bloom the soft-dying day,
>   And touch the stubble-plains with rosy hue;
> Then in a wailful choir the small gnats mourn
>   Among the river sallows, borne aloft
>   Or sinking as the light wind lives or dies;
> And full-grown lambs loud bleat from hilly bourn;
>   Hedge-crickets sing; and now with treble soft
>   The red-breast whistles from a garden-croft;
>   And gathering swallows twitter in the skies.
>   (ll. 23–33)

Imaginary Mirroring and Unity in the Landscape

The impact of this stanza on readers' Imaginary register derives primarily from the status of unity, coherence, and narcissistic security that the description of the landscape confers on readers' bodies. That is, both the total gestalt and the individual details of the landscape offer positions of Imaginary identification (active narcissistic desire) from which readers can experience a fundamental security of the body ego. In relation to the total gestalt of the landscape, the audience's position is that of a transcendent observer, the supreme position of mastery and self-unity.

In relation to the individual details, the audience is also offered a position of corporeal security and well-being: there are no overwhelming or even mildly threatening creatures or landscape features here; all is gentle, soft, and diminuitive. Nor is there any conflict among any creatures or aspects of the landscape. On the contrary, each mirrors the others, either visually (as in the sunlight refracted by the clouds and reflecting off the stubble plains) or acoustically (in the sounds of all the creatures singing, as well as in the alliteration, assonance, and rhymes of the words themselves). Such mirroring and harmony evoke a muted but multiple Imaginary identificatory response from readers that can powerfully reinforce their sense of corporeal well-being in the face of the decline and death intimated in the Symbolic register.

The Voice in the Real

The acoustic mirroring also affects readers at the level of the Real, with the various sounds representing the object a in the form of the voice, which from birth (if not before) provides soothing and reassurance and thus helps to constitute one's sense of being and well-being. The stanza not only *represents* the voice, its rich vowel sounds and soft, steady rhythm also *evoke* the voice, reproducing the soothing, reassuring sounds of the maternal voice and thus allowing readers momentarily to recover this lost object. This evocation of the comfort of the maternal voice functions as a complement for the sense of well-being provided in the Imaginary register by the images of union found, for example, in the choir of gnats and in the simultaneity of the other songs as well as in the unity of the plurality of singers.

These images and fantasies of union and completion prompt readers, on the one hand, to repress the negative, dismembering attributes usually associated with death, and on the other hand, to acquiesce to the presence in the Symbolic register of death itself, which, as commentators have noted, is latent in the songs: the slaughter imminent in the lamb's bleat ("bleed"?)—a fate darkly suggested by the fact that, though still a lamb, this creature is said to have reached the end of its growth—and the signal present in the gathering of the swallows and in the voices of approaching evening (a metaphor for death) and winter, which will bring either literal death or figurative (in the form of departure).

Invoking Death and Revoking Nonbeing in the Symbolic

In the Symbolic register, this intimation of death is combined with a repression of the attributes of nonbeing normally associated with death. The process begins with the question, "Where are the songs of Spring?" No sooner is the issue raised than it is suppressed: "Think not of them," we are told, and we gladly obey. This suppression, however, is only a decoy that functions to distract us from the major repression, which occurs in the locution, "songs of Spring." As a metaphor and metonym for the joyful and exuberant life that gives rise to the song, this phrase tends to repress our awareness of that life per se by substituting "songs" for it. The abundance of life is thus reduced to sound, of which there is also an abundance in Autumn.

A similar effect is produced by the other images in the stanza, each of which functions as a metaphor and/or metonym for death. The first instance, "while barred clouds bloom the soft-dying day," involves numerous metaphoric barrings of death as nonbeing. The most basic occurs in the phrase "soft-dying day." Here the very signifier of death, "dying," is deprived of its sting by being made to function as a metaphor for ending in general, and the ending of a mere day more specifically. Giving "dying" such an innocuous signified deprives this signifier of its alliance in the Symbolic order with attributes of terrible loss and nonbeing, an effect that is reinforced by the linking of "dying" to "soft" in a compound adjective. And there are still other factors of this metaphor that contribute to its trivializing, repressive effect. For one, evening, the signified of the metaphor "soft-dying day," is itself a common, codified metaphor for literal death, the end of the day signifying the end of life. The effect of this added dimension is to create a situation in which signifier and signified seem to switch places, like the duck and rabbit in the gestaltist figure, so that the powerful connection linking death with the annihilation or nonbeing of a living individual is once again cut off.

In addition, the synchronic repositioning of death that results from this metaphoric substitution/repression of nonbeing is reinforced by the syntagmatic position of "dying" as the object of "bloom." This verb, by metaphorically signifying the manifestation of intense, exuberant, and productive life—the antithesis of death as nonbeing—attributes these qualities and the jouissances they entail to "dying" by syntagmatically positioning it as their product—that is, as an attribute of the direct object of "bloom." Similarly, the clouds, which obscure the sun and are thus common (codified) metaphors of decreased joy and vitality, are here positioned as the subject of "bloom," making them agents of exuberant life in their very act of obscuring the source of life (the sun). This effect culminates in the following line, where these same clouds are made the agents of revivification, as they "touch the stubble plains with rosy hue"—a syntagmatic chain that makes the headless wheat (also a common metaphor for death) the bearer of an image of blooming life ("rosy hue").

In the succeeding line, death and the natural human response to it— mourning and wailing, which would in most cases evoke a similar feeling in the audience—are invoked but trivialized, which preempts an empathic response from readers. This trivialization of death and mourning is produced by their being presented as activities of one of the most insignificant creatures imaginable: the gnats, whose insignificance is reinforced by the redundant "small." The gnats remain the focus of the audience's attention and identification[8] in the following two lines, where death is once again evoked and its negativity repressed in several ways. The signifiers "river" and "sallows" are traditional metonyms for death (a tie that is weakened by the naturalistic descriptive function of these signifiers here), and "dies" signifies death explicitly. But here, as in the case of "dying," "dies" is employed metaphorically and thus functions in a preemptive or innoculatory manner, warding off the full emotional impact of death. For "dies" here signifies absence of wind, an absence which is itself a traditional metaphor for death, the absence of spirit (*spiritus* = "wind"). This double metaphor represses the profound negativity normally associated with death and makes death utterly inconsequential. The inconsequentiality is reinforced metonymically by the correlation of "dies" with "lives" via the conjunction "or": whether the wind "lives or dies" is all one; whether the gnats are "borne aloft or sinking"— literally or metaphorically—makes no difference, and through the blurring of distinction between literal death and metaphorical death, this indifference is extended to literal life and death as well.

The Significance of "To Autumn"'s Ideology

The effect of these repressions and displacements of the negativity of death, bolstered by the fantasies of passive narcissistic gratification and the images of mirroring, is unmistakable and is attested to by nearly all

---

[8]As Blackstone notes, 360.

who have written on the poem. Many readers are left at the end of the poem not only reconciled to death but possessed of the positive conviction, "Now more than ever seems it rich to die," thus manifesting their involvement with the jouissance that is beyond and/or inimical to life and that constitutes the aim of the death drive. This state of mind testifies to the alterations, even if only provisional, of the subjective economy of these readers.

The alterations remain invisible to a casual reading of the poem, and when they are exposed by an analysis such as the foregoing, they may at first seem incapable of producing significant changes in the subjective economy. But although each evoked or repressed attribute of death may be connected to the master signifier "death" or the image or fantasy of gratification by a mere thread, the force of all the threads acting together is capable, like the ropes of the Lilliputians, of moving a subject by repositioning the signifiers that represent it in relation to other signifiers, images, and fantasies. It is these subtle but numerous repositionings that explain the changes in thoughts and feelings about death which many readers report upon reading the poem. And it is these repositionings—the repression and evocation not of historical facts but of attributes of identity and objects of desire and jouissance—that constitute the poem's ideology. For such repositionings are what produce different subjects, subjects who think and feel differently and who are thereby disposed to act differently.

What then is the ideological significance of the poem? There are two factors to consider: first, the effect of these repositionings on readers' psychic economies as such and, second, the repercussions of these psychological effects in the social order. Concerning the first factor, the effect of "To Autumn" seems (at first glance, at least) benign: insofar as people who read the poem feel reconciled to death, even desirous of it, the poem produces within the psychic economy a result not only unobjectionable but, one would think, devoutly to be wished: the state of Nietzschean *amor fati* or Hegelian freedom, in which the subject is at peace with and even desirous of necessity (the Real). Escaping from suffering and from the threat of nonbeing is an impulse that we all share and that no one can legitimately gainsay. All other things being equal, one would certainly not begrudge readers this effect, especially if they, like Keats himself, were face-to-face with death.

The problem, of course, is that all other things are never equal, and in the present case, the very positionings that succeed in simultaneously embracing the Real and reducing human suffering also result in an evasion of the task of ameliorating the real human suffering that often pervades life and accompanies death. "To Autumn"'s provision of passive narcissistic gratification, as well as its repression of dismemberment and significations of nonbeing, promotes an attitude which is essentially that of the natural supernaturalism that has been identified as the Romantic ideology: an attitude that turns away from real human finitude and the suffering attendant upon it, and pursues passive narcissistic gratification in all three registers, thus embracing a quietism devoid of motivation to respond actively to real human suffering—one's own as well as that of others.

This passive narcissistic gratification of "To Autumn" and the profound quietism that it promotes will also reinforce the desire for a master that we saw operating in the political sphere. The submission to a master may take the increasingly common form of political apathy, or it may disguise itself as political activism, operating under the cloak of signifiers of mastery, independence, and sovereignty (as in the case of Reagan's supporters) or signifiers of victimization and suffering (as in the case of Jackson's supporters). In addition, the embrace of the death drive promoted by "To Autumn" may well feed into the particular ways that different readers have of courting death that are embodied in a myriad of habits and lifestyle choices involving eating and drinking, working and playing, loving and hating, and so on. It is to all of these hidden, more disturbing ramifications of the predominant audience response that we must be attentive if we want to expose and, in doing so, intervene psychoanalytically in the core of "To Autumn"'s ideology.

EPILOGUE

The most natural reaction to repression and intolerance promoted by the different discourses analyzed in this book might be to avoid these discourses—for example, by criminalizing pornography or choosing not to teach *Heart of Darkness*. The most effective way, however, to undermine the destructive attitudes and behaviors promoted by these discourses is not to ignore the discourses but rather to subject the destructive attitudes to analysis, identifying and exposing the anxieties, identifications, and desires that underwrite them. If this approach is taken, a work such as *Heart of Darkness* can, in certain circumstances, actually be more effective in reducing repression and its comcomitant intolerance and oppression than a more tolerant, "politically correct" work might be.

Especially in the classroom, *Heart of Darkness* or any other work that provokes aversion to another race or sexual orientation with an alien mode of jouissance offers an excellent occasion for the psychoanalytic cultural criticism I am advocating. In eliciting and operating on the most basic forces underlying intolerance (including racism, sexism, and homophobia), such works serve a function similar to that of the transference neurosis in psychoanalytic treatment: they constitute what Freud called a new edition of the analysand's conflict, bringing the subject's unconscious impulses and anxieties into the open in the here and now, where they are susceptible to examination and interpretation and hence transformation. To the extent that readers can be brought to recognize, acknowledge, and work through the unconscious desires and anxieties that such texts evoke in them, the intolerance that is the product of their ego-alien impulses will be undermined.

Analyses of audience response such as those undertaken in this book must not simply be developed and accumulated as scholarly capital. To achieve psychological and social change, they must, like interpretation in psychoanalytic treatment, engage with the living desire of the subject who is being analyzed. Moreover, for optimal results, each subject should have a significant interest in confronting his or her own unconscious desires. Ideally, each should believe that knowledge of one's own unconscious, however disturbing it might be at first, will ultimately be liberating and empowering.

These considerations suggest that at the present time it is in the literature classroom that such analyses have the best chance of producing positive results. But they also suggest that what goes on in the classroom will need to be modified if optimal results are to be obtained. Some of the first changes that need to be considered involve canon and curriculum: rather than selecting texts on the basis of such general standards as "timelessness" or "greatness" or even "representativity" or "diversity" and attempting to instill knowledge of those texts or of their social conditions as an end in itself, teachers would do well to begin with the audience (i.e., the students) and ask what sorts of works are most likely to engage their deepest identifications, desires, and anxieties in ways that can be made apparent to them. Teachers should also ask what sorts of assignments and classroom activities would be most likely to help students become aware of their desires in relation to a given text or discourse and to work through their conflicts concerning these desires. Only when the analytic strategy presented in this book is put to use in the classroom or some other public forum— i.e., outside the rather restricted pale of studies, such as this one, written primarily for other academicians—will it be possible for the psychological and social change aimed at here to occur.

To what degree change can be realized through the analytic strategy and apparatus I have presented is not something that can be determined before they are put into practice. The relative success or failure of any such project will be determined in part by all sorts of other conditions, political and material, prevailing at the time. But the wager of this book is that helping subjects analyze their responses to cultural artifacts and discourses can provide an opportunity for them to begin to work through some of their more debilitating and destructive conflicts of identification and desire, and that such working through can open the way not only to greater jouissance for these subjects but also, through the resulting changes in their attitudes and behavior, to beneficial social change.

That such change will be socially beneficial in every instance cannot be guaranteed. But the fact that intolerance and injustice are underwritten by the unconscious conflicts in identification and desire of both the perpetrators and the victims indicates that reducing the unconscious conflicts will on balance contribute to a more just and tolerant society. In fact, I would go so far as to say that without reducing the unconscious conflicts—whether by individual psychoanalysis, by cultural criticism, or by various other means—the chances of reducing injustice and intolerance are virtually nonexistent.

WORKS CITED

Achebe, Chinua. "An Image of Africa: Racism in Conrad's *Heart of Darkness*." In *Heart of Darkness,* 3d ed., ed. Robert Kimbrough, 250–62. New York: Norton, 1988.

Alcorn, Marshall W., and Mark Bracher. "Literature, Psychoanalysis and the Re-Formation of the Self: A New Direction for Reader-Response Theory." *PMLA* 100 (1985): 342–54.

André, Serge. *Que veut une femme?* Paris: Navarin, 1987.

Arac, Jonathan. Introduction to *Postmodernism and Politics,* ed. Jonathan Arac, ix–xliii. Minneapolis: University of Minnesota Press, 1986.

———. "The Struggle for the Cultural Heritage: Christina Stead Refunctions Charles Dickens and Mark Twain." In *The New Historicism,* ed. H. Aram Veeser, 116–131. New York: Routledge, 1989. Pages 116–131.

Baines, Jocelyn. *Joseph Conrad: A Critical Biography.* London: Weidenfeld & Nicolson, 1960.

Bate, W. Jackson. *John Keats.* Cambridge: Harvard University Press, 1963.

———. *The Stylistic Development of Keats.* New York: Humanities Press, 1945.

Blackstone, Bernard. *The Consecrated Urn.* London: Longmans, Green, 1959.

Bloom, Harold, ed. *John Keats.* New York: Chelsea House, 1985.

———. *The Visionary Company.* Ithaca: Cornell University Press, 1971.

Brantlinger, Patrick. *Crusoe's Footprints: Cultural Studies in Britain and America.* New York: Routledge, 1990.

———. "*Heart of Darkness*: Anti-Imperialism, Racism, or Impressionism?" *Criticism* 27 (1985): 363–85.

Brower, Reuben. *The Fields of Light.* London: Oxford University Press, 1951.

Bush, Douglas. *John Keats.* New York: Macmillan, 1966.

Condit, Celeste Michelle. *Decoding Abortion Rhetoric: Communicating Social Change.* Urbana: University of Illinois Press, 1990.

Conrad, Joseph. *Heart of Darkness.* In *"Heart of Darkness": A Case Study in*

Contemporary Criticism, ed. Ross C. Murfin, 17–94. New York: St. Martin's, 1989.

Cooke, Michael G. *The Romantic Will.* New Haven: Yale University Press, 1976.

Crabbe, Anthony. "Feature-length Sex Films." In *Perspectives on Pornography: Sexuality and Film in Literature,* ed. Gary Day and Clive Bloom, 44–66. New York: St. Martin's Press, 1988.

Crews, Frederick. "The Power of Darkness." *Partisan Review* 34 (1967): 507–25.

Day, Gary. "Looking at Women: Notes toward a Theory of Porn." In *Perspectives on Pornography: Sexuality and Film in Literature,* ed. Gary Day and Clive Bloom, 83–100. New York: St. Martin's Press, 1988.

Eagleton, Terry. *Literary Theory.* Minneapolis: University of Minnesota Press, 1983.

Eco, Umberto. *A Theory of Semiotics.* Bloomington: Indiana University Press, 1979.

Fish, Stanley, *Is There a Text in this Class?* Cambridge: Harvard University Press, 1980.

Fitzgerald, William. "Articulating the Unarticulated: Form, Death, and Other in Keats and Rilke." *MLN* 100 (1985): 949–67.

Ford, Newell F. "Holy Living and Holy Dying in Keats's Poetry." *Keats-Shelley Journal* 20 (1971): 37–61.

Fox-Genovese, Elizabeth. "Literary Criticism and the Politics of the New Historicism." In *The New Historicism,* ed. H. Aram Veeser, 213–24. New York: Routledge, 1989.

Freud, Sigmund. *The Standard Edition of the Complete Psychological Works of Sigmund Freud.* 24 vols. London: Hogarth Press, 1953–74.

Fry, Paul H. *The Poet's Calling in the English Ode.* New Haven: Yale University Press, 1980.

Gallagher, Catherine. "Marxism and the New Historicism." In *The New Historicism,* ed. H. Aram Veeser, 37–48. New York: Routledge, 1989.

Guerard, Albert J. "The Journey Within." In *Heart of Darkness,* 3d ed., ed. Robert Kimbrough, 243–50. New York: Norton, 1988.

Gunn, Giles. "Beyond Transcendence or Beyond Ideology: The New Problematics of Cultural Criticism in America." *American Literary History* 2 (1990): 1–18.

Hartman, Geoffrey H. "Poem and Ideology: A Study of Keats's 'To Autumn.'" In Hartman, *The Fate of Reading,* 124–46. Chicago: University of Chicago Press, 1975.

Hartsock, Nancy. "Postmodernism and Political Change: Issues for Feminist Theory." *Cultural Critique* 14 (1989–90): 15–33.

Hodge, Robert, and Gunther Kress. *Social Semiotics.* Ithaca: Cornell University Press, 1990.

Holland, Norman. *The Dynamics of Literary Response.* New York: Norton, 1968.

———. *5 Readers Reading.* New Haven: Yale University Press, 1975.

———. *Poems in Persons.* New York: Norton, 1973.

Humphries, Reynold. "The Discourse of Colonialism: Its Meaning and Relevance for Conrad's Fiction." *Conradiana* 21 (1989): 107–33.

Hyland, Peter. "The Little Woman in *Heart of Darkness.*" *Conradiana* 20 (1988): 3–11.

Les Identifications et le désir. Actes de L'Ecole de la Cause freudienne. Paris: ECF, 1986.

Iser Wolfgang, *The Act of Reading.* Baltimore: Johns Hopkins University Press, 1978.

Jackson, Jesse. Speech to the Democratic National Convention. Atlanta, 20 June 1988. *Facts on File,* July 22, 1988, 533–34.

Jameson, Fredric. *The Political Unconscious: Narrative as a Socially Symbolic Act.* Ithaca: Cornell University Press, 1981.

Jauss, Hans Robert. *Aesthetic Experience and Literary Hermeneutics.* Translated by Michael Shaw. Minneapolis: University of Minnesota Press, 1982.

Johnson, Richard. "What Is Cultural Studies Anyway?" *Social Text* 6 (1987): 38–80.

Kappeler, Susanne. *The Pornography of Representation.* Minneapolis: University of Minnesota Press, 1986.

Katan, Maurits. "Childhood Memories as Contents of Schizophrenic Hallucinations and Delusions." *Psychoanalytic Study of the Child* 30 (1975): 357–74.

———. "Schreber's Delusion of the End of the World." *Psychoanalytic Quarterly* 18 (1949): 60–66.

King, Martin Luther. "Letter from Birmingham Jail." In *The Norton Reader,* ed. Arthur M. Eastman, 5th ed., 852–66. New York: Norton, 1980.

Lacan, Jacques. "Desire and the Interpretation of Desire in *Hamlet.*" In *Literature and Psychoanalysis,* ed. Shoshana Felman, 11–52. Baltimore: Johns Hopkins University Press, 1982.

———. *Ecrits.* Paris: Seuil, 1966.

———. *Ecrits: A Selection.* Translated by Alan Sheridan. New York: Norton, 1977.

———. *The Four Fundamental Concepts of Psychoanalysis.* Edited by Jacques-Alain Miller. Translated by Alan Sheridan. New York: Norton, 1977. [Seminar XI]

———. *Le Séminaire, Livre III: Les psychoses.* Text established by Jacques-Alain Miller. Paris: Seuil, 1981.

———. *Le Séminaire, Livre VI: Le désir et son interpretation.* Typescript of unpublished seminar, 1958–59.

———. *Le Séminaire, Livre VII: L'éthique de la psychanalyse.* Text established by Jacques-Alain Miller. Paris: Seuil, 1986.

———. *Le Séminaire, Livre IX: L'identification.* Typescript of unpublished seminar, 1961–62.

———. *Le Séminaire, Livre XVII: L'envers de la psychanalyse.* Text established by Jacques-Alain Miller. Paris: Seuil, 1991.

———. *Le Séminaire, Livre XVII,* Unpublished session of June 3, 1970. [XVIIA]

——. *The Seminar of Jacques Lacan: Book I: Freud's Papers on Technique, 1953–1954.* Edited by Jacques-Alain Miller. Translated by John Forrester. New York: Norton, 1988.

——. *The Seminar of Jacques Lacan: Book II: The Ego in Freud's Theory and in the Technique of Psychoanalysis, 1954–1955.* Edited by Jacques-Alain Miller. Translated by Sylvana Tomaselli. New York: Norton, 1988.

Lentricchia, Frank. "Foucault's Legacy: A New Historicism?" In *The New Historicism*, ed. H. Aram Veeser, 231–42. New York: Routledge, 1989.

Liu, Alan. "Local Transcendence: Cultural Criticism, Postmodernism, and the Romanticism of Detail." *Representations* 32 (1990): 75–113.

——. "The Power of Formalism: The New Historicism." *ELH* 56 (1989): 721–71.

London, Bette. "Reading Race and Gender in Conrad's Dark Continent." *Criticism* 31 (1989): 235–52.

Luker, Kristin. *Abortion and the Politics of Motherhood.* Berkeley: University of California Press, 1984.

McClure, John A. "The Rhetoric of Restraint in *Heart of Darkness.*" *Nineteenth-Century Fiction* 32 (1977): 310–26.

McGann, Jerome. "Keats and the Historical Method in Literary Criticism." *MLN* 94 (1979): 988–1032.

Macksey, Richard. " 'To Autumn' and the Music of Mortality: 'Pure Rhetoric of a Language Without Words.' " In *Romanticism and Language*, ed. Arden Reed, 263–308. Ithaca: Cornell University Press, 1984.

Madden, Fred. "Marlow and the Double Horror of *Heart of Darkness.*" *The Midwest Quarterly* 27 (1986): 504–17.

Meckier, Jerome. "The Truth about Marlow." *Studies in Short Fiction* 19 (1982): 373–79.

Mellor, Anne K. *English Romantic Irony.* Cambridge: Harvard University Press, 1980.

Merton, Andrew H. *Enemies of Choice: The Right-to-Life Movement and Its Threat to Abortion.* Boston: Beacon Press, 1981.

Miller, J. Hillis. " 'Heart of Darkness' Revisited." In *"Heart of Darkness": A Case Study in Contemporary Criticism*, ed. Ross C. Murfin, 209–23. New York: St. Martin's Press, 1989.

Miller, Jacques-Alain. "A and a in Clinical Structures." Proceedings of the First Paris-New York Psychoanalytic Workshop. New York, n.d.

——. "*Extimité.*" *Prose Studies* 11 (1988): 121–130.

Montrose, Louis A. "Professing the Renaissance: The Poetics and Politics of Culture." In *The New Historicism*, ed. H. Aram Veeser, 13–36. New York: Routledge, 1989.

Nemoianu, Virgil. "The Dialectics of Movement in Keats's 'To Autumn.' " *PMLA* 93 (1978): 205–14.

Newton, Judith Lowder. "History as Usual? Feminism and the 'New Historicism.' " In *The New Historicism*, ed. H. Aram Veeser, 152–67. New York: Routledge, 1989.

Ong, Walter J. "Truth in Conrad's Darkness." *Mosaic* 11 (1977): 151–63.

Patterson, Annabel M. " 'How to load and . . . bend': Syntax and Interpretation in Keats's *To Autumn.*" *PMLA* 94 (1979): 449–58.

Pearce, Donald. "Thoughts on the Autumn Ode of Keats." *Ariel* 6 (1975): 3–19.

Pecora, Vincent. "*Heart of Darkness* and the Phenomenology of Voice." *ELH* 52 (1985): 993–1015.

———. "The Limits of Local Knowledge." In *The New Historicism*, ed. H. Aram Veeser, 243–76. New York: Routledge, 1989.

Perkins, David. *The Quest for Permanence.* Cambridge: Harvard University Press, 1959.

Pison, Thomas. "A Phenomenological Approach to Keats's 'To Autumn.' " In *Phenomenology, Structuralism, Semiology*, ed. Harry R. Garvin. Lewisburg, Pa: Bucknell University Press, 1976.

Poovey, Mary. "Cultural Criticism: Past and Present." *College English* 52 (1990): 615–25.

Poulet, Georges. "Criticism and the Experience of Interiority." In *Reader-Response Criticism,* ed. Jane P. Tompkins, 41–49. Baltimore: Johns Hopkins University Press, 1980.

Przybylowicz, Donna. "Toward a Feminist Cultural Criticism: Hegemony and Modes of Social Division." *Cultural Critique* 14 (1989–90): 259–301.

Reagan, Ronald. *Abortion and the Conscience of the Nation.* Nashville: Thomas Nelson, 1984.

———. Speech to the Republican National Convention. Detroit, 17 July 1980. *Facts on File,* 18 July 1980, 531–34.

Reeves, Charles Eric. "A Voice of Unrest: Conrad's Rhetoric of the Unspeakable." *Texas Studies in Literature and Language* 27 (1985): 284–309.

Ricks, Christopher. *Keats and Embarrassment.* London: Oxford University Press, 1974.

Rosmarin, Adena. "Darkening the Reader: Reader-Response Criticism and *Heart of Darkness.*" In *"Heart of Darkness": A Case Study in Contemporary Criticism*, ed. Ross C. Murfin, 148–68. New York: St. Martin's Press, 1989.

Ryan, Michael. "Literary Criticism and Cultural Science: Transformations in the Dominant Paradigm of Literary Study." *North Dakota Quarterly Review* 51 (1983): 100–112.

Schwarz, Daniel R. *Conrad: "Almayer's Folly" to "Under Western Eyes."* Ithaca: Cornell University Press, 1980.

Sedlak, Valerie F. " 'A World of their Own': Narrative Distortion and Fictive Exemplification in the Portrayal of Women in *Heart of Darkness.*" *College Language Association Journal* 32 (1989): 443–65.

Shelley, Percy Bysshe. "A Defense of Poetry." In *The Complete Works of Percy Bysshe Shelley*, Roger Ingpen and Walter E. Peck, 7:109–40. New York: Gordian, 1965.

Shumway, David R. "Transforming Literary Studies into Cultural Criticism: The Role of Interpretation and Theory." *Works and Days* 3 (1985): 79–89.

Smith, Johanna M. " 'Too Beautiful Altogether': Patriarchal Ideology in *Heart of Darkness.*" In *"Heart of Darkness": A Case Study in Contemporary Criticism*, ed. Ross C. Murfin, 179–94. New York: St. Martin's Press, 1989.

Straus, Nina Pelikan. "The Exclusion of the Intended from Secret Sharing in Conrad's *Heart of Darkness.*" *Novel* 20 (1987): 123–37.

Tessitore, John. "Freud, Conrad, and *Heart of Darkness.*" *College Literature* 7 (1980): 30–40.

Thomas, Brook. "The New Historicism and other Old-Fashioned Topics." In *The New Historicism*, ed. H. Aram Veeser, 182–203. New York: Routledge, 1989.

——. "Preserving and Keeping Order by Killing Time in *Heart of Darkness.* In *"Heart of Darkness": A Case Study in Contemporary Criticism*, ed. Ross C. Murfin, 237–55. New York: St. Martin's Press, 1989.

Vendler, Helen. *The Odes of John Keats.* Cambridge: Harvard University Press, 1983.

Webb, Peter. "Victorian Erotica." In *The Sexual Dimension in Literature*, ed. Alan Bold, 90–121. New York: Barnes & Noble, 1982.

Williams, Linda. *Hard Core: Power, Pleasure, and the "Frenzy of the Visible."* Berkeley: University of California Press, 1989.

Zita, Jacquelyn N. "Pornography and the Male Imaginary." *Enclitic* 9 (1987): 28–44.

Žižek, Slavoj. *The Sublime Object of Ideology.* New York: Verso, 1989.

INDEX

abortion, 15, 103
  See also discourse: antiabortionist
Achebe, Chinua, 138, 160
advertisements, 31, 39–40, 67
aggressivity, 38, 68–71, 76, 90, 92, 101, 163
AIDS, 167
alienation, 55, 66–74, 78, 97, 127
America, 120–21
anxiety, 64, 66, 70–71, 109–10, 121, 180–81, 190–91
aporia, 144
Arac, Jonathan, 2, 5
Aristotle, 179
Arnold, Matthew, 46
athletic performances, 34

baby, 110, 113, 115
Baines, Jocelyn, 142
Bate, Walter Jackson, 168, 177
being, 123, 148, 153, 172–73, 178–79, 182–83
belief, 104, 147–48, 151, 155–58
  See also knowledge
Bercovitch, Sacvan, 10
Blackstone, Bernard, 169, 187
Bleich, David, 2
Bloom, Allan, 56
Bloom, Harold, 168–69, 182
body, 66, 85, 90, 103, 115, 148–49, 172
body ego, 32–40, 75–76, 111–13, 117, 122, 184
Brantlinger, Patrick, 2, 5–6, 9, 139
Brower, Reuben, 177

bureaucracy, 55
Bush, Douglas, 169, 176

canon, 191
cars, 45
castration, 92, 98–99, 110, 120–25, 135, 152–53
change
  psychological, 12, 14, 16, 21–22, 97–104, 118–19, 146, 163–67, 188–92
  social, 12, 14, 16, 19, 52–80, 83, 97–102, 118–19, 146, 163–67, 188–92
Christianity, 110
Coleridge, Samuel Taylor, 23, 46
collector's object, 44
compromise, 142–44, 147
Condit, Celeste, 103, 105, 111–12
conflict, 46–52, 66, 69, 78, 134, 142, 154, 190, 192
Conrad, Joseph
  Heart of Darkness, 15, 138–67, 190
conservatism, 118
Cooke, Michael, 171
cosmetics, 34
Crabbe, Anthony, 88–89
cultural criticism, ix–x, 1–16, 53–80, 83, 138, 190–92
culture, 1, 13, 16, 19, 56, 97, 138
curriculum, 191

dance, 34
Day, Gary, 89, 92
death, 114–15, 128, 148–49, 153, 157, 159–60, 165, 168–72, 176, 178–89

death drive, 173, 179–82, 188–89
deconstruction, 2, 60, 66–67, 71, 79,
    147
Deep Throat, 89
demand, 41, 77
Derrida, Jacques, 143
desire
    active anaclitic, 14, 21, 29–30, 39, 44,
        85, 95–96, 183
    active narcissistic, 14, 20, 27–29, 32–
        37, 45, 70, 91, 95, 114
    analyst's, 100–102
    in discourse, 10, 14, 19–52
    in the discourse of the analyst, 69–70,
        72–75, 78
    in education, 190–92
    in hysteria, 66–67
    of the Other, 19–21, 77, 87–88, 92–
        93, 95, 116
    passive anaclitic, 14, 21, 30–31, 39–
        40, 44, 183
    passive narcissistic, 14, 20, 23–26,
        37–39, 44–45, 69–70, 76, 91, 105,
        110, 115, 120, 122, 128–37, 174–
        78, 182–84, 187, 189
    phallic, 96–98
    See also recognition
discourse, 12, 14, 53–80, 190
    of the Analyst, 63–64, 67–73, 77–80,
        142
    antiabortionist, 15–16, 74, 103–18
    of the Hysteric, 64–68, 70, 78, 102,
        121, 128, 130, 136, 145–46
    of the Master, 58–66, 78, 120–24,
        127–28, 145
    philosophical, 60, 65
    political, 15–16, 60, 67–68, 74, 119–
        37
    pornographic, 15–16, 74, 83–102
    receiver in, 54
    revolutionary, 58, 62–65
    scientific, 53, 58–61
    sender in, 54
    of the University, 54–59, 66, 69–71,
        78
dogmatism, 118
drives, 40–45, 73, 142–48, 152, 154,
    158, 160–64, 173, 183
drugs, 45, 167

Eagleton, Terry, 2–3, 11
Eco, Umberto, 12
education, 1, 53, 55, 60, 190–92
    See also students

ego, 59, 70–71, 90, 95, 98, 145–46,
    151, 163, 174
    See also body ego
ego ideal
    in analysis of response, 75–77
    changes in, 70–72, 100, 162
    conflict of, with fantasy, 43, 47–51,
        142–47, 151, 157–64
    role of, in fanaticism, 117, 136
    threats to, 105–9, 146–47,
embryos, 107
Emmanuelle, 89
epistemology. *See* discourse: philosophi-
    cal
erotism, 29–30, 39, 42, 44
ethics, 70, 78–80, 101, 104, 131
    See also discourse: philosophical
exhibitionism, 46–47

fantasy
    anal, 177
    in antiabortionist discourse, 114–18
    and death drive, 179
    as defense against lack, 128
    in discourse of the Analyst, 68–80
    in discourse of the Master, 59, 65,
        120
    fundamental, 73, 163
    homosexual, 99
    interpellation through, 40–45
    oral, 176–77
    scopic, 178, 183
    See also ego ideal: conflict of, with
        fantasy
fashion, 34, 40
fatherhood, 109–10
fathers, 115
fellatio, 89
femininity
    and the law, 116, 132
    masculine fear of, 164–65
    in masculinity, 99
    and motherhood, 109–10
    as Symbolic construct, 30–31, 42,
        47–52, 84–87, 94
feminism and feminist criticism, 2, 57–
    58, 62, 65, 67–68, 97, 101, 140
fetish object, 44
fetus, 103–6, 111–12, 115–17
Fish, Stanley, 2, 67
Fitzgerald, William, 176
formalism, 4–5, 10, 21, 57
Foucault, Michel, 62
Fox-Genovese, Elizabeth, 4

Freud, Sigmund, 71
Fry, Paul, 181
fundamentalism, 118

Gallagher, Catherine, 4
gaze, 45, 126–27, 135, 152–53, 178, 183
government, 122–23
Grier, Roosevelt, 50
guilt, 70
Gunn, Giles, 2, 7
guns, 45

H.D., 35
Hamlet, 38
Hardy, Thomas, 45
Hartman, Geoffrey, 168–69, 183
Hartsock, Nancy, 8
hate, 154
Hawkins, Hunt, 138
Hegel, G. W. F., 172, 179, 188
Hemingway, Ernest, 37
Hirsch, E. D., 56
historicism, 5–7, 69, 140
history, 5–7, 69, 140
Hitler, Adolf, 136
Hodge, Robert, 12
Holland, Norman, 2, 12–13
Homer, 21
hommelette, 115
homophobia, 99, 141–42, 163–64, 190
homosexuality, 39, 43, 70–71, 99, 164–66
honor, 123–24
humanities, 1, 56
Humphries, Reynold, 139
Hyland, Peter, 139–40
hypnotism, 136
hysteria, 66–67
See also discourse: of the Hysteric

ideal ego, 32, 69–72, 76–77, 105, 107–9
ideals, 68–74, 77–78, 118, 141, 144–48, 154, 157, 161–63, 171
See also ego ideal
identification, 14, 20, 141, 165
changes in, 69–80, 100–102, 136, 190–92
with characters, 152, 155–59, 166
in discourse, 21–22
with images, 32–38, 91, 111–12, 147–48, 175–85
with objects *a,* 72, 114, 117

with signifiers, 27–29, 72, 120, 124, 128, 146
See also desire: active narcissistic
identity
based in body image, 114, 175
based in knowledge, 150
based in signifiers, 23, 53, 67, 71, 99–100, 104–7, 110, 116, 120–24, 132, 152, 155
change in, 72, 97, 188
and conflict with unconscious desire, 69, 147–48, 158
sexual, 51, 86, 93, 95, 110, 154, 167
threats to, 156
ideology, 9, 15–16, 138, 140–41, 167–71, 174, 178, 180, 188–89
ideology, critiques of, 139–40
images, 23, 29, 31, 74, 93, 154, 161, 174–80, 183–88
of the body, 32–40, 51, 76, 90–91, 111, 149, 181–82
of dismemberment, 38, 111–14, 128, 148, 172–73, 180–81, 189
Imaginary order, 14, 22–23, 31–40
death drive in, 179
desire in, 75–76, 85
identification in, 111–12, 146–48, 180, 182, 184–85
notion of death in, 114, 172, 175
See also body ego; desire; *and* images
imperialism, 138–39
instincts, 115–16, 142, 154
interpellation, 104, 121, 124, 127–32, 140–65
desire in, 10, 14, 19, 65
in discourse of the Analyst, 68, 77–79
conflict in, 46–52
through fantasy, 40–45, 75, 77, 114–18
through images, 31–40, 75–77, 110–14
through signifiers, 22–31, 75–76
intolerance, 190, 192
See also tolerance
irony, 144–46
Iser, Wolfgang, 2, 8, 67

Jackson, Jesse, 15, 68, 74, 119, 127–37, 189
Jameson, Fredric, 2
Jauss, Hans Robert, 8, 21, 141
Johnson, Richard, 3, 11, 13

jouissance, 20, 40, 65–67, 95, 188, 192
  alien, 99–102, 143, 151–54, 162–67, 190
  and being, 124, 178–79, 183
  conflict of, with identity, 69, 146–47, 162
  and death drive, 182, 188
  as factor in discourse, 53, 141
  through fantasy, 73, 77
  limitless, 135–37, 153
  lost or forbidden, 65–67, 74, 99–102, 127, 137, 147, 157
  and the Other, 21, 42–43, 72, 85, 95–96
  through possessing the object *a*, 44
  through possessing a signifier, 29, 94
  and the unconscious, 48

Kappeler, Susanne, 84–85
Katan, Maurits, 98
Keats, John
  "To Autumn," 15, 168–89
King, Martin Luther, 28–29
Klein, Melanie, 98
knowledge, 111, 135, 147–51, 191
  as basis of identity, 150, 155–62
  in cultural criticism, ix, 1, 6–10, 19, 144–46
  in discourse, 53–64, 67, 71–73, 78
  See also belief
Kress, Gunther, 12
Kristeva, Julia, 12–13, 115

lack, 41, 65, 115, 120–21, 125–30, 135, 153, 163, 177
  in the Other, 45–46, 72, 77, 118, 126, 130, 178
law, 59, 73, 92, 109–10, 115–16, 120–26, 135–36, 154, 167
Lefort, Rosine, 98
Lentricchia, Frank, 4
libido, 20, 39, 90, 115–16, 162
lies, 159
life, 105–6, 110, 172–73, 178, 183, 186–87
Liu, Alan, 4–5
London, Bette, 140–41, 164
love, 20, 70, 85, 91, 95–96, 100–101, 105, 110, 114, 116–17, 125, 154, 165–66, 176, 183
Luker, Kristin, 106–9, 111, 117

McClure, John, 143
McGann, Jerome, 169–70
Macksey, Richard, 168, 171–72

Madden, Fred, 143
Marxist criticism, 2–3, 21, 57–58, 62–63, 65, 78
masculinity, 26–27, 29–31, 42, 44, 49–52, 84, 86, 88, 91–95, 102, 107, 164–65
master signifier, 23–31, 47–53, 58–73, 76–79, 91, 104–11, 118–21, 124–25,
masturbation, 89, 97–98
meaning, 71–72, 123–24, 148, 183
meaninglessness, 64, 66, 71
Meckier, Jerome, 143
Mellor, Anne, 168–69
Merton, Andrew, 104, 106, 108, 113, 117
metaphor, 49–52, 105–6, 133–35, 173, 178, 180, 182, 184–87
metaphor, phallic, 94
metonymy, 49–52, 105–6, 133–35, 173, 176, 178–80, 182, 184, 186–87
Miller, Hillis, 144, 146, 155, 157
Miller, Jacques-Alain, 13, 100, 163
mirroring, 175, 184–85, 187
mirror stage, 32–34, 174, 179, 181
models, 37–38
money, 45
Montrose, Louis, 2, 6, 9
moral code, 104, 111
Morgan, Marabel, 47
motherhood, 109–10
mothers, 115
music, 45
Mussolini, Benito, 136

name, 133
narcissism, 101, 104, 118, 121–22, 144, 166, 172, 184
  See also desire: passive narcissistic
nationalism, 44
Nemoianu, Virgil, 176
new historicism, 4–8, 57
Newton, Judith, 8
Nietzsche, Friedrich, 143, 179, 188

object *a*, 40–45, 53–55, 64–65, 69, 71, 100, 114–17, 120, 125–27, 135, 145–48, 151–54, 167, 176–78
obsessional, the, 145–46
oedipal complex, 70, 166
Ong, Walter, 142
ontology. See discourse: philosophical
Other, 137, 159, 163–64, 167, 178, 182–83

Other (*continued*)
  desire of, 19–45, 72, 77, 85–86
  Imaginary, 20, 32–40, 42–46, 90
  Real, 20, 42–46, 77, 88–89
  Symbolic, 20, 23–31, 41–46, 49, 76,
    91–93, 110, 130–32, 172–76
  See also lack: in the Other
outlaws, 104
Owen, Wilfred, 38–39

Paine, Tom, 125
paternal metaphor, 51
patriarchy, 100, 103, 139
Patterson, Annabel, 177
Pearce, Donald, 169–70
Pecora, Vincent, 5, 8, 143
penis, 86, 93, 94
perception, 35–36, 177
Perkins, David, 171–72
personhood, 106–7, 110
personification, 175, 178
perversion, 92
phallic signifier, 120–27, 131
phallus, 86–87, 93–96, 99–100, 109–
    10, 131
philosophy. *See* discourse: philosophical
phobic object, 160
Plato, 21
Playboy, 90
plus-de-jouir, 40–45, 64, 120, 163
poetry, 68
points de capiton, 29, 51, 98
politics, 189
  See also discourse: political
Poovey, Mary, 2–3, 7
pornography, 15, 83–102
  See also discourse: pornographic
Poulet, Georges, 2
power, 62, 131, 136
pregnancy, 108, 167
projection, 160, 162, 165
protest, 66
Przybylowicz, Donna, 7
psychoanalytic theory and criticism, x,
    11–14, 57–59, 62, 74, 78, 101–2,
    143, 190–92
psychoanalytic treatment, 68–73, 78–
    80, 100, 146–47, 163, 190
psychosis, 98

race, 135, 166, 190
racism, 45, 138–42, 163–64, 166,
    190
rape, 86–88, 90, 92–93, 96
Rat Man, 69–72

reader-response analysis, 2, 8, 13, 15–
    16, 23–31, 35–39, 66–67, 74–75,
    141
Reagan, Ronald, 15, 74, 105–6, 113,
    119–27, 130–31, 135–36, 189
Real order, 14, 22–23, 98, 189
  death drive in, 179, 188
  desire in, 40–45, 85, 114–18, 125,
    127, 135–36, 176, 185
  in discourse analysis, 77
  as the non-symbolized, 61, 150–51,
    160
rebellion, 55
reception theory, 8, 10–12, 21
recognition, 23–29, 129–32, 158, 172
  See also desire: passive narcissistic
Reeves, Charles Eric, 145
religion, 70–71, 136
renunciation, 142–43
representation, 8–10, 84, 138–40, 164–
    65, 167, 170, 180
repression, 72–73, 98, 102, 108, 118,
    144, 147, 190
  in discourse, 53, 59, 65, 71, 120, 127,
    134, 173, 175, 183–88
  of drives and jouissance, 151–52,
    157–59, 162, 166
  of the feminine, 99
resistance, 66, 142
restraint, 142–43, 147
revolution, 58, 62–63, 67, 73, 101–2
Ricks, Christopher, 168
Rosmarin, Adena, 138, 140, 155
Ryan, Michael, 11

sacrifice, 124
sadism, 70
sadomasochism, 44
Said, Edward, 2, 9
scenes, 35–37, 75, 148, 168
Schreber, 98
Schwarz, Daniel, 157
science, 60
  See also discourse: scientific
Sedlak, Valerie, 140–41
separation, 68–74, 136
sexism, 140–42, 163–64, 166, 190
Shakespeare, 46
shame, 64, 66, 70
Shelley, Percy Bysshe, 21–22
Shumway, David, 7
signifiers, 23–31, 46–53, 75, 91, 94–
    95, 132–33, 172–73, 175–79
  materiality of, 51, 177
  phallic, 92–93, 95, 98–99, 102

signifiers (*continued*)
 transcendental, 118
 unconscious chains of, 42, 47–52
 See also master signifier
Smith, Johanna, 139, 146
space, 35–37, 76
speed, 45
stars, 45
Straus, Nina, 141, 165
students, 2, 55–56
subject, 13, 84, 95, 122–24, 130, 132,
 137, 171–73, 188
 divided, 41, 53, 64, 55, 71–72, 78,
 132, 146–47, 162
 See also alienation
subjectivity, 11–12, 22, 40, 188
subject position, 7–8, 19, 47–49, 130,
 136, 141, 163
subject presumed to know, 131, 152,
 157–59
sublimation, 166
subversion, 66
Symbolic order, 100, 107, 109, 131–34,
 152, 171–72, 178–79, 185
 castration in, 120–22, 125
 desire in, 23–31, 76, 85, 91–92, 95–
 99
 and the Real, 40–41, 47–48, 65, 98,
 115–16, 146, 152–60, 167
 as one of three registers, 14, 22–23
 See also castration; desire; *and* master
 signifier
symptom, 13, 66–67, 166
system, 55–59, 67, 120, 123, 126–27,
 135, 150–51, 156
 See also knowledge

teaching, 2, 190–92
 See also education *and* students

Tessitore, John, 143
Thomas, Brook, 6, 167
tolerance, 164
 See also intolerance
transference, 131, 135, 158, 162
transference neurosis, 190
truth, 144, 159

unconscious, 43, 47–49, 132, 142, 145–
 47, 161, 163–66, 179, 190–92
undecidability, 144–46

vagina, 86, 94
values, 104, 113, 121–22, 124, 157,
 162–63
 change in, 78–79, 171
 conflict of, with fantasy, 68–73, 146–
 47
 as determinants of subject position,
 10,
 in discourse analysis, 77
 See also ideals *and* master signifier
vel of alienation, 123–25
Vendler, Helen, 176–77, 179
voice, 45, 126–27, 135, 144, 152–53,
 185
voyeurism, 46

Webb, Peter, 86–87, 93
whipping, 86, 96
Whitman, Walt, 36
Williams, Linda, 85, 88–89, 102
Wolfman, 72
women, 139
Wordsworth, William, 23, 43

Zita, Jacquelyn, 83–86, 88–89, 95–96,
 99
Žižek, Slavoj, 40–41, 44

Library of Congress Cataloging-in-Publication Data

Bracher, Mark, 1950–
   Lacan, discourse, and social change : a psychoanalytic cultural
criticism / Mark Bracher.
      p. cm.
   Includes bibliographical references and index.
   ISBN 0-8014-2784-3 (cloth). — ISBN 0-8014-8063-9 (Paper)
   1. Discourse analysis. 2. Language and culture. 3. Social
change. 4. Psychoanalysis and literature. 5. Lacan, Jacques, 1901–
1981. I. Title.
P302.B7   1993   92-31172
401'.41—dc20